Garden
Bugs
of
Ontario

Gardening to Attract, Repel and Control

Leslie Pro
and L

D1292568

LONE
PINE

Lone Pine Publishing

The Publisher: Lone Pine Publishing
10145–81 Avenue
Edmonton, AB
T6E 1W9
Canada

Website: www.lonepinepublishing.com

Library and Archives Canada Cataloguing in Publication

Foster, Leslie Proctor, 1968-
    Garden bugs of Ontario / main author, Leslie Proctor Foster ;
with Ken Fry and Doug Macaulay.

Includes bibliographical references and index.
ISBN 978-1-55105-508-4

    1. Insects—Ontario—Identification. 2. Garden pests—Ontario—
Identification. I. Fry, Kenneth McNichol, 1961- II. Macaulay, Doug,
1975- III. Title.

QL476.F68 2007   595.7'09713   C2007-906015-3

Editorial Director: Nancy Foulds
Project Editor: Gary Whyte
Editorial: Wendy Pirk, Sheila Quinlan, Nicholle Carrière
Technical Consultant: Don Williamson
Illustrations Coordinator: Carol Woo
Production Manager: Gene Longson
Book Design: Heather Markham
Layout and Production: Michael Cooke, Trina Koscielnuk, Megan Fischer
Cover Design: Gerry Dotto
Cover Photo: Monarch larva (JupiterImages Corporation)
Anatomy Illustrations: Frank Burman
Illustrations and Photographs: please see p. 4 for a complete list of credits

We acknowledge the financial support of the Government of Canada through the Book Publishing Industry Development Program (BPIDP) for our publishing activities.

PC: P1

Table of Contents

Acknowledgements

I would like to thank the editorial staff at Lone Pine Publishing, particularly Gary Whyte and Wendy Pirk, for their help and encouragement in preparing this book, and my fellow co-authors Ken Fry and Doug Macaulay for their great bug knowledge. I would especially like to thank my husband Rob and our wonderful boys Tie and Trent for their patience, love and support.

–Leslie Proctor Foster

I would like to thank the excellent editorial and production staff at Lone Pine, my wife for her support and forbearance, and the myriad of insects that serve as an inspiration and source of wonder every day.

–Ken Fry

I would like to thank my family for their loving support and encouragement of my entomology pursuits: my wife Sherri, my parents Allan and Karen, my brothers Stacy and Roger, and my nephew Blake Mackey. Special thanks go to Greg Pohl for his enthusiasm and for inspiring me to pursue this career. From the University of Alberta in my early teenage years, I thank Dr. Ronald Gooding, Dr. John Spence and Gerald Hilchie; and from my entomology studies and summer student work I thank Dr. Lloyd Dosdall, Dr. Jan Volney, Greg Pohl and Dr. Dave Langor. Also, thanks to Charlie Bird, Chris Schmidt, Gary Anweiler, Felix Sperling, Ernest Mengerson, Rob Hughes and other members of the Alberta Lepidopterists Guild for their inspiration and for their continuing work on Alberta Lepidoptera. Thanks to Cal and Charity Dakin for their input and support. Lastly, thanks to my coworkers Toso Bozic and Martine Bolinger who have supported my interest in entomology.

–Doug Macaulay

The Publishers would like to acknowledge the assistance of Maria MacRae early in the project.

Illustration and Photo Credits

Illustrations: **Charity Briere** 24a, 54, 61, 62, 66, 69, 72, 77, 85, 88, 99, 100, 101, 105, 108, 122, 146, 181, 183b; **Frank Burman** 14, 15, 16, 17; **Ivan Droujinin** 21b, 24b, 49, 51, 52, 53, 56, 59, 60, 63, 64, 65, 67, 68, 70, 71, 75a, 75b, 76, 82, 83, 84, 86, 87, 92, 93, 94, 95, 97a, 103, 104, 106, 107, 110, 111, 125, 126, 127, 128, 129, 130, 132, 133, 136, 137, 143, 147, 150, 151, 152, 153, 154, 156, 157, 158, 161, 162, 163, 167, 173, 180, 188a, 188b, 189, 192, 204, 205; **George Penetrante** 131, 134, 148, 166, 168, 169, 170, 171, 172, 177, 179, 190, 200, 201; **Ian Sheldon** 1, 3, 21a, 25, 26, 34, 42, 43, 44, 45, 46, 47, 48, 50, 55, 57, 58, 73, 74, 78, 79, 80, 81, 89, 90, 91, 96, 97b, 98, 102, 109, 112, 113, 114, 115, 116a, 116b, 117a, 117b, 118, 119, 121, 124, 135, 138, 139, 140, 141, 142, 145, 155, 159, 160, 164, 174, 175a, 175b, 176, 182, 183a, 184, 185, 186, 193, 194, 195, 196, 197, 198, 199, 202, 203.

Photography: **Tamara Eder** 15a, 36a, 36b, 123a, 144; **JupiterImages Corporation** OFC, 12, 13, 41, 123b, 165; **Liz Klose** 39; **Doug Macaulay** 20b, 23, 29; **Heather Markham** 20a; **Tim Matheson** 15b, 18a, 31, 32, 47, 73, 74, 113, 120, 178, 187, 206; **Allison Penko** 35; **Laura Peters** 22, 40, 117, 149; **Robert Ritchie** 18b, **Gary Whyte** 191a, 191b.

Quick Reference Guide

Meadowhawks &
Dragonflies, p. 42

Mosaic Darners
p. 45

Spreadwings
p. 46

Bluets
p. 48

Grasshoppers
p. 49

Field Crickets
p. 50

Broad-winged Katydid
p. 51

Ambush Bug
p. 52

Damsel Bugs
p. 53

Plant Bugs
p. 54

Stink Bugs
p. 55

Spined Soldier Bug
p. 56

Lace Bugs
p. 57

Boxelder Bug
p. 58

Minute Pirate Bug
p. 59

Spined Assassin Bug
p. 60

Hairy Chinch Bug
p. 61

Aphids
p.62

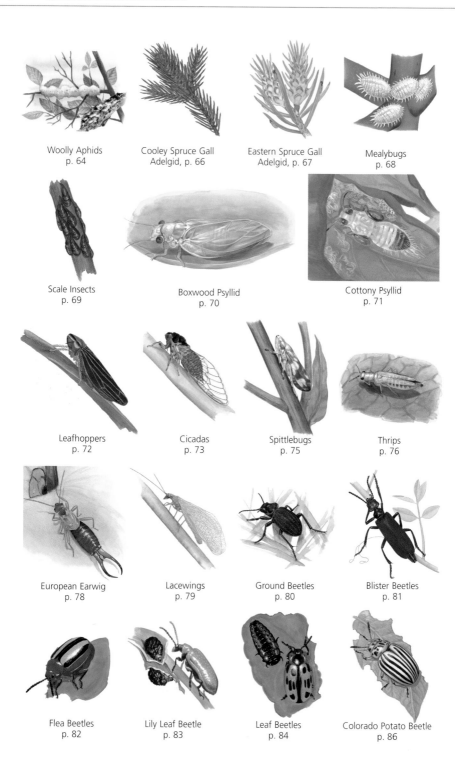

Woolly Aphids
p. 64

Cooley Spruce Gall
Adelgid, p. 66

Eastern Spruce Gall
Adelgid, p. 67

Mealybugs
p. 68

Scale Insects
p. 69

Boxwood Psyllid
p. 70

Cottony Psyllid
p. 71

Leafhoppers
p. 72

Cicadas
p. 73

Spittlebugs
p. 75

Thrips
p. 76

European Earwig
p. 78

Lacewings
p. 79

Ground Beetles
p. 80

Blister Beetles
p. 81

Flea Beetles
p. 82

Lily Leaf Beetle
p. 83

Leaf Beetles
p. 84

Colorado Potato Beetle
p. 86

Sap Beetles
p. 87

Carrion Beetles
p. 88

Click Beetles
p. 89

June Beetles
p. 90

European Chafer
p. 92

Aphodius Beetles
p. 93

Japanese Beetle
p. 94

Lady Beetles
p. 96

Multicoloured Asian
Lady Bird Beetle, p. 98

Bark Beetles
p. 99

Elm Bark Beetles
p.100

Eastern Ash Bark Beetle
p. 101

Strawberry Root Weevil
p. 102

White Pine Weevil
p. 103

Poplar & Willow Borer
p. 104

Rose Curculio
p. 105

Asian Long-horned
Beetle, p. 106

Poplar Borer
p. 107

White-spotted Sawyer
p. 108

Bronze Birch Borer
p. 110

Emerald Ash Borer
p. 111

Tiger Swallowtails
p. 112

Cabbage Butterfly
p. 114

Clouded Sulphur
p. 115

Spring Azures & Eastern
Tailed Blue, p. 116

Mourning Cloak
Butterfly, p. 118

Painted Lady
p. 119

White Admiral
p. 121

Monarch
p. 122

European Skipper
p. 124

Lilac Leaf Miner
p. 125

Peach Twig Borer
p. 126

Peach Tree Borer
p. 127

Raspberry Crown Borer
p. 128

Ash Borer
p. 129

Boxelder Twig Borer
p. 130

Aspen Twoleaf Tier &
Aspen Leafroller, p. 131

Northern Pitch Twig
Moth, p. 132

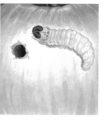

Codling Moth
p. 133

Uglynest Caterpillar
p. 134

Eastern Tent Caterpillar
p. 135

Common Plume Moth &
Many Plumed Moths, p. 137

Luna Moth
p. 138

Polyphemus Moth
p. 139

Twin-spotted Sphinx
p. 140

Snowberry Clearwing
p. 141

Garden Tiger Moth
p. 142

Gypsy Moth
p. 143

Underwing Moths
p. 145

Linden Looper
p. 146

Speckled Green
Fruitworm, p. 147

Armyworm Moth &
Army Cutworm, p. 148

Carpenterworms &
Carpentermoths, p. 150

Sod Webworms
p. 151

Root Maggots
p. 153

Crane Flies
p. 155

Fruit Flies
p. 156

Carrot Rust Fly
p. 157

Tachinid Flies
p. 158

Hover Flies
p. 159

Robber Flies
p. 160

Chokecherry Gall Midge
p. 161

Swede Midge
p. 162

Fungus Gnats & Shore
Flies, p. 163

Mosquitoes
p. 164

Webspinning Sawflies
p. 166

Dogwood Sawflies
p. 167

Willow Redgall Sawfly
p. 168

Raspberry Sawfly
p. 169

Imported Currantworm
p. 170

Birch Leaf Miners
p. 171

Pear Slug
p. 173

Ants
p. 174

Carpenter Ants
p. 176

Honey Bee
p. 177

Solitary Bees
p. 179

Bumble Bees
p. 181

Parasitoid Wasps
p. 182

Yellow Jackets
p. 184

Spruce Spider Mite
p. 188

Eriophyid Gall Mites
p. 189

Spider Mites
p. 190

Blacklegged Tick
p. 192

Crab Spiders
p. 193

Wolf Spiders
p. 194

Jumping Spiders
p. 195

Orbweavers
p. 196

Northern Black Widow
p. 197

Centipedes
p. 198

Millipedes
p. 199

Pseudoscorpions
p. 200

Springtails
p. 201

Harvestmen
p. 202

Sowbugs
p. 203

Gray Garden Slug
p. 204

Earthworms
p. 205

Lacewing

Introduction

No healthy garden is complete without a plethora of bugs—all bugs, including the beneficial, the beautiful, the nasty and the pesky. We even lose sleep as we plot the demise of most of the critters that haunt our minds and our gardens.

If we look closely enough for them and spend some time learning about them, bugs will delight us. Some bugs are like mini-superheroes in the garden, battling the evil pests. Yes, it can be difficult to overcome our fears of some of these little garden beasties, but many gardeners in Ontario realize that having a variety of bugs is good, and that biodiversity in the garden or on the farm is crucial to how well the plants do. It is just a matter of recognizing the good bugs from the bad and understanding the role each one plays. In this book, we hope to welcome you to the world of garden bugs and give you some tools to help you understand, recognize and appreciate them.

What Are Bugs?

The bugs covered in this book belong to three different phyla—the Annelida, the Mollusca and the Arthropoda. The creatures we call bugs—earthworms, slugs, insects and the like—lack backbones (vertebrae). To keep our entomology buddies happy, we should mention that some insects are known as true bugs, from the order Hemiptera, but for all you non-entomologists out there, we refer to "bugs" in this book generically.

Bugs rule the world. They outnumber all other life forms. Even if all the other described species were together in one group, that group would be a small fraction of the total species pie. Arthropods in particular dominate, occupying all areas of the globe—land, air and sea.

Without bugs we are doomed. They are important food sources for many animals such as fish, birds and small mammals. They are pollinators, responsible for the success of many of our crops. They are decomposers, building our soils and filling them with nutrients. Many are predators of pests that would otherwise eat us out of house and home.

Bugs are so successful because of a number of different abilities they have. They are extremely adaptable and have many morphological traits that help them survive most environments on our planet, including freezing temperatures and droughts. If one species can't handle an environment, you can be certain that another species can. Some have tough exoskeletons that behave like suits of armour and resist many conditions that other organisms cannot. Bugs can reproduce prolifically and go from being scarce to quite common in a matter of weeks. Just think of mosquitoes in spring—a few large females survive winter, and their offspring send us running for repellent a few weeks later. Some species are even parthenogenetic, meaning that they do not have to mate to reproduce.

The following sections describe the characteristics of annelids, molluscs and arthropods so we can get to know their strengths and weaknesses.

Phylum Annelida

The phylum Annelida has about 9000 known species and includes earthworms, leaches and polycheate worms. Most annelids are aquatic, but a few, such as the earthworm, are terrestrial. They like moist environments and have soft bodies.

The most noticeable thing about these critters is that they are segmented from one end to the other. This segmentation has made earthworms unique in that they can localize muscle movement with the segments, giving them the ability to move in all directions rather freely. The body wall of annelids is special as well—it has both circular and longitudinal muscles that give earthworms a wider range of motion than many other creatures. Just watch them crawl around—they are quite amazing. These animals maintain their body's rigidity by having a pressurized body cavity. Those of you who have held an earthworm know what I'm talking about; they are like little liquid-filled tubes. Their body is soft to the touch and can compress quite easily, unlike the other bugs covered in this book.

In the garden, a wrong decision could lead to a series of long-lasting consequences such as pest outbreaks, poor crop yields or sterile soil. Losing bug diversity is a bad thing, so when we look at pest management, we want to be sure we are dealing with the problem and not just the symptom.

Annelids have well-developed internal organs. Their digestive system is complete with a mouth, gut and anus. Respiration is through the skin, so they have no true respiratory organs. The circulatory system is closed, with a dorsal vessel and a ventral vessel connected by a series of vessels that pump blood into the dorsal head region. In the anterior, they also have a series of hearts that help circulate blood. The nervous system consists of a ventral nerve cord with a series of ganglia. In the head, concentrations of these ganglia form a small brain.

Reproduction in earthworms is simple: they contain both male and female sex organs. Nevertheless, they do mate with other worms and exchange genetic material. Overall, worms have some pretty neat features. Of the creatures covered in this book, they are the simplest of all the species, but the only phyla with a closed circulatory system.

Phylum Mollusca

The phylum Mollusca, with 50,000 described species worldwide, tends to be primarily aquatic: octopi, clams, snails, slugs and so on. Land-dwelling slugs and snails are in the class Gastropoda. Most have some kind of shell that they retract into when threatened. All are soft bodied and none have exoskeletons, unlike most other bugs in this book.

Gastropods use their muscular foot for creeping along. They are rather smart creatures and are likely the smartest invertebrates in this book. They have a well-developed nervous system, well-developed eyes and a large brain. The digestive system is simple, with a mouth, stomach, intestine and anus. They tend to be grazers and feed on detritus and plant material. The circulatory system is open, with the heart circulating blood into the body cavity. The respiratory system consists of gills that collect oxygen and release carbon dioxide, which is transported in the blood. These terrestrial species

Simple Anatomy of an Earthworm

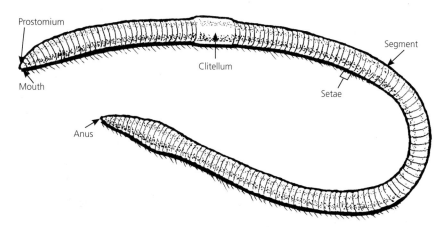

Prostomium

Segment

Clitellum

Mouth

Setae

Anus

Simple Anatomy of a Slug

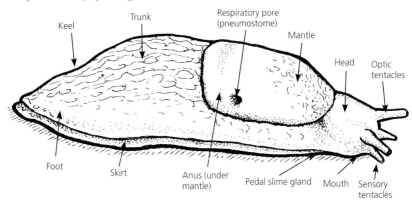

Keel — Trunk — Respiratory pore (pneumostome) — Mantle — Head — Optic tentacles

Foot — Skirt — Anus (under mantle) — Pedal slime gland — Mouth — Sensory tentacles

need to be wet, otherwise their system doesn't work—which is why they are most active on overcast days or at night.

Mollusc reproduction is similar to that of other bugs, with most species tending to be dioecious (either male or female), though our common garden slugs are monoecious (they have both sex organs). In many mollusc species, eggs are fertilized externally and are laid in a sheltered location.

Phylum Arthropoda

The phylum Arthropoda, which dominates the globe, includes insects, spiders, crabs and centipedes. Species in this phylum outnumber species in all other phyla combined. Arthropods

are major contributors to the suffering of humans—it is said that arthropods were responsible for most of the major plagues and famines recorded in history. Therefore, it is important that we learn about the arthropods we are likely to encounter in our gardens.

We cover four classes of arthropods in this book. The largest class is the insects, followed by the arachnids, millipedes and centipedes. The insects are the most successful of the classes and are the most diverse, with around one million described species. Arachnids are next, with around 60,000 known species. The millipedes follow with about 8000 species and the centipedes come in at about 2500 species.

Garden slug

Red Wiggler worms

Arthropods are the most successful phylum for a number of reasons. They are covered in a durable suit of armour made out of a protein matrix called chitin, which gives them an advantage over many other organisms. They are bilaterally symmetrical, so if you cut an arthropod in half from the head downward, you would end up with two virtually identical halves. Arthropod bodies are segmented as well as jointed, with a distinct head, thoracic and abdominal regions and jointed appendages. Most arthropods have ocelli or a series of eyes known as compound eyes; in many cases they have both. They also have a variety of other sensory organs they use to smell, taste, hear and touch their environment.

Their body cavity, or hemocoel, contains their muscles, innards and circulatory system. Arthropod blood is called hemolymph, and a heart circulates it throughout the hemocoel. Their gut or digestive system is complete, not open as is the circulatory system. A nervous system with a simple brain is connected to the central nerve ring, which is connected to the two ventral nerve cords. The respiratory system is unique—tracheal canals are found all over the body and in spiders are connected to the lungs, which are gill-like and known as book lungs.

The arthropod reproductive system is one of the most advantageous of all living things and is one of the reasons arthropods dominate. Some members of this phylum can be monoecious, and others are dioecious. Fertilization of eggs is mostly internal, and most species lay eggs, which develop by going through different growth stages.

Simple Anatomy of a Spider

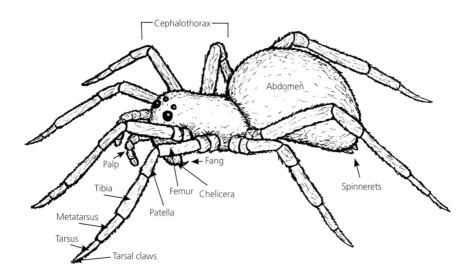

In higher insects such as butterflies and moths, the caterpillar transforms into a very different-looking adult. This transformation, which takes place in the pupa, is called complete metamorphosis. However, many other arthropods, such as grasshoppers, hatch already looking like miniature adults and go through a series of growth stages until they reach maturity. This type of development is known as incomplete metamorphosis.

The external body structure—the exoskeleton, often called the cuticle—is one of the strongest parts of an arthropod's body. It has three layers—a thin outer layer and two thicker inner layers—made up of chitin, which gives it strength. The outer layer is a hard, waxy armour. This layer is the strongest. It is what makes the insects rigid and gives them that crunching sound if they are stepped on. As

Some chemical companies have produced insecticides that disrupt moulting hormones. As well, a biological control called diatomaceous earth, made of sharp particles of fossilized algae, cuts up many arthropods' cuticles, creating wounds that are often fatal. Diatomaceous earth is recommended for species such as ants.

immature arthropods grow, they must shed this outer layer and form a new, larger one.

A hormone called ecdysone triggers the moulting process, during which a new outer layer forms underneath the old one, and moulting fluid is produced. This fluid digests part of the outer layer, which is then absorbed. Once this phase of moulting is complete, another hormone is released, and the outer layer cracks and is shed. At this time, the arthropod often swallows water or air to cause expansion that assists in

Simple Anatomy of an Insect

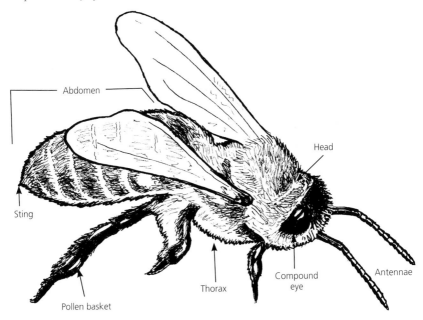

Caterpillar on roses

Beetles

the shedding. Under the old cuticle is a soft, new cuticle that will eventually expand and harden. Meanwhile, the bug is vulnerable to predators and the elements. Insects often wait until it is warm and sunny before they begin the moulting process—it is best not to moult during a rainstorm. Some organisms have many growth stages, called "instars," with the final stage being a transformation into a sexually mature adult.

Arthropods need oxygen to breathe. The main difference between arthropods and other animals is that the arthropods' respiratory system, known as the tracheal system, is completely separate from the circulatory system where oxygen is transported in the blood. Two types of tracheal systems occur: an open system, which is found in most terrestrial garden arthropods, and an enclosed system, which has gills

and is found in aquatic species. The open tracheal system is a series of canals that run from the outer cuticle into the inner system. The outer openings are called spiracles and can be observed using a microscope. These air-filled canals are branches that join larger canals and then split into smaller ones. Oxygen travels from the outer spiracle into the canals and then into the tiny branches that are attached to muscles and organs. Carbon dioxide produced in the muscles and organs is transported out through the canals and then the spiracles.

This open system has disadvantages, and predators or parasites of many insects use them to advantage. Creatures such as parasitic mites can get into the system through spiracles and can reduce the vigour of many susceptible insects—the tracheal mite, for example, has become a pest for beekeepers. Fungal spores can also penetrate these canals when conditions are right. Insecticides disrupt this system as well, and substances such as oils can coat the outer cuticle and block the spiracles.

Arthropods do have blood, but it is different than ours. Most arthropods have an open circulatory system, meaning the blood basically circulates freely around and among the organs. The blood of insects is responsible for transporting materials such as nutrients, hormones, wastes and a few other things. It does not carry oxygen to tissues as it does in other animals. The blood is clear, sometimes with a yellowish or greenish colour. It travels along the dorsal blood vessel located on the top of the body chamber. The vessel runs from the end of the abdomen to the head. The pulsating of the heart, which is the central region of the dorsal vessel, moves the blood by pushing and pulling it through the dorsal vessel. Blood is dumped into the head region and flows back through the body chamber toward the abdomen, where it is then sucked back into the dorsal vessel in the abdomen. Body muscle contraction also aids in the movement of blood through the body. The blood, or hemolymph, does have some blood cells. These vary in shape, size and function and make up about 10 percent of the blood volume. Many parasites of bugs live in the hemolymph, where they feed on tissues and nutrients. Sometimes the insect's immune system will build a cyst of blood cells around the unwelcome guest and may even be successful in killing it, but more often than not the parasite persists.

Eating is the favourite pastime of garden arthropods, so it is important that we understand their digestive system. As with most animals, insects have a mouth during at least one stage in their life, and this mouth varies in shape, size and function. The mouth region has appendages that help the insects grab, suck or chop up their food. Digestive juices are even pumped onto food in many instances to help soften things that would otherwise be too tough to swallow.

Once food is swallowed, it travels into three main sections of the bug before returning to the outer world. First it enters the foregut, then it goes to the midgut and finally the hindgut. The foregut's job is to grind, soften and macerate the food into smaller, more manageable particles. So, a particle of food enters the mouth, travels into the pharynx, and then goes into the esophagus. The pharynx is the chamber located immediately behind the mouth, and the esophagus is the canal that travels inward to the crop. Behind the crop is a chamber called the proventriculus, which contains a valve that separates the midgut from the foregut. This separation is important because the proventriculus acts like a gizzard and sometimes contains teeth that grind up the food more and prepare it for the

When using biological insecticides—and in fact for most biologicals that involve viruses and bacteria—such as Bacillus thuringiensis (B.t.) *in your garden, cover the bugs' food source thoroughly. It is more important to coat the foliage the insects are feeding on rather than the insects themselves. Note that the younger the insect's stage, the less food it needs to consume, and therefore the better this biological control is going to work.*

journey. The proventriculus valve opens periodically and releases food into the midgut. The midgut is like the stomach, where food is digested and bombarded with enzymes. After digestion, nutrients in the far reaches of the stomach are absorbed into the body. The digested food eventually travels along the stomach and into the hindgut, where it begins its journey outward. The intestine and the rectal region continue to extract valuable material, and the rectum sucks out more water. Finally, the solids are passed out the anus. With some species that eat food with a high water content, such as aphids, much of the liquid is excreted; for other species, water is much more valuable and most of it is retained.

For many bugs, the digestive system is their biggest weakness and is how they contract many diseases. Harmful bacteria, viruses and other deadly micro-organisms are gobbled up and enter the insect's mouth, then travel into the stomach where they become active and infect the insect. The year following a tent caterpillar outbreak, for example, the entire population crashes because viruses and bacteria have taken advantage of this digestive weakness.

One of the arthropods' best assets (and the reason they outnumber all other creatures on Earth combined) is their ability to reproduce. It all starts with the egg, but not always with a male and female. All arthropods produce an egg, and many species have both males and females.

Reproductive organs of garden arthropods often occur near the rear of their bodies, so when sexing these creatures, start by looking there. Males have a set of external claspers, whereas females often have an egg-laying ovipositor. This ovipositor can be quite elaborate and long, as it is in some parasitoid wasps. Once eggs are fertilized, they can be deposited in a mass or individually. In rare cases, the insects hold onto the fertilized eggs. For example, some parasitic tachinid flies hang on to the fertilized eggs until they hatch and then deposit live larvae onto hosts.

Snails can cause a lot of chewing damage to plants.

Primary pest (Lilac Leaf Miner damage)

Integrated Pest Management

Integrated Pest Management (IPM) is a method of dealing with pests. It is in widespread use in agriculture and horticulture. Its origins can be traced back to the dawn of agriculture, around 10,000 BCE. Many different definitions of IPM exist, but we will adopt the following definition from *Concepts in Integrated Pest Management* (Norris, et al., 2003):

> A decision support system for the selection and use of pest management tactics singly or harmoniously coordinated into a management strategy, based on a cost benefit analysis that takes into account the interests and impacts on producers, society and the environment.

IPM requires you to gather information and develop a plan with objectives. It requires knowledge of the ecology of the system and is informed or determined not just by profitability, but also by impacts on the environment and society.

Migrant pest (Painted Lady butterfly)

Occasional pest (Western Flower Thrips)

What is Ecology?

Ecology is the study of organisms, their relationships with each other and with their biotic and abiotic (nonliving) environments. You need to understand your plants, not just the pests. You also need to understand the interactions of the plant with the soil, sun, water and other plants. You must take a systems approach to understanding and managing the landscape. Nothing grows in isolation. All organisms, water, air and nutrients—everything in your yard—are connected, and action taken to affect one component will affect each of the others.

What is a Pest?

A pest is commonly defined as anything that is detrimental to or interferes with human activities and desires. Here, a pest is not restricted to the traditional definition, in which an organism affects yield; instead, nearly any organism that negatively affects humans is considered a pest.

For a pest to negatively affect humans, all four of the following conditions—known as the pest tetrahedron—must be met. First, the host plant or plant part has to be present for the insect to feed on; you do not have problems with leaf-feeding insects when there are no leaves. Second, the pest must be present.

Third, the weather conditions must be right; it cannot be too hot or too cold for either the pest or the plant. And fourth, it must be the right time of year. Some pests only feed in spring, whereas others do most of their damage in autumn. You must know what is required of the plant and the pest to diagnose a problem and address it in a timely and efficient manner.

Types of Pests

Not all pests are present year-round or every year. And not all pests are pests

Cabbage Root Maggots on radishes

all the time. There are *primary pests* that you can set your clock by; they come back every year and damage the same plants. Examples include aphids on nearly everything, Colorado Potato Beetles on potato plants and leaf miners on birch.

Insects that are present year in and year out but do not cause substantial damage are called *minor pests.* Many of the showy moths with large caterpillars are considered minor pests. For example, the Spurge Hawkmoth feeds on cushiony spurge. Such caterpillars rarely, if ever, cause significant harm to the landscape.

Some insects are a problem only if the conditions are right. These are potential or *secondary pests,* and they flare up if you plant their preferred host (e.g., hawthorn will be infested by the Apple Maggot). These secondary pests do not harm your primary crop or plant of interest—they sneak up on you from other hosts (in this case the crop or plant of interest is apple and the alternate host is hawthorn). Secondary pests might be waiting for you to change a growing practice to favour them. For example, the Yellow-headed Spruce Sawfly does not affect a white spruce in the middle of a forest, but when you plant just one white spruce, and it is the only tree around, exposed to full sun, then look out—the Yellow-headed Spruce Sawfly will feast on it. Sometimes the weather is ideal for some secondary pest outbreaks (e.g., grasshoppers thrive under drought conditions); otherwise, they lurk in the background, barely noticed.

Secondary pests happily munch away in your yard in relative obscurity. They are often out-competed by primary pests and do not reach the high numbers needed to do much damage or be immediately noticeable. But if the primary pest is eradicated or the secondary pest's community of natural enemies is eliminated by the use of pesticides, then the secondary pest can fill in the gap left by the primary pest or increase to primary pest status because of the lack of natural control.

Two other types of pests common in Ontario are the *migrant pest* and the *occasional pest*. An example of a migrant pest is the Painted Lady butterfly. This butterfly flies up from the southern United States in years of great abundance down there. Several generations may occur in Ontario, but all die out come winter. In years following a season when weather is favourable and food is abundant, a mass migration northward occurs, and it seems as though every other butterfly you see is a Painted Lady.

Occasional pests, including thrips and leafhoppers, are blown in with storms from as far south as Florida.

Types of Damage

A pest can affect a plant in many ways. In agriculture, reduction in yield is usually the main measure of damage by a pest. In home gardens, "yield" might be measured by visual appeal, enjoyment by your children or how many birds are attracted to your yard. If we know the types of damage that exist, we can learn what might have caused the damage. We can then assess the threat the insect poses to our plants and act accordingly. Damage can be characterized in the following ways.

Physical damage harms the plant, compromising structural integrity and allowing entry of pathogens.

Ants and aphids

An animal can be the prey of a predator. If you know a particular insect is prey, you may be able to introduce its predator to help manage its population. Predators are usually generalists, feeding on many different kinds of insects. For example, lady bird beetles will feed on aphids, thrips and spider mite eggs, scale insects and mealybugs, among others.

Wood-boring beetles can weaken branches and stems. Leaves shredded or holed by leaf beetles allow fungi and bacteria in. Roots chewed by weevil grubs expose the plant to invasion by fungi.

Cosmetic damage includes lesions, chewed holes or frass deposits, all of which reduce the aesthetic value of the plant without leading to its death.

Vectoring is when the pest transmits diseases such as phytoplasmas (bacteria-like organisms that infect plants) and viruses, bacteria or fungi. The most commonly known plant phytoplasma is aster yellows, notoriously transmitted by leafhoppers.

Direct contamination is when whole insects, body parts or cast exuviae

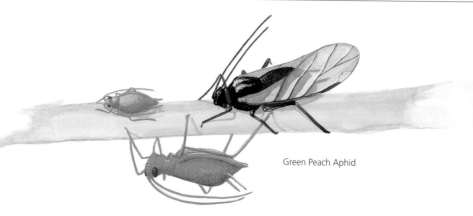

Green Peach Aphid

contaminate the plant, reducing its appeal. For example, lady beetles can spoil a fruit harvest, or black widow spiders can live in a grape cluster.

Economic damage includes the cost of management measures such as equipment and products applied to manage the pests (think of the cost of this book or a session at a horticultural show). Training in the correct use of pesticides is included here as well.

Eastern Tent Caterpillar larvae

Environmental and social costs broadly include groundwater contamination from excess pesticide run-off, or real or perceived harm to a neighbour from exposure to pesticide application.

In addition, insects and their relatives can cause damage, known as arthropod-specific damage which differs from disease or abiotic causes in the following ways:

Biting/Chewing/Boring: Plant material is removed, either in bite-size chunks or by skeletonizing the leaf.

Mining: A form of biting/chewing that takes place within a leaf.

Piercing/Sucking: Fluid is removed, or individual plant cells below the epidermis are digested and removed.

Protection of Other Insects: Some species of ants protect aphids while the aphids feed. The ants collect honeydew from the aphids in return for this protection.

Frass: In some cases (e.g., aphid honeydew) frass causes or contributes to the development of disease. More often, frass reduces the visual appeal of the plant without directly harming its health.

Ecological Roles

To appreciate the influence of pest and plant biology, we need to approach pest management from an ecological perspective. Ecology ranges from the individual to populations (a group made up of members of the same species), communities (assemblages of different species in a geographic area), ecosystems (community and abiotic factors), ecoregions (areas of similar ecosystems) and finally the biosphere we call Earth.

Basic principles or characteristics in ecology allow us to make informed decisions based on simple observations. Organisms can be classified into specific roles in the environment. If we can assign an arthropod to a role, then we will know something about it and how to deal with it. For example, a plant or arthropod can be a host—it is fed on or parasitized by other animals. A plant can be a host to a plant-eating insect. An insect can be a host to a parasitoid. Knowing a plant is host to a particular insect means you will have to manage for that insect.

Parasitoids are insects that kill their host. They are different from parasites, which benefit from their host without killing it. Parasitoids deposit eggs onto or in their host, and the resulting larva(e) devours the host from the inside out. In general, parasitoids are very host-specific, attacking one or just a few different species. If we know the pest in question is host to a parasitoid, we can use the parasitoid to control the pest.

Selectivity of Feeding

Insects exhibit a range of selectivity when it comes to food choice. An insect may have a very narrow range of acceptable food types. It may even feed on only one species of plant or animal. For example, the Monarch Butterfly feeds only on milkweed. An insect might have a moderate range of food preferences; e.g., the Cabbage Butterfly feeds on plants in the family Brassicaceae. Other insects have a wide range of acceptable foods. For example, during an outbreak, the Forest Tent Caterpillar will consume the leaves of nearly any woody plant.

Food Webs

If we look at the energy flows of organisms, we can see what is commonly called a food web. Note that we use the term food web instead of food chain. "Food chain" implies a linear relationship, but in nature, relationships are often much more complex. An insect may help us by preying on a pest but harm us by feeding on plant material in the absence of its prey. If we disrupt one

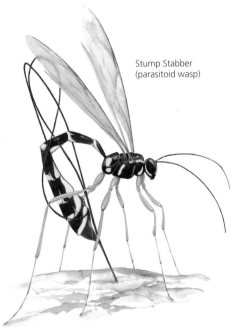

Stump Stabber
(parasitoid wasp)

part of the food web, say by removing a predator, we risk upsetting the equilibrium in our yard. We should recognize that weeds or other plants can serve as alternate hosts for pests and, therefore, should be managed to reduce pest numbers. We can exploit the food web by including plants in our yard that attract beneficial bugs. Parasitic wasps and predatory hover flies need nectar to fuel their flight. You can entice these beneficial bugs into your yard by planting many nectar-bearing flowers.

Why Some Bugs Are So Good at Being Pests

Being short-lived, producing large numbers of offspring and having poor competitive ability doesn't make some bugs better pests; rather, it means they do not like to reside in established ecosystems where they have to duke it out with many other species. Instead, most pests generally tend to exploit a recently disturbed site, such as the artificial landscape in a yard or garden, where there is likely to be few if any competitors. These organisms become pests because they get in fast and eat as much as they can until competitors arrive and push them away. Adults invest very little in their offspring, and the species relies on high numbers of offspring rather than quality of parental care to ensure its survival. The populations can build up rapidly, overwhelming the host plant and the suppressive action of natural enemies. For example, many weeds are well adapted to invading disturbed sites, and aphids and spider mites are well adapted to exploiting annual plants and disturbed sites.

Bugs with the opposite survival strategy are long-lived, have few offspring, are good competitors and prefer to live in stable environments. This strategy is characteristic of many predators. They require a reliable source of prey to be successful. Because they have a high-quality food source (i.e., other insects), they do not need to produce as many young to ensure survival of the species.

Cabbage Butterfly

IPM Decision-Making Process

Development of a sound Integrated Pest Management plan depends on several pieces of information that together are used to make a management decision. The following are the critical steps to take when making IPM decisions.

1. Pest Species Identification. Correctly identifying the pest to ecological role, feeding habit or order, family or genus level is the first priority. If the pest is not properly identified, information on biology and ecology will be incorrect and could lead to a damaging decision. For example, if you have a tree with wood-boring damage, you then know that the pest is likely a beetle or moth, that the immature stage is doing most of the damage and that the adult stage is the one that can be monitored outside of the tree. You have options on whether to treat the host, prevent the adult from attacking the host, or deal with the larva directly.

2. Understanding the Biology of the Pest and Host. You need to characterize, or put into context, what the pest is doing. What is the pest population size? Is it high enough to warrant action? Is the pest population increasing, steady or decreasing? Is there potential for future harm?

What about beneficial arthropods? Are they present? Are there enough to suppress the pest population without you taking action?

What is the status of the host plant? Is it stressed, diseased or in otherwise poor condition? A stressed plant is less able to compensate for insect damage or attack and is therefore more susceptible.

Lastly, you must consider the economics of the plants that need to be protected. Are they expensive, publicly displayed plants you can justify spending effort and money to protect? Or are they tucked away in a low-visibility area, which would allow for a higher tolerance for damage? It is a good idea to prioritize the areas of your yard by deciding which areas need immediate attention or management and which areas are fine just being green—a bit chewed up maybe, but still green.

3. Evaluate the Potential for Damage. Will this pest cause damage? Is the pest density greater than the economic or action threshold for that pest? The economic or action threshold (discussed in detail later) is the go/no-go point for taking action against a pest. If the pest is not an immediate or future threat, there may be no need to act. However, IPM is about being proactive, not just reactive. Although a pest population may be low, allowing it to increase may cause a much bigger problem in following years. Therefore, it might be prudent to manage the pest when you first notice it.

4. Evaluate Available Tactics. Determine which management methods will be best for this pest and situation. Consider cost (including labour), effectiveness and environmental impact. If one method is not satisfactory alone, consider combining two or more methods to achieve your goals.

5. Evaluate Possible Interactions. Is the pest the key pest? By suppressing this pest, will you free up other secondary pests to take its place? Will the tactic negatively affect other members of the ecosystem, such as beneficial arthropods or pollinators? This step is crucial to "Integrated" Pest Management.

6. Legality. Once you have chosen a tactic, make sure it conforms to regulations in your community. Many municipalities have pesticide bans.

7. Decide. If the pest population size does not warrant action, then you can decide to take no action at all. We should not live by the credo "see bug, kill bug." For example, a little pruning can make the plant stronger by stimulating it to grow more leaves or send out more shoots, or it can cause the plant to release defensive chemicals.

You can reduce pest vulnerability by changing some aspect of plant culture. For example, make sure the plant is well watered or fertilized, or spaced far enough away from other plants to encourage air flow.

You can reduce the pest population size directly by releasing biological control agents, spraying with an insecticide or hand picking the pest.

In most circumstances, you will likely choose a combination of options. IPM relies on integrating multiple tactics for the best effect and the least negative impact. When considering the economics of a plan, keep in mind that short-term loss may be acceptable to prevent total loss in the future or if multiple seasons are taken into account.

If steps 5 and 6 are omitted, problems often arise with insecticide resistance, resurgence of a pest, environmental contamination or illegal pesticide residues.

8. Measure Success. Make sure you evaluate whether a given tactic or method worked. Did it have a short-term or lasting effect? Were there side effects? Was it worth the time and effort? Knowing how well or poorly a tactic works feeds back into steps 4 and 5 so that you can make a better decision next time.

Monitoring or Scouting for Insects

How do we know there is a problem in the first place? How do we find the pest if there is a problem? We need to monitor the landscape to detect problems before or as they arise. Monitoring requires a sampling plan. There are two different pest-specific variables to be measured: pest stage present (egg, larva/nymph, pupa or adult) and pest density (how many insects there are in a given area).

What else is there to measure? To put pest stage and pest density into context, we also need to measure developmental events of the plant and pest. Phenology is defined as the sequence of growth and development of an organism over time. We can track phenology by observing plants and animals, or we can predict phenology by monitoring degree-days.

In cold-blooded animals such as arthropods, and in plants, outside temperatures regulate the rate of metabolism or physiology. There are lower and upper thresholds to development (too cold or too hot to grow or develop), and you can predict an organism's development rate based on heat units accumulated. A degree-day is defined as $°D = temp 1° (C or F)$ above the lower threshold for 24 hours, and is calculated using the following formula: $°D = ([Max + Min]/2) - T_{low}$, where Max is the daytime high temperature, Min is the overnight low temperature and T_{low} is the lower developmental temperature threshold for the organism in question.

You can use weather information from Environment Canada to calculate degree-days, but it is best to use data collected on-site using a dedicated weather monitoring station. If you do not know the lower developmental threshold for a pest, use the default value of 10° C.

With degree-days known, you can predict what life stages a pest and a plant are in or when to take action to manage a pest. Degree-day models have been developed for many agricultural pests. You can record degree-days beginning April 1 and see for yourself when various insects emerge. This way you track what goes on in your yard, and you will be prepared each year when a specific pest arrives.

How Many Are There?

To determine the population density, count the number of pests. There are two different counts that can be made: absolute and relative. An absolute count is a measure of pests per unit area (for example, the number of aphids per leaf or beetles per branch). A relative count is a measure of pests per sampling unit (for example, the number of thrips per sticky card).

Insects are usually distributed in the environment in clumps corresponding to their food source. Often, if you see one insect, you will see others nearby. Patches of insects are difficult to detect because there are often large gaps between patches. To overcome this obstacle, you can go through your yard in a systematic fashion, inspecting each plant individually. This inspection will take you a long time. Alternatively, you can sub-sample your yard by inspecting every fifth plant, or some similar fraction. Be sure to inspect a representative of each species of plant in your yard because different insects specialize in different plants.

Because many insects can fly, they can invade your yard from distant infestations. The following are some points to ponder regarding where you may find pests:

- a point-source infestation will look patchy in the early establishment stage
- arthropods are distributed differently on the edge of an area than they are in the centre (there are alternate food hosts near the edges and usually an increase in relative humidity and temperature at the centre of a group of plants)
- prevailing winds and windbreaks may affect how or where flying insects enter your yard or move around in it
- soil conditions can affect how well ground insects will spread in your yard or garden.

Pest density

Monitoring Methods

When deciding which of the monitoring methods you are going to use, ask yourself the following questions:

• Do you require actual numbers or just need to know presence/absence?
• What time were the samples taken? Are the insects of interest active at that time of day?
• What is the weather like (rainy, windy, cold, warm) and will it affect the activity level of the insects?
• What is the phenology of the plant and the pest? Was the damaging stage of the pest present at the time you did your sampling? Is the susceptible stage of the plant (flowers, fruit) present?
• Will surrounding plants act as a refuge for the pest or as a source of re-infestation?

There are four categories of monitoring methods: direct observation, damage evaluation, trapping and soil sampling.

In *direct observation*, you are looking for the pest itself, which is best accomplished by inspecting the plants.

With *damage evaluation*, you are looking for indirect evidence of the pest. You can look for stunted plants, mottled or yellowed leaves, curled leaves, necrotic spots, wilted plants, swollen or galled plant parts or other forms of physical injury. You may also observe a reduction in yield or in the number of blooms.

A less labour-intensive method is to use a trap to collect samples. *Trapping* works well to determine whether the pest is present but it is not always reliable for population numbers. Traps can be affected by wind, and they may be inaccurate because they catch pests in transit and not on the plant. Traps can come in many forms and can be passive or active. Passive traps do not attract the pest. Active traps have some form of attractant such as visual cues (colour or shape) and can be baited with host odours or pheromones. Active traps tend to reduce the amount of by-catch (unintended victims).

Lastly, you can *sample the soil* in a region, a method that is particularly useful when detecting overwintering populations or root-feeding pests.

Monitoring Methods

Method	Target
Visual inspection	Foliage feeders
Frass counting	Non-nest building caterpillars
Honeydew patch counts	Aphids, psyllids
Pheromone traps	Adult moths, bark beetles
Sticky traps	Psyllids, winged aphids, adult thrips
Double sticky tape	Crawler stage of scale insects
Foliage beating	Beetles, mites, thrips, plant bugs, leafhoppers
Burlap bands	Gypsy Moth larvae
Boards/refugia	Snails, weevil adults
Degree-day models	Indicator of when to begin monitoring

The mobility of a pest will affect how and when you monitor. How fast the pest disperses from an alternate host will determine how often you have to resample your yard to ensure you detect the pest at the earliest moment.

Knowing where the pest is likely to come from can help you determine where you should begin your sampling. Does a neighbouring area have the pest and could it serve as a source of infestation?

The timing of your sampling effort is important. When should you sample to be assured the pest is there to be captured? The frequency of your sampling will depend on how rapidly a pest population can change. You must sample for many-generation insects such as aphids far more often than single-generation insects such as white grubs or lygus bugs.

Record Keeping

It is important to maintain records of your monitoring. Records allow you to track trends in populations and determine if they are increasing or decreasing, and they let you see whether your management methods are working. Do you see a long-term upward or downward trend?

You should record the site of collection (where on the plant, where in the landscape); the number of pests in the sample and their life stage; the condition of the host plant; the weather, date and time; and whether any beneficial arthropods are present.

Paying attention to trends will allow you to predict future pest infestations so you can prepare accordingly. You should also keep an eye on what is going on in your neighbour's yard or around your block to be aware of what may enter your yard in the future.

Sticky pheremone traps are useful for monitoring insect populations.

Thresholds

Once you have determined pest identity, pest density and pest and plant phenology, you can make a pest management decision. When an insect causes little or no damage, the impact on the plant is usually low. If the pest causes low levels of cosmetic damage, the plant is considered to tolerate the pest. At slightly higher levels of attack, some plants exhibit "compensatory" behaviour—they increase growth or physiological activity to compensate for what was damaged or lost. Beyond this tolerance or compensation, we observe real damage and loss.

Lygus bug on cosmos flower

The necessity of defining acceptable levels of damage has led to the development of thresholds. The concept of low densities of pests resulting in low levels of damage is central to pest management. It is assumed that a few pests will cause only a little damage, and with increasing density comes increasing damage.

There are different kinds of thresholds. The most basic threshold is that of discovery. If you can detect the insect, at least you know that you have a situation that demands a decision be made. You may take an extreme position by choosing to act on this threshold because you cannot tolerate any damage at all. Often you and your plants can tolerate a wee bit of damage, and just because the pest is present is no cause for alarm. Recall that there are likely beneficial insects around to suppress the pest.

Another type of threshold is called the economic injury level. This threshold is the pest density at which you lose money because of damage caused by the pest. If you take action above this threshold, you may prevent or reduce further loss, but you will have lost more than if you had acted earlier.

The threshold most commonly used is called the economic or action threshold. At this threshold, you must take action to prevent the pest population from reaching the economic injury level. Although you are spending time, effort or money to treat the plants, if you act at this threshold, the cost of the treatment is much less than what you would lose if you did not act. This threshold is lower than the economic injury level because with any tactic you use, there will not be a 100 percent reduction in the pest, and it follows that injury will continue to occur after the management action is taken.

There are limitations to using thresholds. Environmental conditions may change threshold levels from year to year or region to region. For example, drought or wet years affect thresholds.

A strategy of pre-emptive release (releasing the predator or parasitoid before you detect the pest) is commonly used with biological control agents. When this strategy is used, there is usually no need of a threshold because you have already taken action.

Thresholds are of no use when there are no effective tactics available to treat or react to the pest. In this case, prevention is the only option. Thresholds are also of little value in cases where once the pest has reached a detectable stage, it is too late for action. For example, cyclamen mites are usually detected after the damage is done.

Tactics

There are several ways you can manage a pest. The tactics or methods to choose from fall under one of three categories:

• *Pest manipulation*—when you directly target the pest using prevention, pesticides, biological control, behavioural control or physical control.

• *Plant manipulation*—when you indirectly affect the pest by using cultural methods (agronomy) or by modifying host-plant resistance.

• *Environmental manipulation*— when you modify the environment to indirectly affect the pest. It can be on a micro scale (humidity within the canopy, plant thinning, etc.) or on a macro scale (shelterbelts).

Managing Beneficial Insects in the Landscape

A "natural enemy" is defined as any organism that directly suppresses another organism. For the purposes of this book, only beneficial organisms that affect pest species will be considered. A natural enemy can be a predator, parasitoid or disease. Natural enemies should not be ignored when developing an IPM plan because they can contribute significantly to pest management. In this book, we distinguish between natural enemies and biological control organisms. Biological control organisms are commercially produced for use in an IPM program; natural enemies are predators, parasitoids or pathogens that occur naturally in the environment. Natural enemies and commercially obtained biological control organisms can be considered synonymous depending on their use within an IPM program. For example, strategies such as conservation, augmentation and habitat diversity can be applied to enhance the effectiveness of natural enemies and commercial biological control organisms.

Natural enemies can be manipulated in several ways to enhance their impact. The principle method is through conservation of pre-existing natural enemies. Local populations can be increased through augmentation and by various physical and cultural practices.

1. Conservation is the practice of preserving pre-existing populations of natural enemies in a local area. The most effective method of conservation is to limit or eliminate the use of broad-spectrum chemical pesticides. Indiscriminate pesticide use will kill many of the pests; however, those that survive do so because they have a genetic resistance to the pesticide. These resistant survivors will reproduce, resulting in a pesticide-resistant pest population. Natural enemies usually do not have the same degree of chemical resistance as do their prey or hosts and are therefore more susceptible to pesticides. By spraying narrow-spectrum pesticides only when action thresholds have been surpassed and only in areas where absolutely necessary, you contribute to the conservation of natural enemies by limiting their direct exposure to pesticides and pesticide residues.

Another conservation strategy is to provide for the successful reproduction and overwintering of natural enemies.

Convergent Ladybug adult

Provide plants that offer shelter and nectar for adult feeding, and use mulches and hedgerows to provide overwintering sites.

2. Augmentation is the process of supplementing existing natural enemies with releases of wild-collected natural enemies. Augmentation can be achieved in two ways: inoculation or inundation. The practice of inoculation involves introducing natural enemies to an area where they were not originally present or were wiped out. The homeowner relies on the natural enemy to increase its population by reproducing on its own. The introduced natural enemy and its offspring help suppress the pest species. For example, when you clear your yard of old turf and later reseed it, you could collect predatory beetles and reintroduce them into the newly planted turf for control of white grubs and other pests.

Inundation is the practice of repeated introductions of a natural enemy with reliance on only the enemies released for pest suppression. There is no expectation that the introduced natural enemy will reproduce and increase its population. The season may not be long enough for the natural enemy to reproduce, or it may be incapable of surviving winter. You can purchase insects from suppliers, and this option may work for large acreages.

Augmentation may be required after natural enemies have been reduced or eliminated because of pesticide use. Most natural enemies have not been selected for resistance to pesticides. As a result, pest species' populations often explode after pesticide use because of the lack of natural controls. A common example of this phenomenon can be seen in spider mite outbreaks on fruit trees after pesticides are directed at the mites or other pests. The pesticides severely reduce predatory mite populations, allowing pest mite populations to increase. Another example is the loss of predatory rove beetles and ground beetles when a soil drench is used against white grubs.

3. Habitat diversity enhances pest management and adds to the beauty and longevity of the landscape. A uniform or large planting of only one or a few plant species is not ideal for recruiting or maintaining natural enemies. Planting several different species of vegetation provides for multiple hosts, nectar and pollen sources, and microhabitats for resting or overwintering. Use caution when selecting food or habitat plants to ensure the pest does not also feed on that plant. Keep an eye on which bugs are eating what and adjust your plants accordingly to achieve a landscape populated by "selective food plants." A complex canopy with many available layers, heights and textures will usually result in increased success in recruitment and overwintering of natural enemies.

In some instances, natural enemies can prey on alternate hosts, feeding on the secondary planting and then switching to the pest on the primary planting. This phenomenon is called using "banker" plants in biological control. It is an effective method for maintaining natural enemies in the absence of the primary pest. Natural enemies can be lured to a landscape, or the probability of their survival can be increased, by adding organic matter such as manure.

Habitat diversity must also be considered in the context of time. Choose plants that provide resources to natural enemies throughout the growing season. Pay particular attention to early-flowering plants to provide the bugs with a head start in spring.

4. Impact of Management Practices. The use of pesticides can kill off natural enemies. If you wipe out these enemies, the pest species may come back in much greater numbers—a phenomenon called resurgence. Timely and careful use of pesticides limits their impact on natural enemies. Opt for soft or narrow-spectrum pesticides

Beneficial bugs: ladybug (above), ladybug larvae (below)

5. Impact of Maintenance and Cultivar Selection. Many maintenance and cultural practices directly affect pest and natural enemy performance. Excessive fertilization promotes succulent growth, resulting in rapid pest build-up, which in turn may lead to pest species populations that are too large for the natural enemies to control. By setting the blades higher on your lawn mower, you will reduce pest problems by providing a refuge for natural enemies. Selecting resistant cultivars will help suppress disease and keep pests at levels with which natural enemies can cope.

Consider that almost any action taken will have an impact on the plant, its pests and their natural enemies. A good gardener observes what these impacts are and adjusts accordingly.

The garden and yard are every bit as complex and vibrant as any natural area. Protecting your yard and garden is a challenging but rewarding task. To best prevent, reduce or eliminate pests, an integrated management approach is warranted. The objective is to obtain a balanced and healthy landscape ecosystem that will ensure long-term plant health. You don't have to eliminate pests, but instead reduce stress of any sort to the plants and maintain individual pests at levels below an injurious or economic threshold. All sorts of pests are present at all times, whether in the soil, on the plant or in neighbouring areas; therefore, a program based on eradication is not sustainable and rarely, if ever, achievable. An IPM program can be used successfully to maintain a healthy ecosystem.

and apply at the lowest concentration recommended on the product instruction label.

Alternatives to pesticides, such as mechanical or physical practices, can also affect natural enemies. Traps, barriers, screens and other physical methods may reduce or inhibit natural enemies. The use of steam or other temperature-related management practices may reduce natural enemy populations. To offset some of these potential impacts, alter the time or duration of the practices to allow natural enemies to re-colonize or escape the threat. Alternatively, apply the measure when the target pest is most vulnerable and not when natural enemies are.

Pesticides

Synthetic pesticides are a relatively recent innovation in pest management. Inorganic chemicals such as sulphur and arsenicals have been used for centuries, but synthetic organic chemicals have only been used since the middle of the 20th century. Synthetic organic pesticides were quickly and widely adopted because of their ease of use and effectiveness in areas where there were no inorganic pesticides owing to worker safety or phytotoxic (harmful to plants) effects.

There are, arguably, some advantages to using pesticides. They come in handy when all else fails, but they need to be used sparingly and carefully. Pesticides really reduce the amount of effort required when compared to manual weeding. They provide rapid remedial action and typically do not require detailed knowledge of plant and pest biology. But most commonly, gardeners remark that pesticides provide a relatively predictable level of control.

There are three main types of pesticides: *inorganic, organic* and *biopesticides*. There may be some confusion surrounding organic and inorganic pesticides. Inorganic pesticides contain elements such as sulphur, arsenic or mercury. "Organic" is a term applied to any compound that is carbon-based. Therefore, many of the pesticides in use today, such as organophosphates, chlorinated hydrocarbons and carbamates, are organic. Organically certified pesticides, on the other hand, are of organic, inorganic or biological origin, have been evaluated by a regulatory body and are "certified" to meet the standards of that body.

Biopesticides are pesticides that are made up of or are derived from living organisms. Examples include living systems such as bacteria (*Bacillus thuringiensis* var. *kurstaki* [B.t.k.] for use against caterpillars), fungi (*Streptomyces griseoviridis* for protection of plant roots from root rot), nematodes (*Steinernema* spp. for use against white grubs in lawns), fermentation products (isolated proteins from *Bacillus thuringiensis* or *Saccharopolyspora spinosa*) and botanicals (pyrethrum from the petals of *Chrysanthemum coccineum*, rotenone from *Derris* spp. or neem from neem trees).

Regardless of whether a product is referred to or labelled as "conventional" or "organically certified," it is still a chemical. Use it according to the label instructions and only when absolutely necessary; improper use of pesticides can create pest problems such as resistance, resurgence or secondary pests.

There are many different kinds of insecticides, including compounds that attack the nervous, respiratory or digestive systems, disrupt chitin synthesis or development or cause physical damage to the surface wax layer or thin cuticle. The active ingredient (the chemical that is responsible for killing the insect), can be the same in many different brands of insecticide. Read the product label to help you decide which product to use to ensure insecticide resistance does not occur.

Prolonged use of the same active ingredient regardless of manufacturer or formulation (powder, spray) often results in the insect developing resistance to the product. When you

Active Ingredients and Modes of Action

Active Ingredient	Mode of Action	Notes
Traditional Synthetic Insecticides		
Organophosphate, e.g., malathion	Nerve poison, Ach (short for acetylcholinesterase) inhibitor	Mildly persistent, broad spectrum, toxic to vertebrates
Carbamate, e.g., carbaryl	Nerve poison, Ach inhibitor	Broad spectrum, not as toxic to vertebrates
Pyrethroids, e.g., deltamethrin	Nerve poison, sodium channel inhibitor	Low persistence, highly toxic to aquatic organisms
Organotins	Affects energy production	Specific for mites
Neonicotinoids, e.g., imidacloprid	Nerve poison, Ach inhibitor	More specific for insects therefore less toxicity to humans
Biological Insecticides – isolated from micro-organisms		
Bacillus thuringiensis	Stomach poison	Toxin derived from a soil bacteria, specific for caterpillars (B.t.k.) or flies (B.t.i.)
Spinosad	Nerve poison, Ach inhibitor	Derived from a soil fungus
Avermectin	Nerve poison, chloride channel activator	Derived from a soil bacteria
Growth/Development Regulators		
Chitin synthesis inhibitors	Block production of chitin	Slow acting, non-toxic to humans but toxic to other invertebrates (e.g., shellfish)
Insect Growth Regulator	Block action of developmental hormones, check for specific hormone blocked	Specific to insects
Botanicals – isolated from plant material		
Pyrethrum	Nerve poison, sodium channel modifier	Very short persistence
Rotenone	Affects energy production	From Derris and Lonchocarpus, highly toxic to fish
Nicotine	Nerve poison, Ach inhibitor	From tobacco, highly toxic to mammals
Limonene	Nerve poison, Ach inhibitor	From citrus, non-toxic to mammals
Azidiractin	Block action of developmental hormones	From neem, non-toxic to mammals
Oils and Others		
Mineral oil	Suffocation	Dormant oils can harm plants, summer oils less harmful to plants
Sulphur	Contact poison	Effective against mites
Boric acid	Contact poison	Do not allow contact with skin
Diatomaceous earth	Abrasive	Do not inhale
Potassium salts of fatty acids, e.g., insecticidal soap	Desiccation, strips surface wax off insect	Non-toxic to mammals, most effective on soft-bodied insects

spray an insecticide, it kills most of the insects that are susceptible to the poison. Insects that have a pre-existing mutation that allows them to survive the poison and live on to reproduce. This phenomenon results in a pest population with an increasing number of individuals that are no longer harmed by the poison, rendering the poison less and less effective. Eventually, you might just as well hit the insects with the insecticide container for all the harm it does to the resistant pests.

An insect is considered resistant to a pesticide if it has the ability to prevent entry of the chemical, can rapidly bind up or excrete the poison, or has changed the nature of the site of action of the poison such that the poison no longer has any effect. One strategy to avoid selecting for resistant members of a pest population is to rotate among insecticides that have different modes of action; that is, target different sites or systems in the insect. Be careful though—different active ingredients can have the same mode of action.

Chief among the disadvantages to pesticide use are what are called non-target effects. A responsible gardener will take great care in selecting the products he or she uses. How specific a pesticide is has a bearing on how damaging it can be to the environment. In general, the more specific the action of the product, the fewer non-target organisms will be affected. More discriminating pesticides, such as insect growth regulators, interfere with how an insect moults. These pesticides are specifically targeted to insects, although some other arthropods can also be affected. Some insecticides affect only a narrow range of insects. B.t.k., for example, only affects caterpillars.

Dill with sunflowers and others

Conversely, the less specific the product, the more collateral damage there is, with potentially toxic effects to the applicator or bystanders. If a product kills indiscriminately, there is the potential for toxic effects to humans—the weakness of many of the conventional insecticides is that they are nerve poisons; they affect insect and human alike. Toxicity to the user is a primary health concern. Residues on plants and vegetables can affect not only the applicator but also anyone who comes in contact with the product. The chemicals may move outside of your yard and into ground or surface water or into the air. They can also move up the food chain in a process called bioaccumulation. Pesticide residues may accumulate on food and ornamentals, posing a risk to you, your family and your pets. However, if used according to the label instructions, the risk of exposure to residues should be minimized.

An insecticide's effect on non-target organisms can have a huge impact on beneficial insects and other organisms, reducing their ability to suppress pest insects. The result may be a situation in which the pest resurges to a level much higher than it was before you applied the insecticide. In this case, you may be irrevocably tied to the pesticide treadmill, where no other option will suffice unless you are willing to allow the pest population to build up until it crashes and something resembling normality returns (i.e., natural enemies return to your yard and resume their role as guardians).

Your overall goal should be to limit or eliminate the use of pesticides. You should consider the use of insecticides as a last resort. Responsible use of pesticides (i.e., least toxic or most narrowly targeted compounds, applied only when and where the pest is doing damage and only when necessary) will result in less harm to the environment and you, and will also lead to the preservation of the community of natural enemies in your yard.

A Final Word

Overall, bugs are pretty amazing creatures. They have all sorts of adaptations that make them successful. If we learn to understand them, we can learn to appreciate them in our gardens. The more we know about bugs, the better we can prevent or manage outbreaks.

This book is a tool to help you identify bugs and understand them better. Learning about Integrated Pest Management will help you analyze potential pest problems so you can make the right decision for controlling pests or leaving them alone. The key is to create a place where bug diversity is high and balanced so that the opportunity for pest outbreaks is limited. A garden with a great diversity of insects is a wonderful and healthy place.

Garden Bug Directory

Meadowhawks & Whiteface Dragonflies

Sympetrum spp., *Leucorrhinia* spp.

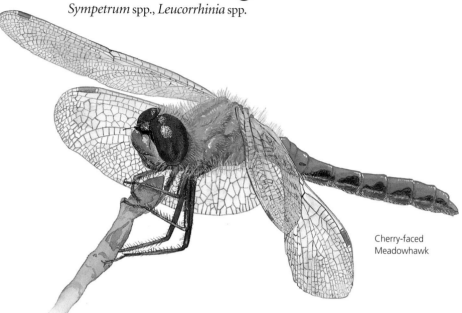

Cherry-faced
Meadowhawk

Meadowhawks and whitefaces are beautiful, beneficial predators of many smaller insects, especially pests such as mosquitoes. These small, bright red or yellow dragonflies are difficult to miss when they are perched on flowers or skimming over a flowerbed and are welcome additions to any garden. The two genera are easy to tell apart.

Whitefaces, as their name suggests, have white faces, whereas meadowhawks do not. Some common species found in Ontario include the Cherry-faced Meadowhawk *(S. internum)*, Variegated Meadowhawk *(S. corruptum)*, Saffron-winged Meadowhawk *(S. costiferum)*, Black Meadowhawk *(S. danae)*, Belted Whiteface *(L. proxima)* and Hudsonian Whiteface *(L. hudsonica)*.

ID: *Adult:* long, narrow body marked with red, black or yellow; wide, double wings. *Nymph:* brownish overall; large eyes; retractable mandible; looks alien-like but resembles wingless dragonfly with compressed abdomen; tiny, bud-like wings protrude slightly from thorax.

Size: *Adult:* 3–4 cm. *Nymph:* variable, but no larger than about 3 cm.

Habitat and Range: Sunny openings in gardens, often near ponds or slow streams, and woodlands.

Scouting: Look for adults perched in the garden or cruising for prey. Whitefaces are present in spring, whereas meadowhawks appear much later, in summer.

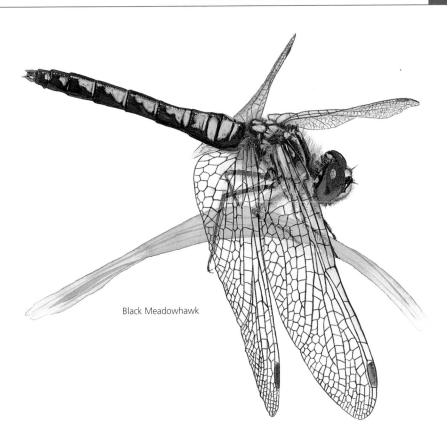
Black Meadowhawk

Dragonflies and damselflies undergo incomplete metamorphosis during their lifetime. Females lay eggs in the vegetation or soil around a pond. Female whitefaces often deposit eggs in floating mats of vegetation, while many meadowhawks drop or fling their eggs into emergent vegetation. Nymphs later hatch from these eggs and begin feeding on anything that is smaller than them. This includes free-swimming insects such as mosquito larvae, other dragonfly and damselfly nymphs and,

as the dragonfly nymphs get bigger, sometimes even tadpoles. The nymphs of all dragonflies and damselflies are aquatic and need wetlands to complete their life cycle.

The nymphs go through a number of moults, growing and changing a little with each one. This stage can last anywhere from several weeks to several years depending on the species of damselfly or dragonfly. Once nymphs mature, they climb out of the waterbody onto emergent

How to Attract: If you live close enough to a natural wetland, you may not have to do anything to attract dragonflies; otherwise you can build a dragonfly pond. They are about 6 m across and at least 60 cm deep in the centre, with shallow edges and a few flat rocks along the edge. Also, support the protection of riparian areas in your neighbourhood.

Meadowhawks & Whiteface Dragonflies (continued)

Hudsonian Whiteface

vegetation and begin a process called transformation, in which they turn into adults. The nymphs swallow air continuously and split the larval skin, slowly rising out of the shell, which is known as an exuviae. Once the nymphs are out, their new body hardens and their wings inflate.

These newly hatched individuals, also known as tenerals, feed until they are sexually mature. This is when adults are seen in gardens, especially away from wetlands. Sexually mature adults later return to the shorelines, patrolling for a mate. Males are often seen guarding their small territories when they are courting females. Mating pairs can be observed flying in tandem, though some species perch while mating. The males also stay nearby or, in some cases, remain connected to the females while the females lay their eggs. Adults live for only a few months.

Dragonflies have many predators. Eggs are attacked by foraging critters such as mice, birds and beetles, and are even parasitized by wasps. Birds and other dragonflies prey on adults, especially tenerals. It is also common to see adults with mites attached to their bodies. These red mites drink the dragonflies' blood.

One study revealed that on average, one adult female meadowhawk eats about 14% of its body weight each day, the equivalent of about 6 mosquitoes per day. An entire squadron can devour hundreds every day.

Mosaic Darners

Aeshna spp.

Variable Darner

One of the swiftest insects on the planet, dragonflies can reach cruise speeds of up to 34 kilometres per hour. These voracious predators eat any smaller insect, especially flies. Horseflies are often victims of darners. On cool mornings, darners can be seen basking on fences or tree trunks as they warm their muscles before their daily activities. Darners occasionally land on a chest or shoulder thinking it is a nice place to bask in the sun. Common species seen in our gardens include the Lake Darner *(A. eremita)*, Variable Darner *(A. iterrupta)*, Shadow Darner *(A. umbrosa)* and Rush Darner *(A. juncea)*.

Darners require wetlands to complete their life cycle but, unlike many other dragonflies, can travel far from water. Females use their ovipositor to insert their eggs into the vegetation or soil around a pond. In ponds without fish, *Aeshna* nymphs are at the top of the food chain, eating everything within reach. *Aeshna* nymphs and nymphs of the genus *Anax* have long, slender abdomens. Other genera's nymphs tend to be stouter.

ID: *Adult:* swift flier; long, narrow, blue or green patterned body; wide double wings; face has dark, T-shaped spot called a "T-spot." *Nymph:* brownish overall; large eyes; retractable mandible; looks alien-like, but resembles wingless dragonfly with compressed abdomen; tiny, bud-like wings protrude slightly from thorax.

Size: *Adult:* 7–8 cm. *Nymph:* variable, but no larger than about 5–6 cm.

Habitat and Range: Sunny openings in gardens throughout Ontario, often near ponds or slow streams.

Scouting: You may see darners cruising over gardens in search of prey or perched on fence posts, higher up on tree trunks or even on garage walls.

How to Attract: If you do not live near a natural wetland, consider constructing a dragonfly pond (see p. 43).

Spreadwings
Lestes spp.

Northern Spreadwing

The spreadwing is one of our most elegant damselflies and is often observed resting in garden vegetation. It can be easily separated from other garden damselflies by the position of its wings. When perched, it holds its wings half spread, hence its name. Unlike its bigger relatives, the dragonflies, this little guy hunts within the garden vegetation rather than patrolling for prey above the garden canopy. It is beneficial to gardeners because it preys on insect pests such as grasshopper nymphs and lygus bugs. The commonly observed species in Ontario are the Northern Spreadwing (*L. disjunctus*) and the Spotted Spreadwing (*L. congener*).

ID: *Adult:* dragonfly-like, with slender, delicate, blue or brown body; metallic emerald or bronze markings on thorax and along abdomen; 2 pairs of narrow wings, held half spread when resting. *Nymph:* slender; brownish overall; large eyes; retractable mandible; feather-like gills at end of abdomen; looks alien-like but resembles wingless damselfly with elongated abdomen; tiny, bud-like wings protrude slightly from thorax.

Size: *Adult:* approximately 4 cm. *Nymph:* variable, but no larger than about 4 cm.

Habitat and Range: Throughout Ontario, in gardens near wetlands.

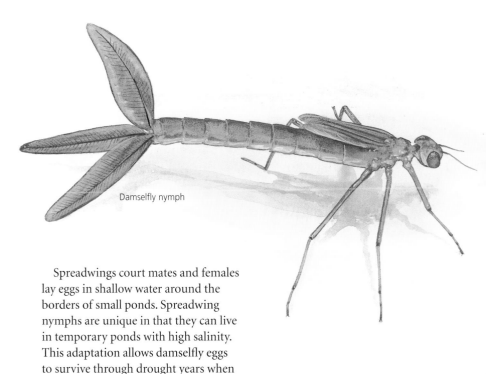

Damselfly nymph

Spreadwings court mates and females lay eggs in shallow water around the borders of small ponds. Spreadwing nymphs are unique in that they can live in temporary ponds with high salinity. This adaptation allows damselfly eggs to survive through drought years when these ponds are absent. When the water returns one or two years later, from either snowmelt or heavy rains, the eggs hatch. However, if these dried-up areas are cultivated or disturbed, the eggs are often killed, and spreadwing populations can be decimated. The protection of these riparian areas during droughts is vital to this species' survival.

Damselflies and other members of the order Odonata change body colour when it is cold. Although it is not known exactly why they do this, scientists suspect the darker colour absorbs more sunlight and makes them less visible to predators.

A favourite environment of spreadwings

Scouting: If your garden is by a wetland, you may find these damselflies among shoreline vegetation and in bordering garden plants. They especially like wet sedge meadows.

How to Attract: Avoid mowing, spraying or clearing the native sedges and cattails near bodies of water. If you do not have a wetland, you can construct one (see p. 43).

Bluets

Coenagrion spp., *Enallagma* spp.

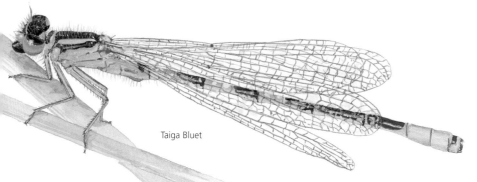

Taiga Bluet

If you see a slender, blue insect zipping through your garden, it is probably a bluet. This mighty hunter is often observed perched among the flowers, munching on little flies. The bluet is considered a typical damselfly; it perches with its wings held over its back. Some of our common species are the Taiga Bluet *(C. resolutum)*, Prairie Bluet *(C. angulatum)*, Boreal Bluet *(E. boreale)* and Northern Bluet *(E. cyathigerum)*.

The bluet inhabits areas bordering wetlands. It inserts its eggs into emergent plant tissue. Nymphs hatch within four weeks. Most Odonate nymphs have a retractable mandible (labium) they use to snatch prey.

Nymphs sit motionless and ambush prey. Damselfly nymphs can be easily separated from dragonfly nymphs because they have external feather-like gills at the end of their abdomens. The nymphs swim differently than dragonfly nymphs, basically wiggling their bodies and using the gills to propel them through the water. Nymphs often complete their transformation around the same time.

Damselflies and other Odonates don't produce their own body heat and therefore need sunlight to fly—that's why we don't see them on cloudy and cooler days.

ID: *Adult:* dragonfly-like with slender, delicate, blue body and black markings on thorax and abdomen; 2 pairs of narrow wings, held over back when resting. *Nymph:* slender; brownish overall; large eyes; retractable mandible; feather-like gills at end of abdomen; looks alien-like but resembles wingless damselfly with elongated abdomen; tiny, bud-like wings protrude slightly from thorax.

Size: *Adult:* approximately 3.5 cm. *Nymph:* variable, but no larger than about 4 cm.

Habitat and Range: Along shorelines of wetlands across southern Ontario.

Scouting: Look in the vegetation along shorelines and among plants in gardens that border wetlands.

How to Attract: Avoid mowing, spraying or clearing the bordering native sedges and cattails near a body of water. If you do not have a wetland, you can construct one (see p. 43).

Grasshoppers

Camnula pellucida, Melanoplus spp.

Migratory Grasshopper

All grasshoppers chew plant material and are capable of stripping plants bare. Common Ontario grasshoppers include the Clear-winged Grasshopper *(C. pellucida)*, which is mainly a grass feeder, preferring Kentucky bluegrass; the Two-striped Grasshopper *(M. bivittatus)*, which feeds on grasses and broad-leaved plants including trees and shrubs; and Packard's Grasshopper *(M. packardii)*, which prefers herbs over grasses. The Migratory Grasshopper *(M. sanguinipes)* is one of our most successful species and is found throughout Ontario. It favours weedy fields, cropland, pastures and gardens— basically anywhere that has grass and weeds growing together.

Grasshoppers produce one generation per year. The eggs are laid in the soil beginning in late July and continuing into autumn. They overwinter in the soil and hatch from late April to late June. Hatching is correlated with soil temperature and occurs after the soil containing the eggs accumulates 200 hours of 15° to 16° C temperatures. The young progress through five to six nymphal instars in 35 to 55 days (depending on species and temperature) before becoming adults. They are capable of dispersing great distances, even up to 1000 kilometres!

A grasshopper's ears are on its hips— specifically, on the side of the abdomen behind the back legs.

ID: *Adult:* dark brown to green or light yellow overall; biting/chewing mouthparts; enlarged hind legs adapted for jumping. *Nymph:* miniature representative of adult but lacks developed wings.

Size: *Adult:* up to 4 cm. *Nymph:* 5 mm to 4 cm.

Habitat and Range: Found throughout Ontario in grasses, pastures and crop fields.

Scouting: Grasshopper populations increase through spring and peak in July and August, declining until the killing frosts of autumn. They are particularly abundant in dry years.

Cultural/Physical Control: Drenching early season rains during egg hatch damage grasshopper populations most. Turn over soil in autumn to expose deeply buried eggs.

Biological Control: Beetles, small mammals and birds prey on grasshoppers, and velvet mites, ground beetles, rove beetles, bee flies and immature blister beetles eat grasshopper eggs. Nymphs are susceptible to parasitism by a tachinid fly and to several natural fungal diseases.

Field Crickets

Gryllus spp.

Spring Field Cricket

The Spring Field Cricket *(G. veletis)* and the Fall Field Cricket *(G. pennsylvanicus)* can occasionally become problems in the garden, feeding on a variety of plants including tomato foliage and fruit. Feeding is restricted to nighttime; field crickets seek shelter under vegetation and debris during the day. They may move in from weedy areas in August and September and occasionally enter houses to feed on natural fibres such as cotton or wool and synthetics.

Field crickets produce one generation per year. The eggs are laid in damp soil in autumn, where they overwinter and hatch in May. The nymphs mature through July and August, moulting eight or nine times.

Field crickets are considered to be "right-handed" because they fold their right wing on top of the left wing.

ID: *Adult:* predominantly shiny black, but may have brown at wing base; antennae as long or longer than body; 2 sensory appendages (cerci) arise from posterior abdomen; female has long ovipositor. *Nymph:* identical to adult, only smaller and without wings.

Size: *Adult:* 2 cm. *Nymph:* 0.5–2 cm.

Habitat and Range: Throughout most of Ontario in wild grassy or weedy areas.

Scouting: Field crickets are nocturnal, so catching sight of these elusive creatures is difficult. Listen for the males' mating calls as they chirp by rubbing their forewings together.

Cultural/Physical Control: Field crickets are beneficial because they feed on grasshopper eggs and moth and fly pupae. However, should you want to control their populations, remove debris they can hide under during the day. To prevent them from entering your house, ensure weather stripping under doors and screens on windows are intact.

Biological Control: A variety of predators prey on crickets, including many species of birds.

Broad-winged Katydid

Microcentrum rhombifolium

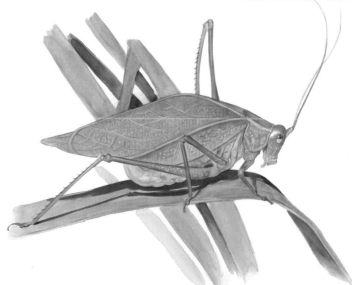

Katydids belong to a group known as long-horned grasshoppers. They are generally flattened sideways like grasshoppers and have very long antennae like crickets. Although well camouflaged and not often seen, the Broad-winged Katydid is often heard calling in the evenings. The adults and nymphs feed on the lower foliage of trees and shrubs, rarely causing any noticeable damage.

Katydids produce one generation per year. The distinctive, flattened, greyish brown eggs are laid in a row along the leaf margin or inserted into the edge of the leaf in late spring or early summer. The nymphs mature during July and August.

In the southern United States, katydids often defoliate young trees and feed on citrus, causing large, smooth, sunken spots on developing fruit.

ID: *Adult:* bright green; biting/chewing mouthparts; long, thin jumping hind legs; widely separated, long antennae; wings are longer than body. *Nymph:* resembles adult, but lacks developed wings.

Size: *Adult:* up to 6 cm. *Nymph:* 5 mm and larger.

Habitat and Range: Throughout Ontario around low-foliage trees and shrubs.

Scouting: Katydid populations increase throughout spring and peak in July and August, declining until the killing frosts of autumn.

Cultural/Physical Control: Control is rarely needed because damage is usually minimal; hand pick katydids and the leaves housing eggs to reduce numbers.

Biological Control: Beetles, small mammals and birds prey on katydids, and velvet mites, ground beetles, rove beetles, bee flies and immature blister beetles eat katydid eggs. Nymphs are susceptible to several natural fungal diseases.

Ambush Bug

Phymata pennsylvanica

These small bugs are ferocious hunters. They lie in wait in the flowers of weeds and garden vegetation for passing insects, which they grasp with their large, pincer-like front legs. They pierce their prey with their mouthparts, injecting a fluid that paralyses it and liquefies its insides, then they suck out the contents. Although they prey on some insect pests, they can do harm by consuming pollinators such as honey bees, bumblebees, butterflies, flies and wasps. Beekeepers consider them a damaging pest.

Ambush Bugs are true bugs, members of the family Phymatidae. Adults are often seen feeding and mating in late summer and early autumn, especially on goldenrod, daisies or sunflowers. Eggs overwinter and hatch in early spring. Nymphs go through five instars and hunt and feed like the adults. There is one generation per year.

ID: *Adult:* flat body; large, pincer-like front legs; triangular-shaped abdomen with wide, yellowish flare on either side; brown markings on head, thoracic shield and abdomen. *Nymph:* oval, almost triangular abdomen; pale to yellowish green.

Size: *Adult:* 10–12 mm. *Nymph:* 1–6 mm.

Habitat and Range: Gardens, meadows and weedy areas throughout southern Ontario.

Scouting: Look for adults in flowers in late summer and early autumn. They are well camouflaged and lie quite still, so they can be hard to spot unless they are feeding on prey.

Cultural/Physical Control: Controls are not usually necessary in a garden or landscape unless populations are very high. If there is one flower they really go for, consider growing something else to reduce the impact on pollinating bees.

Biological Control: Sometimes eaten by birds, rodents, praying mantids, spiders and even other assassin and ambush bugs.

Damsel Bugs

Nabicula spp., *Nabis* spp.

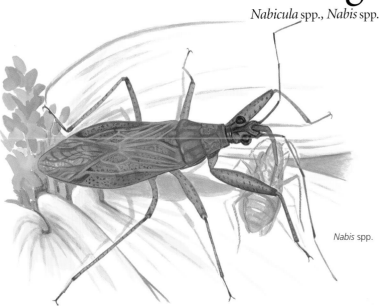

Nabis spp.

Damsel bugs are beneficial predators of small insects. The most common damsel bugs found in Ontario are in the genera *Nabis* and *Nabicula*.

Adult damsel bugs overwinter in leaf litter or anywhere they can find protection from the elements. In spring, they emerge to mate and lay eggs in plant tissue. There are five nymphal instars lasting approximately 8 to 12 days each. There is usually only one generation per year with peak abundance later in summer, around July and August. Damsel bugs are among the last predators to colonize pest infestations; however, there is good evidence to suggest that these beneficial bugs have a major impact on aphids and other crop pests.

Primarily predators, damsel bugs will feed on plant tissue if no other food source is available, though the damage is negligible. If they are really starved, they will feed on each other!

ID: *Adult:* has raptorial forelegs adapted to grasping prey. *Nabis* spp.: slender, elongate, light brown to yellowish bug with protruding eyes. *Nabicula* spp.: shiny black body is more bulbous toward rear than *Nabis* spp., and wings are smaller. *Nymph:* resembles adult but lacks wings.

Size: *Adult:* 5–11 mm. *Nymph:* 3–7 mm.

Habitat and Range: Widespread throughout Ontario; common in field crops, orchards, urban landscapes and gardens.

Scouting: You can often find these bugs in the lawn or garden and actively stalking prey in shrubs and trees.

How to Attract: These bugs are beneficial generalist predators that feed on Meadow Spittlebugs, Tarnished Plant Bugs, leaf beetle eggs and larvae, caterpillar eggs and larvae, leafhoppers, aphids, spider mites and sawflies. Reduce or eliminate the use of insecticides to protect these insects, and maintain diverse plants to encourage them to colonize your garden.

Plant Bugs

Lygus spp., *Tropidosteptes amoenus*

Tarnished Plant Bug

The Tarnished Plant Bug is an introduced pest from eastern Europe. There is a research program currently underway in Canada to introduce parasitoids to help suppress this pest.

Plant bugs pierce and suck plant fluids from leaves, fruit and stems. Common Ontario plant bugs include the Tarnished Plant Bug *(L. lineolaris)* and the Ash Plant Bug *(T. amoenus)*. There are many other plant bugs, but these two are the most often encountered and the most damaging.

Tarnished Plant Bugs overwinter as adults in leaf litter and other protected habitats. The adults emerge in spring to feed on weeds, mate and then move into crops and emerging garden plants. Once in the new food, the females lay their eggs into plant tissue. There are five nymphal instars that develop over the course of the summer, with adults active in August. There is only one generation per year.

Ash Plant Bugs overwinter as eggs inserted into the bark of ash trees in autumn. In spring, the eggs hatch and the five nymphal instars feed on the undersides of emerging leaves. A second generation appears in July, with adults active from late summer until the first killing frost in autumn.

ID: *Adult: Tarnished Plant Bug:* bronze overall with white triangle just behind pronotum or shoulders. *Ash Plant Bug:* similar in size and shape but tan overall. *Nymph:* wingless early on and has developing wingbuds in later instars; moves very rapidly. *Tarnished* and *Ash plant bugs:* more greenish overall.

Size: *Adult:* 3–5 mm. *Nymph:* 1–3 mm.

Habitat and Range: *Tarnished Plant Bug:* found everywhere on trees, shrubs, flowers and vegetables. *Ash Plant Bug:* predominantly on green ash.

Scouting: Common symptoms of Tarnished Plant Bug feeding include yellowing of leaves and "cat-facing" in strawberries. Ash plant bug feeding causes leaves to turn yellow or appear mottled or burned (much like leafhopper burn), and in extreme cases, there may be premature leaf drop.

Cultural/Physical Control: Remove weeds early in the season to deprive Tarnished Plant Bugs of food. Use repeated applications of strong jets of water to remove Ash Plant Bugs.

Biological Control: Many generalist predators attack plant bugs. Maintain a diverse landscape to conserve and possibly attract beneficial insects to suppress plant bugs.

Stink Bugs

Acrosternum hilare, Elasmucha lateralis

The Green Stink Bug *(A. hilare)* is common on leaves, fruit and flowers of trees and shrubs across Ontario. The Parent Bug *(E. lateralis)* feeds mainly on birch and willow.

Stink bugs overwinter as adults in sheltered areas, emerging in spring to lay barrel-shaped eggs in neat rows on the underside of leaves of weeds, trees and shrubs. Adult female stink bugs tend to their eggs until the eggs hatch, ensuring maximal survival of their broods. The nymphs typically feed on weeds during their five nymphal instars before moving on to feed on leaves of shrubs and trees as adults. There is only one generation of stink bugs per year in Ontario.

Stink bugs are aptly named; they really do stink! They have glands on their underside that secrete a foul liquid to discourage predators.

Green Stink Bug

ID: *Adult: Green Stink Bug:* green with broad shoulders; large, triangular scutellum. *Parent Bug:* yellowish brown body. *Nymph: Green Stink Bug:* lightly coloured with black markings, becoming increasingly green in later instars. *Parent Bug:* newly emerged nymph is bright red, becoming increasingly green in later instars.

Size: *Adult:* 8–12 mm. *Nymph:* 3–8 mm.

Habitat and Range: Prefers wooded areas and treed landscapes across Ontario.

Scouting: Piercing/sucking causes yellowing or mottling of leaves, sometimes resulting in uneven bumpiness. Fruit and flower buds are also attacked. Tomatoes can look like they were stabbed, with a dark pinprick surrounded by a yellow or light green halo.

Cultural/Physical Control: High population densities are rare. Keep plants healthy and eliminate weeds to reduce their impact. Dislodge adults from trees with pressure sprays of water.

Biological Control: Generalist predators, including birds, feed on the nymphs and adults. Parasitoids attack stink bug eggs. Look for infested eggs, which tend to be black instead of green.

Spined Soldier Bug

Podisus maculiventris

The Spined Soldier Bug is a predatory stink bug that preys on Colorado Potato Beetles, hornworms, Cabbage Loopers, webworms and any other garden and crop pests. It subdues large prey by impaling them with its piercing, sucking mouthparts.

The Spined Soldier Bug lays several hundred cream-coloured, barrel-shaped eggs in clusters. Nymphs begin to feed four to five days after hatching and continue to attack prey as they mature over the next 30 days. Adults live for two to three months. There are probably two or three generations per year.

In one season, an individual Spined Soldier Bug can consume more than 100 late instar armyworm larvae.

ID: *Adult:* brownish overall; pointed shoulders. *Nymph:* Resembles adult, only smaller.

Size: *Adult:* 10–11 mm. *Nymph:* 5–10 mm.

Habitat and Range: Throughout Ontario in gardens and crops.

Scouting: Spined Soldier Bugs do not usually exist naturally in high numbers. They may be found hunting for prey on their favourite crops such as onions, sweet corn, tomatoes, potatoes, and beans.

How to Attract: Spined Soldier Bugs may be purchased and released into gardens. Also, there is a commercially available pheromone that can be used to attract them to the garden. Spined Soldier Bugs are very susceptible to some insecticides and are in fact more vulnerable to them than most of their prey.

Lace Bugs

Corythucha spp., *Stephanitis* spp.

Lace bugs are so called because of their broad, lacey wing covers. Ontario has several species of lace bug, but some of the most common are the Rhododendron Lace Bug *(S. rhododendri)* and Azalea Lace Bug *(S. pyrioides)*, both of which feed on rhododendron and azalea. Several *Corythucha* species feed on a wide range of broadleaf trees and woody ornamentals including sycamore, chokecherry, alder, poplar, birch and willow.

Lace bugs are members of the family Tingidae. Like all true bugs, they have sucking mouthparts. Adults and nymphs puncture the underside of leaves and suck out plant juice. These feeding wounds appear as numerous light-coloured flecks on the upper leaf surface. The damage is generally cosmetic, but high populations can cause leaves to dry, curl, yellow and drop. Severe infestations over a few years can lead to decline of shrubs and trees.

Lace bugs that attack evergreen broadleaf shrubs overwinter as eggs on leaves. Lace bugs that attack deciduous trees overwinter as adults under the bark. Most female lace bugs insert their eggs along a leaf vein and seal the hole

Corythucha spp.

with shiny, dark excrement. Eggs hatch in April or May, and the nymphs go through five instars. Adult populations generally peak in July. Most lace bugs have two generations per year.

ID: *Adult:* flat body with lace-like wing covers. *Nymph:* spiny, black or dark-coloured body; often feeds in groups.

Size: *Adult:* 3–3.5 mm. *Nymph:* 1–2 mm.

Habitat and Range: Usually found on the underside of tree and shrub leaves, flowers and weeds.

Scouting: The first signs of lace bugs are usually numerous small, white or yellow flecks on leaves. Look for cast skins and dark, shiny, varnish-like excrement on the underside of the leaves, especially along the veins. Look for adults and nymphs on the underside of

leaves from April to early September. On evergreen hosts, leaf feeding is often apparent on older leaves long after the bugs are gone.

Cultural/Physical Control: Hose nymphs off leaves with a strong jet of water in spring.

Biological Control: Lacewings, predatory mites and bugs attack lace bugs, but not usually in large enough numbers to prevent damage. Insecticidal soap will kill lace bugs if sprayed on the underside of leaves where they will come into contact with it, and it is not damaging to beneficial predators and parasites. More than 1 application is usually needed.

Boxelder Bug

Boisea trivittatus

The Boxelder Bug is a piercing/sucking bug that causes lesions to leaves and seeds of box elder (also known as Manitoba maple). The Boxelder Bug is also known as the Eastern Boxelder Bug, not to be confused with the Western Boxelder Bug (*B. rubrolineata*), which is not found in Ontario. The Boxelder Bug overwinters as an adult, often aggregating in the tens and hundreds in houses—some people dislike this insect because of this unnerving habit. Normally, adults overwinter in a sheltered area outside, emerging in spring, when the female lays her eggs in leaves of the Manitoba maple. The nymph undergoes five instars, feeding on the underside of leaves and on developing seeds. The adult is present from July onward. There is only one generation per year.

Although related to plant bugs and stink bugs, this species does not have any scent glands and therefore does not use an offensive odour as a defensive mechanism.

ID: *Adult:* predominantly black with red outlining pronotum and basal half of wings. *Nymph:* bright red with increasing amounts of black in later instars.

Size: *Adult:* 8–12 mm. *Nymph:* 3–8 mm.

Habitat and Range: Across Ontario on Manitoba maple.

Scouting: Look for nymphs and adults on the underside of leaves or on seeds. Adults often bask in sunny areas such as south-facing walls and fences.

Cultural/Physical Control: Damage is negligible but you can use a jet of water to flush these bugs from their reverie. If large numbers are entering your home, seal gaps and holes, weather stripping and any place utilities enter through the outer wall.

Biological Control: Many generalist predators attack Boxelder Bugs.

Minute Pirate Bug

Anthocoris spp., *Orius tristicolor*

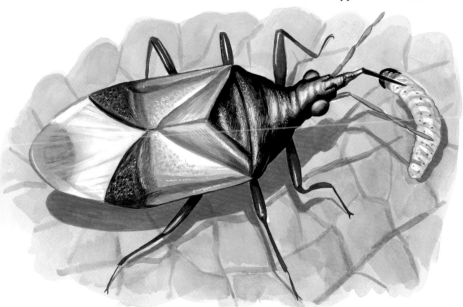

The Minute Pirate Bugs' family name, Anthocoridae, means "flower bug." These generalist predators have piercing/sucking mouthparts, but unlike damsel bugs, they do not have raptorial forelegs for grasping their prey. The most common pirate bugs in Ontario belong in the genus *Orius.*

Adults overwinter in leaf litter. They are among the earliest of the predators to emerge in spring. Eggs are laid in plant material but do not cause any lasting harm. Nymphs go through five instars in approximately 20 days under warm conditions. There can be as many as four generations in a season.

The Insidious Flower Bug (O. insidiosus) and the Minute Pirate Bug (O. tristicolor) are available commercially for thrips and spider mite control in greenhouse crops.

ID: *Adult:* predominantly black; moderately elongate with white markings at base and tips of wings. *Nymph:* reddish brown to yellowish; has more bulbous abdomen than adult, making it pear shaped.

Size: *Adult:* 2–5 mm. *Nymph:* 1–2 mm.

Habitat and Range: Widespread across Ontario in grasses, flowers, vegetables, trees and shrubs.

Scouting: In early spring, pirate bugs are abundant in weeds and early emerging plants.

They venture into your garden as the season progresses. In the absence of any prey, pirate bugs feed on foliage and pollen but are not considered a problem.

How to Attract: These little fellows feed on spider mite eggs, nymphs and adults, aphids, leaf beetle eggs, thrips, psyllids and caterpillar eggs and early instars, so do what you can to diversify the flowers available throughout the season.

Spined Assassin Bug

Sinea diadema

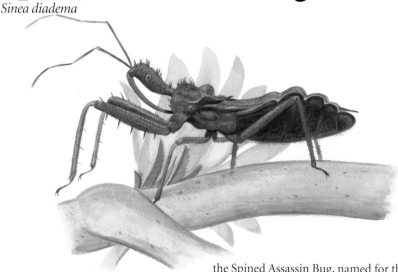

Assassin bugs are elongate in form and have a large snout that holds the stylet mouthparts. Most assassin bugs, like true predators, move slowly through trees, shrubs and flowers looking for prey, which they attack with lightning speed, often taking down prey several times their own size. Adults and larvae feed on over 50 types of prey, mostly larvae of beetles and moths. Assassin bugs are sometimes found inside houses, and several species can inflict a painful bite. Some are predators of bed bugs, flies, caterpillars and other insects. A common assassin bug in Ontario is the Spined Assassin Bug, named for the spines on its head, thorax and front legs. They are often found on flowers, where they wait to capture a visiting bee or fly.

Assassin bugs mate in autumn. Females lay hexagonally shaped clusters of 40 to 190 eggs on hard surfaces including tree trunks and houses. The tiny nymphs hatch in early May.

Many species of assassin bugs will bite humans. People who are sensitive to bites experience burning pain, intense itching and swelling with a rash and welting. Some bites can even cause heart palpitations, nausea, faintness and shortness of breath.

ID: *Adult:* brown, narrow, angular, rough body; head, thorax and front legs are covered with spines. *Nymph:* similar to adults, but smaller and wingless.

Size: *Adult:* 20 mm *Nymph:* 5 mm

Habitat and Range: Open areas such as fields, roadsides and railways where there are many wild flowers throughout Ontario.

Scouting: Nymphs and adults are often spotted laying in wait for their prey on flowers. Spined Assassin Bugs are valuable predators of many plant pests but this particular species of Assassin Bugs will not bite humans.

Cultural/Physical Control: Assassin bugs fly at night and are attracted to lights. Ensure screening around doors and windows is adequate and gaps around openings are caulked. Do not handle assassin bugs with unprotected hands.

How to Attract: They are naturally present in the garden. Keep them around by adding organic mulch around plants and plant alfalfa, carrots, oleander and members of the daisy family.

Hairy Chinch Bug

Blissus leucopterus hirtus

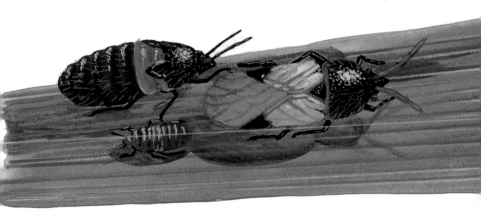

The only species of the group known as chinch bugs found in Ontario is the Hairy Chinch Bug *(B. leucopterus hirtus)*, which pierces and sucks fluid from grasses.

Chinch bugs overwinter as adults in tufts of grass, under litter or on leaves at woodland margins or other protected areas. Adults emerge in spring, fly to nearby turf and mate. The females lay eggs on leaves, roots and soil for two to three weeks, with the eggs beginning to hatch in mid- to late June. The bugs pass through five nymphal instars over 30 to 90 days, with only one generation per year. From August to October, adults begin to migrate to nearby overwintering sites.

It is not so much the fluid withdrawal by chinch bugs that harms plants; rather, it is the toxin in the insects' saliva that causes damage, turning the grass blade yellow.

ID: *Adult:* black body; white wings have dark triangle on outer margin. *Nymph:* pale grey with reddish brown abdomen; darkens as it matures; wingless.

Size: *Adult:* 4–5 mm. *Nymph:* 1–3 mm.

Habitat and Range: Attacks all lawn grasses, but prefers sunny, undisturbed areas.

Scouting: These insects are most active during periods of hot, dry weather. Infestations begin in June and last until October. Adults are present in early spring and from August to October; nymphs are present from early to midsummer until late August or early September. Watch for patchy dead or yellowing grass.

Cultural/Physical Control: A healthy lawn is your first defence against this pest. Heavy rains can drown nymphs and bury eggs. Light or no snow cover can result in high overwintering mortality. Remove excessive thatch.

Biological Control: The principle predator is the Big Eyed Bug (*Geocoris* spp.). This cute little bug can be seen prowling through the lawn in search of chinch bugs, sod webworms and other turf-inhabiting insects. There is also a natural fungus, *Beauveria globulifera*, which occurs under moist conditions and attacks chinch bug larvae.

Aphids

Acyrthosiphon caraganae, Hyadaphis tataricae, Myzus persicae

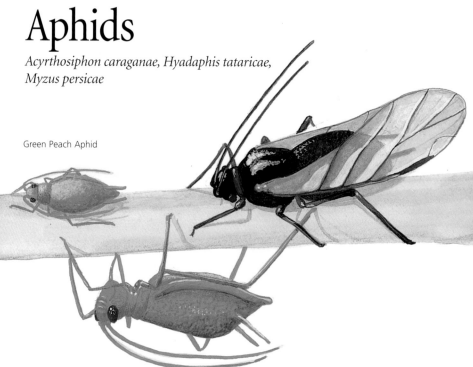

Green Peach Aphid

Generally, aphids can be found sucking plant juices from the growing tips and undersides of leaves or on the stems and roots. The most common aphid you will encounter is the Green Peach Aphid *(Myzus persicae)*. It feeds on more than 200 species of herbaceous plants. The Potato Aphid *(Macrosiphum euphorbiae)*, Smoky-winged Poplar Aphid *(Chaitophorus populicola)*, Caragana Aphid *(A. caraganae)*, Honeysuckle Aphid *(H. tataricae)*, Conifer Aphids *(Cinara* spp.) and Poplar Vagabond Gall Aphid *(M. vagabunda)* are all named for their food preference.

Some aphids have very complex life cycles, which involve more than one host plant species, migratory winged and stationary wingless forms, and summer asexual and autumn sexual generations. In summer, all aphids give birth to live young without mating. Some aphids, such as the Green Peach

ID: *Adult:* soft-bodied and pear-shaped; can be winged or wingless; usually green but can be yellow, white, bronze, dark brown, black or pink; cornicles on posterior end. *Nymph:* identical to adult, but smaller; if adult is winged, you will see wingbuds on nymph.

Size: *Adult:* 2–4 mm. *Nymph:* 1–2 mm.

Habitat and Range: Common in grassy areas, on shrubs and in trees province-wide.

Scouting: Aphids prefer warm, humid conditions. They do the most damage in spring to growing tips and new shoots. The high level of nutrient drain caused by feeding aphids often distorts plant tissue, making it become curled, puckered or discoloured. Heavy infestations can cause a plant to lose vigour. Aphids excrete "honeydew," a sticky fluid that favours sooty mould development and may attract ants, wasps and flies. Look at the underside of leaves, growing points and stem tips. Yellow sticky traps can be used to monitor winged adults.

Giant Conifer Aphid

Aphid, reproduce asexually all summer long on herbaceous hosts but produce males in autumn for sexual mating, resulting in an egg that overwinters on a woody host.

The Poplar Vagabond Gall Aphid forms a gall that accommodates the aphids growing and feeding inside. This woody growth persists all season long on the stems of poplars. The aphids leave the gall to feed on loosestrife during summer.

One common feature of aphids is their ability to rapidly increase in population, in extreme cases up to 12-fold within one week.

Some aphids give birth to daughters that are themselves pregnant!

Cultural/Physical Control: Because of the enormous potential for population growth, take action upon first detection. Limit weeds that serve as alternate hosts. Heavy rainfall or high winds dislodge aphids, so try using a hard spray of water to wash them off. Soapy water acts like an insecticide. Hand pick or prune infested leaves or galls. Use sticky bands on tree trunks to prevent ants from tending to aphids.

Biological Control: Many invertebrates, including lady bird beetles, hover fly larvae, lacewing larvae and midge larvae, feed on aphids. Parasitic wasps can have a huge impact on aphid populations; if these wasps are active in your yard, you will see grey-brown parchment-like remains of aphids.

Woolly Aphids

Eriosoma spp.

Woolly Apple Aphid colony

The Woolly Elm Aphid *(E. americanum)* and the Woolly Apple Aphid *(E. lanigerum)* alternate between white elm in early spring and autumn and *Amelanchier* species (Woolly Elm Aphid), or apple, hawthorn, crab apple and mountain ash (Woolly Apple Aphid) during summer.

Both species of aphid overwinter as eggs on the bark of the elm host. The eggs hatch before leaf buds open, and the stem mother invades the buds. As the leaves open, the aphids reproduce and feed, causing the leaves to form a "pseudogall." Unlike a true gall, a pseudogall has no abnormal

ID: *Adult:* soft-bodied; blue to purple overall, covered in white, waxy material; winged forms are black. *Nymph:* does not produce wax.

Size: *Adult:* 3 mm. *Nymph:* 1–2 mm.

Habitat and Range: Anywhere white elm and the alternate hosts co-exist.

Scouting: Pseudogalls appear shortly after leaf-out. The Woolly Apple Aphid's pseudogall is an unsightly mass of leaves, whereas the Woolly Elm Aphid pseudogall is composed of only 1 leaf. On the alternate host, waxy material is the most striking feature.

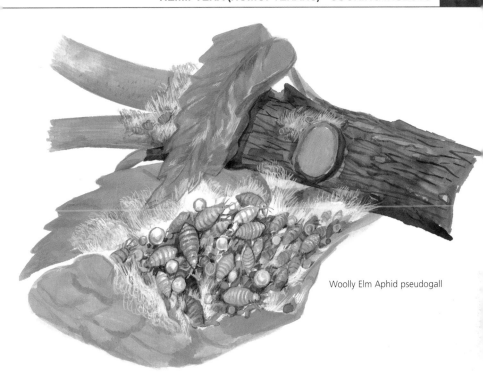

Woolly Elm Aphid pseudogall

woody growth; instead, the leaves curl downward, enclosing the aphids. The aphids feed in these pseudogalls until late June or early July. Winged forms then migrate to their alternate host to produce wingless feeding forms that cause galls at the feeding site. The Woolly Elm Aphid infests the roots, and the Woolly Apple Aphid infests roots and stems, especially water shoots. Several generations will pass on the alternate host. In autumn, winged forms of both species return to elm trees to produce wingless males and females that mate to produce an overwintering egg.

These aphids feed by sucking fluid out of the buds and leaves. The damage they cause on elms is unsightly but does not seriously harm the trees. Aphids feeding on the summer host can kill young seedlings or stunt mature plants. The honeydew these aphids produce can cause sooty mould to form on underlying leaves.

The aphid that emerges from the overwintering egg is referred to as the "stem mother" and is well adapted to produce many offspring, ensuring successful colonization of the leaves.

Cultural/Physical Control: In spring, prune or hand pick pseudogalls or galls off the alternate host. Use a strong jet of water to knock the Woolly Apple Aphid off the alternate host.

Biological Control: Many natural predators such as lacewings, flower flies and ladybugs prey on woolly aphids.

Cooley Spruce Gall Adelgid

Adelges cooleyi

The Cooley Spruce Gall Adelgid is one of a few woolly aphids that feed on conifers. This insect resembles an aphid and feeds in a similar manner by piercing the plant and sucking out phloem sap. On white spruce, a gall forms in response to the feeding at the tip of new growth. The gall usually kills the new shoot and can persist for several years. This insect rarely causes serious damage, but the galls can be unsightly, and persistent infestations can stunt growth.

Some woolly aphids may live on only one host, whereas other species require two hosts to complete their life cycle. The Cooley Spruce Gall Adelgid alternates between white spruce and Douglas-fir, or it can survive on either host alone. A free-living stage that feeds on the lower surface of Douglas-fir needles begins the cycle. Winged and wingless forms develop, with the wingless form producing long strands of wax, referred to as flocculence. Winged forms migrate in summer to white spruce to lay eggs that develop into wingless males and females. These aphids mate and lay eggs at the base of old bud scales. Once the eggs hatch, the nymphs feed for a while and then move to the stem below a bud to overwinter. In spring, the awakening nymphs feed, which spurs the plant to produce a gall. The overwintered females lay a new batch of eggs, and the hatching nymphs enter the developing gall to feed in relative safety. Winged females emerge from the galls later in summer to fly back to a Douglas-fir to lay eggs, the nymphs of which hatch out to overwinter and begin the cycle again.

ID: *Adult:* soft-bodied; winged or wingless; black overall; wingless adults covered in white waxy material. *Nymph:* soft-bodied; bluish purple overall.

Size: *Adult:* 2–4 mm. *Nymph:* 1–2 mm.

Habitat and Range: Across the northern U.S. and southern Canada; alternates between spruce and Douglas-fir.

Scouting: In early summer, look for white, waxy material on needles near the branch tips. In midsummer, look for swollen branch tips that progress in colour from light green to brown. Galls form only on spruce, whereas flocculence can be seen on both spruce and Douglas-fir.

Cultural/Physical Control: Prune galls while still green or purple to prevent adult emergence. In spring, use a strong jet of water to wash off nymphs feeding on needles.

Biological Control: Many insects prey on adelgids, including lady beetles, minute pirate bugs and lacewings.

Eastern Spruce Gall Adelgid

Adelges abietis

The Eastern Spruce Gall Adelgid was introduced to North America from Europe. It feeds on the leaves and roots of *Picea* spp. including white, red, black and blue spruce and, importantly in Ontario, the traditional Christmas tree, Norway spruce. Feeding nymphs inject saliva into the tree, which induces the tree to produce characteristic small, green to pink, pineapple-shaped galls at the base of the new shoots. The galls prevent proper twig growth; however, affected terminals often are not killed. The galls can disfigure ornamental and Christmas trees and result in significant economic losses for those industries.

Unlike some adelgids, the Eastern Spruce Gall Adelgid requires only one host to complete its life cycle. In early spring, overwintering nymphs become adults and deposit eggs at the bases of the new shoots. As the buds break, the nymphs hatch and begin to feed, causing the leaf bases to enlarge and enclose the nymph in the waxy gall. Each gall may contain up to a dozen nymphs. In August, the galls break open, and winged adult females emerge and fly to new needles on the same or different tree to lay eggs. Only females are produced. They die shortly afterward, leaving the eggs protected underneath their bodies. Look for white, cottony spots over winter.

The Grape Phylloxera (Daktulosphaira vitifoliae) *is a close relative that can be very destructive to grape vines because it forms galls on leaves and roots, causing premature defoliation, reduced shoot growth and reduced yield of fruit. When this North American species was introduced to Europe in the 19th century, it devastated the wine industry. A partial solution was to graft susceptible European vines to resistant North American rootstock.*

ID: *Adult:* soft-bodied and pear-shaped; winged; green overall with long antennae; no cornicles on abdomen. *Nymph:* wingless; soft-bodied; green overall.

Size: *Adult:* 2–4 mm. *Nymph:* 1–2 mm.

Habitat and Range: Across the northern U.S. and southern Canada in forests containing spruce trees.

Scouting: In early summer, look for green and then pink, pineapple-shaped galls at the base of the new shoots. Galls form only on spruce.

Cultural/Physical Control: Prune galls while green or pink to prevent adult emergence.

Biological Control: Many insects prey on adelgids, including lady beetles, minute pirate bugs and lacewings.

Mealybugs

Planococcus citri, Pseudococcus longispinus

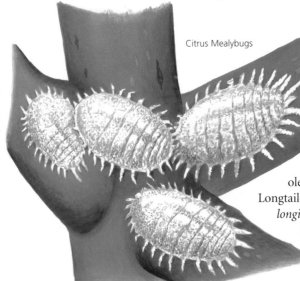

Citrus Mealybugs

The Citrus Mealybug feeds on a wide range of hosts including African violet, begonia, cactus, citrus, coleus, fuchsia, gardenia, geranium, impatiens, oleander and poinsettia. The Longtailed Mealybug *(Pseudococcus longispinus)* prefers dracaena but can be found wherever the Citrus Mealybug feeds. Most mealybugs undergo gradual metamorphosis, with females able to lay up to 600 eggs in wax-covered clusters. The Longtailed Mealybug gives birth to live young, and Citrus Mealybug eggs hatch into mobile first instar "crawlers" that are the primary stage for dispersal. Older nymphs and adults will slowly disperse among plants. Nymphal instars last two to three weeks, and there can be several generations each year.

Mealybugs are pests of houseplants and greenhouses. They suck out plant juices, and the saliva of the Citrus Mealybug *(Planococcus citri)* has a toxic effect on some plants. While they feed, mealybugs produce a liquid waste that may contribute to growth of black, sooty mould. Mealybug infestations are unappealing, and the fluid drain can stunt the plant.

ID: *Adult:* flattened, bluish, wax-covered body. *Longtailed Mealybug:* 2 or more long, waxy filaments arise from the rear. *Nymph:* identical to adult, only smaller.

Size: *Adult:* 2–5 mm. *Nymph:* 1–3 mm.

Habitat and Range: Eggs, all 3 nymphal instars and the adults live on the undersides of leaves, along veins or in the leaf axils on greenhouse and house plants.

Scouting: Look for waxy build-up and sooty mould in dense infestations. Also watch for browning of leaf midribs in coleus.

Cultural/Physical Control: The wax provides protection, and their habit of penetrating into leaf axils makes this insect difficult to manage. Control light infestations by hand washing or wiping leaves with cotton swabs dipped in rubbing alcohol. For heavy infestations, remove the entire leaf.

Biological Control: A very small lady beetle, the Mealybug Destroyer *(Cryptolamus montrouzier)* and a parasitic wasp (effective against only the Citrus Mealybug) are commercially available. The lady beetle is not as effective against the Longtailed Mealybug, which will out-compete the Citrus Mealybug to become the dominant species present.

Scale Insects

Chionaspis spp., *Lepidosaphes ulmi*, *Parthenolecanium corni* and others

Oystershell Scale

Armoured scale insects pierce and suck plant cell contents, whereas soft scale insects feed on plant fluids. Injury to the plant resulting from scale insect activity includes reduced host plant vigour, defoliation, dieback and the unsightly presence of the scales themselves. Soft scales produce honeydew, which may result in sooty mould.

Armoured scales produce a hard protective covering. They are flattened and may be elongate, whereas soft scales are hemispherical. All life stages can be present on the host plant at the same time. Some armoured scale species have winged males, whereas others are parthenogenic. Immature male armoured scales are usually smaller and more elongate than the females. Adult male armoured scale insects do not feed.

In both groups of scale insects, the female lays the eggs beneath her, using her body as a protective cover. All of the scales mentioned below overwinter in the egg stage with the exception of the European Fruit Lecanium *(P. corni)*, which overwinters as a nymph. The only dispersal stage is when first-stage crawlers emerge and move about for several days before settling down to feed. There is typically only one generation per year.

ID: *Adult: Pine Needle, Scurfy* and *Oystershell scales:* elongate; white to grey overall. *San Jose Scale:* circular with white centre. *European Fruit Lecanium:* brown to black rounded hump. *Nymph:* identical to adult, only smaller.

Size: *Adult:* 1–8 mm. *Nymph:* 1–5 mm.

Habitat and Range: Common armoured scale species in Ontario: *Pine Needle Scale (C. pinifoliae):* on pine, Douglas-fir and cedar but most often on white and Colorado spruce. *Scurfy Scale (C. furfura):* on ash, aspen, dogwood, elm and willow. *Oystershell Scale (L. ulmi):* on ash, birch, cotoneaster, elm, fruit trees, lilac and poplar. *San Jose Scale (Quadraspidiotus perniciosus):* on ornamentals and mountain ash. Common soft scale species in Ontario: *European Fruit Lecanium:* on ash, birch, dogwood, elm, fruit trees and roses.

Scouting: The crawlers are very small and are often overlooked. Scales tend to cluster together and, at first glance, resemble rough bark.

Cultural/Physical Control: Inspect plant material before planting out. Prune infested limbs or treat with horticultural oil in early spring to suffocate the eggs.

Biological Control: Scale insects have several predators including lacewings and lady beetles.

Boxwood Psyllid

Cacopsylla buxi

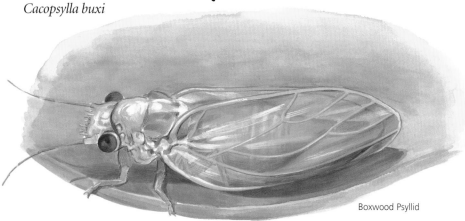

Boxwood Psyllid

Jumping plantlice or psyllids are small, sucking insects in the family Psylloidea. They are related to aphids, lace bugs and whiteflies. The nymphs are covered with a white, waxy substance that makes them look like little tufts of white wool or sugary deposits on leaves. There are over 3000 known species of psyllids worldwide. The Boxwood Psyllid is commonly seen in gardens and landscapes in Ontario.

Boxwood Psyllid adults and nymphs suck plant sap from new shoots and leaves, resulting in leaf cupping and distortion. Leaves also become covered with honeydew and black, sooty mould. Boxwood Psyllids overwinter as eggs in protected areas on the plant. Nymphs appear in white, woolly tufts on boxwood leaves in early July. Nymphs go through five instars, and winged adults emerge in early August. There is one generation per year.

Psyllids produce acoustic signals or "songs" during mating, specific to each species. These sounds range from honks, croaks and burps to wailing and whining.

ID: *Adult:* greyish green body with wings. *Nymph:* flat, grey body covered with white, cottony "wool."

Size: *Adult:* 3 mm. *Nymph:* 1–2 mm.

Habitat and Range: Throughout southern Ontario.

Scouting: Look for leaf curling and white, woolly tufts on boxwood leaves in spring and early summer; leaves often appear dirty as a result of honeydew and sooty mould.

Cultural/Physical Control: Keep boxwood hedges healthy, pruned and vigorous. Boxwood can sustain quite a lot of psyllid feeding without permanent damage. These psyllids generally disappear in August.

Biological Control: Some naturally occurring predatory bugs such as *Dicyphus* and *Orius* (available commercially for greenhouse use) and parasitic wasps attack psyllids, but they have not been evaluated for control on outdoor plants. Spray insecticidal soap on the underside of leaves where the insects will come into contact with it. Usually, more than 1 application is needed. Use a spray with dormant oil and lime sulphur in winter or early spring to kill eggs.

Cottony Psyllid

Psyllopsis discrepans

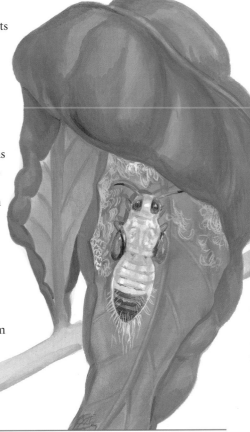

The Cottony Psyllid pierces and sucks plant fluid, resulting in plants with stunted growth, leaf curl and premature leaf drop. This species is an introduction from Europe. Records of the Cottony Psyllid in eastern Canada date back to 1921.

The Cottony Psyllid has only a single generation in Europe but has two generations in Ontario. It overwinters as an egg at the base of terminal leaf buds. The egg hatches in spring coincident with leaf flush, and the nymph feeds on the newly developing leaves. There are five nymphal instars, which last from 9 to 11 days each. The instars mature into adults by July, feeding on tender stem tissue. Another round of egg laying occurs with a second generation of nymphs emerging in late July and persisting into September. Females from this generation lay an overwintering batch of eggs in August or September.

ID: *Adult:* light green to yellow with black markings; female is paler than male. *Nymph:* greenish yellow, flattened body; often has waxy filaments originating from posterior abdomen.

Size: *Adult:* 3–4 mm. *Nymph:* 1–2 mm.

Habitat and Range: Throughout Ontario; feeds only on Manchurian and black ash; Manchurian ash will have many more nymphs per leaf than black ash but will not suffer as much damage.

Scouting: Examine terminal branches for yellowish, rice-shaped eggs at the base of the buds. Nymphs can be found in rolled-up leaves. Initial damage appears as downward curling and mild yellowing of the leaves.

Late-stage damage appears as tightly curled leaves with white, waxy material sticking out. Premature leaf drop and dieback of branches may occur in severe infestations. Adult feeding stunts growth of branches.

Cultural/Physical Control: Tree health is the best defence against this pest. Use a strong jet of water or insecticidal soap to penetrate the curled leaves early in leaf development. Treat plants with horticultural oil to smother the eggs before leaf flush.

Biological Control: Many generalist predators attack the Cottony Psyllid, including minute pirate bugs, lady bird beetles and lacewing larvae.

Leafhoppers

Edwardsiana rosae, Graphocephala coccinea, Macrosteles fascifrons and others

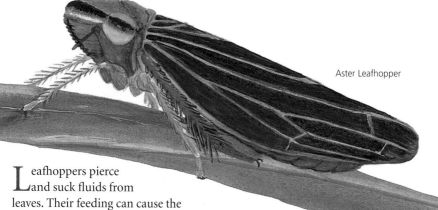

Aster Leafhopper

Leafhoppers pierce and suck fluids from leaves. Their feeding can cause the leaves to curl, wrinkle or wilt. In some cases, the leaves turn brown, giving them a scorched appearance—hence the term "hopperburn." Some species are capable of transmitting viral and phytoplasma diseases. Common Ontario leafhoppers include the Candy-stripe Leafhopper (*G. coccinea*) on leaves of woody shrubs; the Aster Leafhopper (*M. fascifrons*) on grasses, lettuce, and carrots; *Empoasca* leafhoppers on potato and beans; and the Rose Leafhopper (*E. rosae*) on roses. There are several hundred other species of leafhopper that feed on deciduous trees and shrubs with the exception of ash and cedar.

Leafhoppers produce one to four generations per year. Some species, such as the Rose Leafhopper and many that feed on trees, overwinter as an egg inserted into the host plant. Other species, such as the Aster Leafhopper, overwinter in the Gulf of Mexico and only arrive in the north as adults in late spring. These migrants lay eggs in the host plant, and the hatching and development of the nymphs progress as for the resident species. Nymphs are wingless initially but develop wingbuds as they moult from instar to instar. Leafhoppers are very agile and spring away at the slightest disturbance.

ID: *Adult:* ranges from pale white to black with vivid red stripes; bluntly rounded head tapers toward posterior; folds wings tent-like over body. *Nymph:* pale overall.

Size: *Adult:* 4–8 mm. *Nymph:* 1–4 mm.

Habitat and Range: Many species are blown in from the south with weather systems in spring, whereas others successfully overwinter throughout Ontario.

Scouting: Look for leaf curling or "hopperburn." On a disturbed plant, you

are not likely to miss the leafhoppers living up to their name—hopping away.

Cultural/Physical Control: Knock these insects off your plant by syringing with a strong water stream. Suppress leafhopper numbers by eliminating grasses that serve as alternate hosts.

Biological Control: Generalist predators, such as birds and lady beetles, feed on leafhoppers.

Cicadas

Okanagana spp., *Tibicen pruinosa*

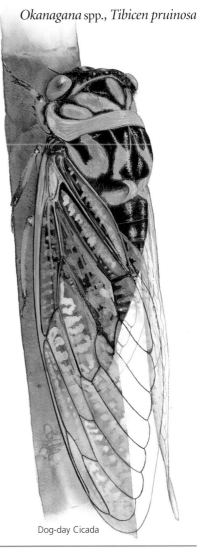

Nymphal cicadas pierce and suck plant sap from the roots of trees but do not cause any appreciable damage to the host plant. Adult cicadas are not known to cause any damage by feeding. However, their habit of inserting eggs into twigs and stems can allow diseases to enter or the twigs to splinter. The Dog-day or Annual Cicada *(T. pruinosa)* is the largest cicada in North America. It feeds on many different deciduous trees. Say's Cicada *(O. rimosa)* is found on aspen, jack and lodgepole pine. The Canadian Cicada *(O. canadensis)* feeds on pine and has the northernmost range of any cicada in the world.

Eggs are laid in twigs and stems of host plants. The nymphs hatch in summer and drop to the ground,

Dog-day Cicada

ID: *Adult:* blunt-headed; stout body with large, thick-veined clear wings. *Dog-day Cicada:* black with greenish highlights on wings and body. *Canadian Cicada:* black with yellowish tan markings. *Nymph:* tan coloured.

Size: *Adult:* 30–55 mm. *Nymph:* 20–30 mm.

Habitat and Range: mixed-wood forests throughout southern Ontario.

Scouting: Listen for the male's "song" and look for splintered twigs and branches caused by egg laying.

Cultural/Physical Control: Unnecessary because neither nymph nor adult causes noticeable damage.

Biological Control: Adult cicadas make a fine meal for many birds and insectivorous rodents.

Cicadas (continued)

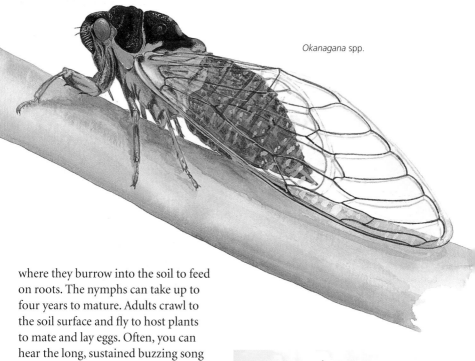

Okanagana spp.

where they burrow into the soil to feed on roots. The nymphs can take up to four years to mature. Adults crawl to the soil surface and fly to host plants to mate and lay eggs. Often, you can hear the long, sustained buzzing song of the male as he calls for the female. Although a nymph may take two to five years to mature, there are overlapping generations; therefore, you will see cicadas every year.

In the eastern United States, the Periodical Cicada (Magicicada septendecim) has a synchronized emergence every 17 years! The next ear-splitting racket is expected in 2021.

Spittlebugs

Aphrophora gelida, Philaenus spumarius

Spittlebugs are piercing/sucking insects that feed on xylem fluids. Many species occur in Ontario and can be found feeding primarily on woody plants. However, the Meadow Spittlebug *(P. spumarius)* feeds on a wide variety of decorative flowering plants as well as strawberries and peas. The adult Boreal Spittlebug *(A. gelida)* feeds on pine, spruce and Douglas-fir; the nymphs feed on goldenrod, fireweed and other forbs. All spittlebugs in the nymphal stage produce a spittle mass, a combination of excess plant sap, air and mucus, which is thought to protect the nymph from predators and from drying out.

Eggs are laid in small masses in cracks and crevices on the host plant. Nymphs hatch out in spring and feed on stems, where they produce the spittle mass. Adults fly to new hosts in late spring or early summer and continue feeding throughout summer. Overwintering eggs are laid on host plants in autumn.

Meadow Spittlebug nymph

Meadow Spittlebug adult

The spittlebug's prominent, "Klingon-esque" face houses the many muscles needed for the strong sucking pump used to draw in plant sap.

ID: broad, pointed head; wings taper to a point. *Adult: Meadow Spittlebug:* tan to brownish overall. *Boreal Spittlebug:* mottled, with pale patch on wings. *Nymph:* light green to yellowish overall.

Size: *Adult:* 7–15 mm. *Nymph:* 1–8 mm.

Habitat and Range: Widespread throughout Ontario.

Scouting: Look for the spittle mass of the nymphs on stems. Adults are difficult to spot.

Cultural/Physical Control: Hose off spittle masses in spring and eliminate or suppress weedy alternate hosts.

Biological Control: Birds and yellow jacket wasps prey on spittlebugs.

Thrips

Frankliniella spp., *Thrips* spp.

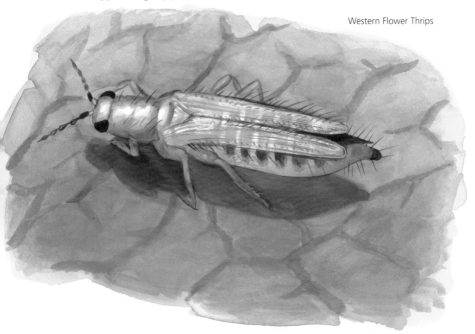

Western Flower Thrips

Thrips are unusual in that they have asymmetrical mouthparts—they lack one mandible. This asymmetry results in a form of feeding called "punch and suck," in which thrips use their sole mandible to punch a hole in a plant cell and then form a mouth cone with the remaining mouthparts to suck out the cell contents, leaving a void in the tissue. There are many thrips in Ontario, but the most damaging and commonly encountered are the Western Flower Thrips (*F. occidentalis*), Eastern Flower Thrips (*F. tritici*), Onion Thrips (*T. tabaci*) and a species with no common name, *T. vulgatissimus*.

Thrips are capable of having many generations per year. Most thrips can reproduce asexually by parthenogenesis (there are no males and the female

ID: elongate body with short legs; slightly protruding antennae. *Adult:* delicate wings with long fringe of hairs on trailing edge. *Western Flower and Eastern Flower thrips:* yellow overall. *Onion Thrips:* pale overall. *T. vulgatissimus:* dark black overall. *Nymph:* usually light yellow.

Size: *Adult:* 2–3 mm. *Nymph:* 1–2 mm.

Habitat and Range: Widespread throughout Ontario; can be found in vegetables, flowers, shrubs and trees; prefers drier habitat; often found in association with spider mites, and feeds on their eggs; larvae are usually found on leaves, and adults can be on leaves or in flowers.

Scouting: Look in flowers, under leaves and on stems of plants in dry or exposed areas. Some species of thrips form galls, whereas others feed on surface tissues, causing irregular patches of dead cells or streaks (a

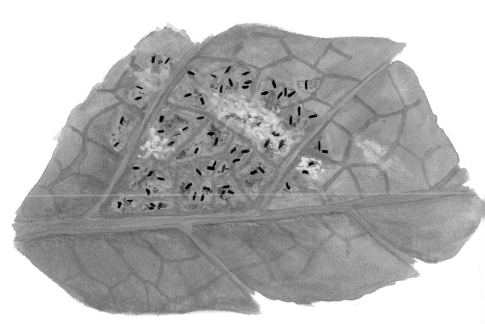

produces clones of herself). The Onion Thrips reproduces in this manner. The Western Flower Thrips will produce females if mated and males if unmated in a form of reproduction called haplodiploidy. If no males are around, she makes some—how handy is that?

Adult thrips lay eggs into a slit in the host plant. First and second instar thrips punch and suck, feeding on surface tissues, often on the undersides of leaves. Non-feeding prepupal and pupal stages are usually spent in the soil, though some species pupate on the plant. Adults can fly but prefer to walk or hop around on the plant surface.

Adult Western Flower Thrips and Eastern Flower Thrips prefer to feed on pollen within the protective confines of a flower. The life cycle from egg to adult can take as little as three weeks in warm weather.

"Thrips" is both plural and singular, just like "moose."

result of cell death and subsequent growth of surrounding tissue). Flower thrips can cause deformed leaves and flowers by feeding at the bud stage.

Cultural/Physical Control: Encourage vigorous plant growth. Dislodge larvae with a jet of water. Remove weeds: they serve as an alternate food source.

Biological Control: Although they feed on spider mite eggs, which is beneficial, thrips do more harm than good. Fortunately many generalist predators feed on thrips, including lady bird beetles, pirate bugs, damsel bugs and some predatory mites.

European Earwig

Forficula auricularia

Earwigs are active during the night and hide in dark, damp places during the day. The best identifying feature is the pair of pincers (cerci) on the end of the abdomen, which are used for mating, for manipulating food and for defence. The European Earwig, like most earwigs, is omnivorous. It eats plant material, including flower petals and leaves, insects such as aphids and insect eggs. The adults have wings that are folded under short wing covers; however, they rarely fly. The European Earwig was introduced to North America in the early 1900s on the west coast; it has spread rapidly and is now found throughout most of North America.

In autumn, adult males and females dig a small nest in the ground. The pair will stay in the nest until late winter, when the female forces the male out of the nest. She lays her first batch of eggs and guards them. Once they hatch, she cares for them for several weeks. In late spring, a second, smaller batch of eggs is laid. Owing to cool spring days, the first batch of eggs takes 70 days to hatch, while the second takes only 20 days. European Earwigs exhibit one generation per year.

ID: *Adult:* elongated, reddish brown body; pair of bowed (male) or almost straight (female) cerci at end of abdomen. *Nymph:* whitish miniature of adult.

Size: *Adult:* 16 mm. *Nymph:* 5–12 mm.

Habitat and Range: Widespread and abundant in shady places, under wood, stones, etc.

Scouting: Earwigs can be found in high numbers under boards, in tree holes or wherever it is damp and dark.

Cultural/Physical Control: Eliminate hiding places, including piles of leaves. Reduce populations by using traps. Grooved boards or corrugated cardboard strips can be set in hedges and around trees. Remove traps weekly; shake out and destroy earwigs.

Biological Control: A tachinid fly *(Bigonicheta spinipennis)* is a natural predator.

Lacewings

Chrysoperla spp., *Chrysopa* spp. and *Hemerobius* spp.

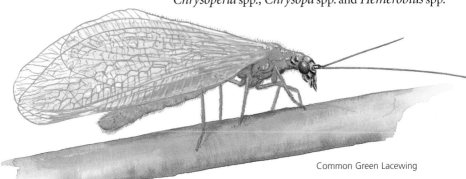

Common Green Lacewing

All larval lacewings are predators of soft-bodied insects. Adult green lacewings in the genus *Chrysoperla* are pollen and nectar feeders, whereas adult green lacewings in the genus *Chrysopa* and adult brown lacewings in the genus *Hemerobius* feed on insects, pollen and nectar. The most common lacewings observed in Ontario are the green lacewings in the genus *Chrysoperla;* the Common Green Lacewing *(Chrysoperla carnea)* and the Goldeneyed Lacewing *(Chrysopa oculata)* are widespread throughout Canada. Brown lacewings are less common, found mostly in wooded areas, with *H. humulinus* distributed across Canada.

Adults overwinter in leaf litter. They emerge in spring to lay several hundred eggs on leaf and stem surfaces. Green lacewing eggs are supported on a long, silken stalk, whereas brown lacewing eggs are laid directly on the plant surface. The larvae hatch in four to seven days, undergo three larval instars and pupate in the open on the plant surface (green lacewing) or in protected places (brown lacewing) in a silken cocoon. There may be several generations per year, depending on temperature.

Lacewings readily come to light, so they are often found flitting about in homes in the evening.

ID: *Adult: Green lacewing:* delicate light green with lacy wings. *Brown lacewing:* similar to green lacewing but smaller and brown. *Immature:* flattened, elongate and bulging in middle; pair of long, curved, pointed mandibles on head used to skewer prey. *Larva:* often mottled white and brown or white and green.

Size: *Adult:* 12–20 mm. *Larva:* <1–8 mm.

Habitat and Range: *Green lacewing:* found throughout Ontario. *Brown lacewing:* limited to wooded areas.

Scouting: Adults rest during the day but will fly if disturbed (they are clumsy fliers and are quite comical to watch). Larvae are voracious predators that can be found patrolling leaves, fruit and stems for prey.

How to Attract: Flowering plants that provide nectar and pollen for the adults will attract lacewings into your yard. Lacewing larvae are known as aphid-lions for their prowess at feasting on aphids. However, they also feed on eggs and soft-bodied insects such as caterpillars, psyllids, spider mites, thrips and leafhoppers.

Ground Beetles

Calosoma spp., *Carabus* spp., *Pterostichus* spp.

Fiery Hunter

Larval and adult ground beetles are predators of insects and other arthropods, earthworms and slugs. Common Ontario ground beetles include the Purple-rimmed Carabus *(Carabus nemoralis)*, Fiery Hunter *(Calosoma calidum)* and European Carabid *(P. melanarius)*. Among many others are *Elaphrus* spp. around bogs, *Bembidion* spp. along shorelines, *Agonum* spp. near bodies of water, and *Patrobus* spp. in forested areas and cultivated lands.

Ground beetles overwinter as pupae or adults, with adults often living two or three years. Eggs are laid in soil or, with some species, in mud cells attached to plants. Larvae go through four instars in the shallow soil or on the soil's surface. Pupation occurs in the soil. Adults emerge in June and July and are active until autumn. Adults are typically nocturnal, though if disturbed they will be visible during the day.

Some ground beetles are capable of consuming their own weight in insects every day.

ID: *Adult: Purple-rimmed Carabus:* black with protruding head; flared pronotum; broadly oval abdomen tapers to a point; elytra and pronotum are rimmed with purple. *Fiery Hunter:* similarly shaped but with red spots on elytra. *European Carabid:* not as curvy; uniformly shiny black. *Larva:* yellowish brown; elongate, tapering toward posterior.

Size: *Adult:* 12–22 mm. *Larva:* 5–15 mm.

Habitat and Range: *Purple-rimmed Carabus* and *Fiery Hunter:* widespread in urban areas throughout Ontario. *European Carabid:* originally from Europe but now widespread in urban areas and slowly spreading to rural habitats.

Scouting: The Purple-rimmed Carabus and the Fiery Hunter are arboreal hunters, feasting on caterpillars. The European Carabid is more earthbound. Although most active at night (you can often hear them rustling through leaves after sundown from June onward), they also crawl around during the day.

How to Attract: These insects are beneficial and, despite their conspicuously large size, should not be feared or harmed. Ground beetles are among the most abundant predators in the landscape. They are diligent and seemingly inexhaustible in their pursuit of prey. These beetles thrive in undisturbed areas, so try to leave some earth undisturbed.

Blister Beetles

Epicauta spp., *Lytta* spp.

Adult blister beetles chew on leaves and flowers of plants. There are many species, but the showiest is Nuttall's Blister Beetle *(L. nuttalli)*. The name blister beetle is not an idle label; the beetles produce a chemical called cantharidin that causes blistering when it comes in contact with moist skin. Males produce the chemical and pass it to the female during mating.

Nuttall's Blister Beetle

The adult blister beetle emerges in June and July to feed on foliage and mate. The female lays her eggs in soil near a source of food such as grasshopper eggs or ground-nesting bumble bee nests containing bee larvae. The first instar larva is an active crawler that searches out leafcutter bee and bumble bee nests or grasshopper egg batches, upon which subsequent larval instars feed. The larva overwinters, pupating the following spring.

A European species of blister beetle, L. vesicatoria, *is ground up and sold as a cure-all and aphrodisiac known as Spanish Fly. It isn't just snakes (and their oil) that are flogged as a panacea for your ills.*

ID: *Adult:* elongate and colourful with soft elytra; often iridescent or metallic green, purple or blue; rounded pronotum usually narrower than head or abdomen. *Larva:* brownish to whitish grub.

Size: *Adult:* 12–25 mm. *Larva:* 5–13 mm.

Habitat and Range: Widespread throughout Canada; naturally occurs on wild legumes such as vetches; predominantly a pest of field crops such as alfalfa and canola, but one species, *L. viridana*, feeds on caragana.

Scouting: Adults chew on young leaves and flowers and are most abundant 1–2 years after a grasshopper infestation. Immatures are soil dwellers that do not affect plant material.

Cultural/Physical Control: It is unlikely that these beetles will cause enough damage to be a concern.

Biological Control: Here we witness the Jekyll and Hyde nature of this beetle. The adult is a nuisance in the garden, but the larva feeds on grasshopper and cricket eggs. Unfortunately, the larva also attacks eggs and larvae of leafcutter bees and bumble bees.

Flea Beetles

Disonycha xanthomelas, Epitrix cucumeris, Phyllotreta spp.

Spinach Flea Beetle

Flea beetles have large hind legs, which they use for jumping to escape from predators.

Adult flea beetles feed on foliage, and larvae feed on roots and tubers. Common Ontario flea beetles include the Potato Flea Beetle *(E. cucumeris)*, Crucifer Flea Beetle *(P. cruciferae)* and Striped Flea Beetle *(P. striolata)*. A flea beetle that lives its entire life on spinach is the Spinach Flea Beetle *(D. xanthomelas)*.

Flea beetles that develop below ground typically overwinter as adults in sheltered areas or leaf litter and emerge in spring to feed on weeds and emerging crops. Females lay eggs in the soil near food plants and die soon after. One to two weeks later, larvae hatch and feed on roots and tubers or, for the Spinach Flea Beetle, on foliage. The larvae pass through four instars and then pupate in the soil, except the Spinach Flea Beetle, which pupates on the leaf surface. Adults emerge and feed throughout summer and into autumn. Most species have only one generation per year.

ID: *Adult:* shiny, metallic beetle with jumping hind legs; most are blue to black. *Striped Flea Beetle:* 2 wavy yellow stripes along elytra. *Spinach Flea Beetle:* yellow pronotum. *Larva:* elongate, brown to whitish body; 3 pairs of legs near head; head capsule is usually distinct.

Size: *Adult:* 2–3 mm. *Larva:* 1–2 mm.

Habitat and Range: Throughout Ontario.

Scouting: The Potato, Crucifer and Striped flea beetles feed on newly emerging host plants in spring, especially the cotyledons, where severe damage can occur. In July and August, they feed on mostly the upper but also the lower surface of leaves. Feeding is characterized by pitting or a shot-hole appearance. Spinach Flea Beetle adults and larvae feed on the leaf surface. Early instar

larvae feed in groups, skeletonizing the leaf surface; later instar larvae and adults cause characteristic pitting and shot-hole damage.

Cultural/Physical Control: Remove weeds because they serve as alternate food hosts. Flea beetles overwinter in litter near food plants, so rotate or move your crucifers and potatoes around the garden to escape the beetles. Plant early emerging varieties as "trap crops" that can be treated with insecticide, thereby limiting the need to spray your food crop. Flea beetle adults prefer to feed in open, sunny, warm areas, so try to shade your plants wherever possible.

Biological Control: Natural enemies abound but do not have a substantial impact on large populations of flea beetles.

Lily Leaf Beetle

Lilioceris lilii

The beautiful Lily Leaf Beetle is native to Europe and North Africa. It was first found in 1945 in Montreal and has since been reported throughout Ontario wherever lilies are grown. This beetle is considered a pest to lily growers; it feeds on all lily species, lily of the valley, Solomon's seal and *Fritillaria* spp. Both adults and larvae feed on leaves, but in heavy infestations they will also eat flowers, seed capsules and stems.

The beetle overwinters as a pupa in soil and debris. Adults emerge in early spring and mate, and the females lay 200 to 300 eggs in rows on the underside of leaves. When the larvae hatch, they begin to eat on the underside of leaves. As the larvae mature, they begin to feed on the upper surface of the leaves. The larva stage lasts 16 to 24 days, during which time the larvae keep themselves covered under a protective layer of their own excrement. The larvae bury into the soil, make a protective cocoon and pupate. After 20 to 25 days, the adults emerge. In Ontario, there may be two or three generations per year.

ID: *Adult:* bright red elytra; black antennae, eyes, head, legs and underside. *Larva:* covered in own slimy, black excrement.

Size: *Adult:* 6–8 mm. *Larva:* 8–10 mm.

Habitat and Range: Throughout Ontario wherever its hosts grow.

Scouting: Beginning in late spring, look for eggs and small larvae on the underside of host plants and adults and large larvae on the upper surface of leaves.

Cultural/Physical Control: Hand pick the adults and larvae and destroy the eggs. Avoid introducing this insect to a new location by being sure any new plants you bring in have no sign of it.

Biological Control: A least 4 species of parasitic wasps in Europe lay their eggs in the larvae.

Leaf Beetles

Acalymma vittatum, Calligrapha multipunctata multipunctata and others

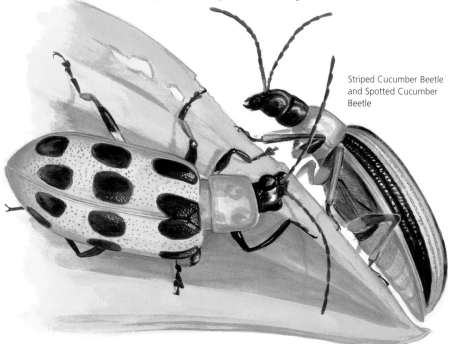

Striped Cucumber Beetle and Spotted Cucumber Beetle

Adult and larval leaf beetles chew leaf material and, in extreme cases, can strip a tree bare. There are many leaf beetles across Ontario but the following are a few of the commonly encountered species: the Cottonwood Leaf Beetle *(Chrysomela scripta)*, Aspen Leaf Beetle *(Chrysomela crotchi)* and Willow Leaf Beetle *(Calligrapha multipunctata multipunctata)*. In the same family, Chrysomelidae, the Striped Cucumber Beetle *(A. vittatum)* is associated with vegetables instead of trees.

In general, leaf beetles overwinter as adults in leaf litter near host trees. They emerge in spring to feed on flushing leaves and tender bark. Females lay

ID: *Adult:* head and pronotum roughly equal in width, with wider elytra that is often brightly coloured or marked with lines or spots. *Willow Leaf Beetle:* white with black spots. *Cottonwood Leaf Beetle:* white with black stripes. *Striped Cucumber Beetle:* black with light stripes. *Aspen Leaf Beetle:* black with red sides. *Larva:* black to yellowish or reddish; elongate, clearly segmented and rough looking, almost like a little alligator.
Size: *Adult:* 10–12 mm. *Larva:* 3–10 mm.

Habitat and Range: Widespread throughout Ontario on broadleaved trees; most leaf beetles are named for their preferred host plant including willow *(Willow Leaf Beetle)*, poplars *(Cottonwood Leaf Beetle)*, cucumbers *(Striped Cucumber Beetle)* and trembling aspen *(Aspen Leaf Beetle)*.

Scouting: Leaf beetles typically scrape away the surface tissue on leaves. Later instars chew small holes in leaves. Adults skeletonize the leaves but cause much less damage

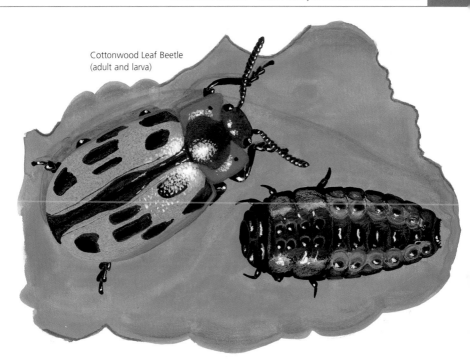

Cottonwood Leaf Beetle
(adult and larva)

eggs in clusters on the underside of leaves. Larvae feed in groups in the early instars and spread out to feed singly in later instars. After two to three weeks, they pupate on the underside of leaves, on the stem of the tree, at the base of grasses or in the soil, depending on the species. There may be two or more generations per year depending on temperature and food availability.

There are over 35,000 species of leaf beetles in the family Chrysomelidae alone. Chrysomelids are well known for being very colourful and decorated and are often used in jewellery. Apart from their beauty, they often have various chemical defenses, which they derive from the plants they eat. The San Bushmen of the Northern Kalahari in Africa use a toxin found in the Arrow Poison Beetle larvae on the tips of their arrows.

than do the larvae. Striped Cucumber Beetle adults feed on foliage and are especially damaging to cotyledons and seedlings, while the larvae feed below ground on the roots of cucumber, squash and other cucurbits.

Cultural/Physical Control: Prune egg masses and use pressure sprays of water to reduce the impact of tree-feeding species. The Cottonwood Leaf Beetle prefers to attack saplings, and controlling the beetle on these plants greatly reduces pressure on older trees. Rotate crops or plant in various areas to limit the damage done by the Striped Cucumber Beetle; early suppression is important because it is a vector of bacterial wilt and cucumber mosaic virus.

Biological Control: Generalist predators attack the eggs and early instar larvae.

Colorado Potato Beetle

Leptinotarsa decemlineata

This species originated in the eastern high plains of the U.S. portion of the Rocky Mountains and has spread across Canada and to Europe and Asia.

Adults and larvae bite and chew leaf material. Adults overwinter deep in the soil and emerge in May and June to feed on potato, eggplant and tomato. Females lay barrel-shaped orange eggs in groups of 10 or more on the underside of a leaf, eventually laying up to 500 eggs in their lifetime. Four larval instars feed on foliage alongside the adults. The larvae then drop to the soil surface and burrow 5 to 10 centimetres down to pupate. There may be one or two generations per year.

This beetle is a major concern for potato producers. Considerable research has gone into evaluating biological control using bacteria and fungi.

ID: *Adult:* roundish body; orange head and pronotum; yellowish elytra with parallel black stripes running lengthwise. *Larva:* orange, hump-backed body with 2 rows of black dots along side.

Size: *Adult:* 8–12 mm. *Larva:* 5–10 mm.

Habitat and Range: Across Ontario; found primarily on potato but also on tomato, eggplant and nightshade.

Scouting: Adults and larvae co-occur all season. Larvae make a ragged wound on leaves and often soil the leaf surface with their excrement. Adults feed by taking notches out of leaf margins. Look for batches of eggs on the underside of leaves. Feeding activity by the insect before the plant has bloomed stresses the plant and reduces the resources available to devote to reproduction (the bloom) or tuber growth. Feeding after the plant has bloomed usually does not have a serious impact.

Cultural/Physical Control: The easiest and most effective means of suppressing this beetle is to remove the egg masses in May and June. If you overlook some eggs, hand pick the larvae and adults in June and July.

Biological Control: Parasitism and predation by ground beetles, stink bugs and lady bird beetles rarely control this pest when it is present in high amounts.

Sap Beetles

Glischrochilus quadrisignatus, Carpophilus lugubris

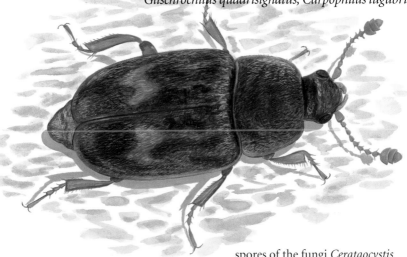

These little beetles don't bite and are generally harmless, but they are strongly attracted to ripe berries, fermenting fruit, alcohol and fresh paint. They bore into ripe tomatoes, apples and pears, and can be nuisances around garbage cans. Some species feed on and breed in carrion, and some in flowers, where they consume petals and pollen. Larvae of most species feed on fungi, but a few are predators of other insects. Some species' larvae eat developing kernels of sweet corn ears and are also known to spread the spores of the fungi *Cerataocystis fagacearum*, which causes oak wilt disease.

Adults and larvae overwinter in plant debris. Females emerge in late spring and lay eggs typically in rotting fruit. Larvae feed through four or five instars before pupating in the soil. There are two or three generations per year, depending on the species, and numbers generally peak in late June or July. Populations are often cyclic; every few years a high population develops then crashes because they are an attractive food for predatory insects and birds.

ID: *Adult: G. quadrisignatus:* black with yellow or reddish orange spots on elytra. *Dusky Sap Beetle* (Carpophilus lugubris)*:* dull dark grey with short wing covers. *Larva: G. quadrisignatus:* white with dark brown head. *Dusky Sap Beetle:* slightly flattened body; white with brown head and dark area on hind segment.

Size: *Adult:* 3–12 mm. *Larva:* 2–10 mm.

Habitat and Range: Widespread throughout the province.

Scouting: Look for sap beetles in June or July on ripe berries, fruit, sweet corn silks, petals and pollen.

Cultural/Physical Control: Pick fruit before it becomes overripe. Keep cull piles far away from producing crops. Bury and turn compost piles regularly. There is no effective control for sap beetles on corn silks or berry crops, but in small gardens they can sometimes be trapped using banana peels or muskmelon rinds. Check traps every 3 or 4 days and replace frequently. Adding pineapple scraps or a bait made from stale beer, yeast, vinegar, molasses and water may help attract them.

Biological Control: Many natural predators, including birds, feed on sap beetles.

Carrion Beetles

Nicrophorus spp.

Spinach Carrion Beetle larva

Carrion beetles, also called burying beetles, aid in the decomposition of dead animals. These beetles feed at night and, if disturbed, drop to the ground and rapidly seek cover under clumps of soil.

Adults overwinter in leaf litter and protected areas. They emerge in early May and mate. Females then lay eggs in the soil or in a dead animal. Larvae emerge a week later and start to feed on the dead carcass, or, in the case of the Spinach Carrion Beetle *(Silpha bituberosa)*, on the leaves of young plants. In a few weeks, the last instar larvae tunnel two to five centimetres into the soil to pupate, with adults emerging two to four weeks later. There is only one generation of Spinach Carrion Beetle per year, but other species may have two to three generations.

Carrion beetles are necessary to reduce dead animals to a state where bacteria and fungi can finish off the decomposition process. Crime scene investigators may use the instars of carrion beetle larvae, along with that of fly maggots, to estimate time of death.

ID: *Adult: Carrion* beetle: shiny black body with 4 orange spots on elytra. *Spinach Carrion Beetle:* dull black body with raised edges on elytra. *Larva:* shiny black, elongate, flattened and tapered toward posterior end.

Size: *Adult:* 10–12 mm. *Larva:* 3–10 mm.

Habitat and Range: Widespread in Ontario.

Scouting: Feeding damage results in ragged edges and holes on the leaves. Damage does not affect yield substantially.

Cultural/Physical Control: Remove weeds, which are food sources early in May. Hand pick when beetles are active at night.

Biological Control: Generalist predators consume the larvae.

Click Beetles

Conoderus spp.

Western Eyed
Click Beetle

Larval click beetles or wireworms shred roots and crowns of plants. More than 880 species of click beetle are in North America; as many as 24 different species may affect crops.

Adults emerge from pupation in April and May. Females prefer to lay eggs in loose, moist soil. Eggs hatch in three to seven weeks, and the larvae persist for 4 to 11 years before pupating. Pupae overwinter, and adults emerge the following spring. Adults expire the season they emerge.

You can place a potato a few centimetres under the soil in your garden and dig it up in a few weeks to see how many wireworms are there. Newly hatched larvae feed near the surface when it is cool and moist and move farther down to find moisture when it is hot and dry.

The name "click beetle" refers to the adult's ability to arch its thorax against its abdomen and snap into the air to startle predators or to right itself if it has been overturned.

Also Known As: Wireworms

ID: *Adult:* elongate; characterized by having 2-pointed corners on rear of protothorax. *Larva:* elongate, cylindrical and hardened body; progresses from white to tan to dark brown as it matures.

Size: *Adult:* 8–12 mm. *Larva:* 5–20 mm.

Habitat and Range: Throughout Ontario, often resting on trees and shrubs.

Scouting: Look for adults on plants while larvae live in the soil; they form tunnels when feeding in potato tubers and shred plant material instead of biting and chewing. The inner leaves of the plant wilt first.

Cultural/Physical Control: Most wireworm larvae die shortly after emerging from the egg because of changing moisture content, bacterial disease and predation. Consistently moist soils favour the larvae. Remove grasses near your vegetables, don't seed too early and encourage rapid germination to reduce the impact of wireworms.

Biological Control: Larvae are eaten by ground beetles and rove beetles.

June Beetles

Phyllophaga spp., *Polyphylla decemlineata*

May Beetle

Larval June beetles feed on roots of grasses, whereas the adults either do not feed or feed on leaves of trees and shrubs. There are several *Phyllophaga* species of June beetle in Ontario. The distinctive Ten-lined June Beetle (*Polyphylla decemlineata*) is slightly larger.

June beetle adults emerge from the soil in June, except the Ten-lined June Beetle, which emerges in July. Females lay their eggs in soil below turf that is near a light. Larvae develop through three instars over three years. First instar larvae hatch in June and feed until September, moult to second instar

ID: *Adult:* brownish and robust; antennae resemble a stack of long, thin pancakes impaled at one end on a stick. *Larva:* large, C-shaped grub with well-developed head and thoracic legs; underside of rear end has characteristic elongate V-shaped pattern of hairs.

Size: *Adult:* 15–20 mm. *Larva:* 5–30 mm.

Habitat and Range: Throughout Ontario; larvae feed on native grasses and on grass species used for lawns.

Scouting: The larvae inhabit the soil or subsurface layer of turf beneath the thatch in open fields, lawns, pastures, tree and shrub nurseries and cultivated fields. Larval damage, consisting of irregular patches of dead turf, occurs throughout summer. The larvae cut the roots; loosened sod can be rolled up like a carpet. Adults readily come to lights, and it is common to find stunned adults flailing about on their backs below street and porch lights.

Ten-lined June Beetle

and burrow down to overwinter. The following spring, the larvae return to the root zone to feed until autumn, when they again burrow deep for winter. In spring of the third year, the third instar larvae return to the root zone to feed for a short while and then burrow down to pupate. The adults develop in autumn and stay in the soil until the following spring. There can be overlapping generations with adults and all three instars present in one season.

The Ten-lined June Beetle is the largest scarab in Ontario. Members of the family Scarabeidae, or scarabs, are more commonly known as dung beetles. If it were not for the introduction of the lowly dung beetle into Australia, the Aussies would be hip deep in dry dung and worthless range land owing to the foreign nature of dung from cattle brought over by Europeans. Recall that Australia originally had no native ungulates (cows and the like), only marsupials to fill the ecological niche of grazer.

Cultural/Physical Control: The best defence is a well-maintained lawn. Weekly deep watering will help turf tolerate low levels of infestation. Remove excessive thatch. Control of adult beetles is not practical.

Biological Control: Ground beetles, birds and small mammals feed on the grubs. Crows and skunks tearing up your lawn is a good sign you have white grubs. Manage the white grubs and you should not have any problems with the vertebrates. Use nematodes (*Steinernema* and *Heterorhabditis* spp.) to treat the grubs if soil temperatures are above 20° C and there is adequate moisture.

European Chafer

Rhizotrogus majalis

Many animals, such as crows and skunks, will tear up your lawn in search of these juicy grubs.

The European Chafer beetle is an introduced species relatively new to North America. In the middle of June, large mating swarms of adults may be seen on trees around dusk. They cause only minor chewing damage along the margins of some leaves. Most damage is done in late summer by the larvae that feed on the roots of grasses and some shrubs. In fact, European Chafer larvae seem to out-compete Japanese Beetle larvae where the soil is sandy. Larvae feeding on grass roots seriously damages lawns across Ontario.

A one-year life cycle predominates, but a small percent of European Chafers require two years to complete their development. Eggs hatch around mid-July, and the larvae moult twice over the next eight weeks. The larvae are well adapted to cool, moist conditions and remain underground within five centimetres of the surface. During winter, they dig down farther to overwinter until April, when they once again come toward the surface and begin to feed and pupate. Adults emerge in May and mate, and the females burrow into the soil and deposit 20 to 30 eggs in earthen cells.

ID: *Adult:* oval, stout, light brown body. *Larva:* white overall; C-shaped.

Size: *Adult:* 9–11 mm. *Larva:* 1.5–33 mm.

Habitat and Range: Throughout Ontario where there are lawns.

Scouting: Larvae stay in soil beneath thatch lawns, grasslands and pastures. Damage, occurring in late summer and autumn, consists of irregular patches of dead turf. Larvae eat the roots, causing sod to loosen in large patches. Adults can be found in large aggregations feeding on host leaves during the day.

Cultural/Physical Control: Feed and water your lawn regularly to keep it healthy. To check for grubs, cut out a 30 cm x 30 cm piece of turf 5 cm deep, and look under it. If you find more than 20 grubs, control is needed.

Biological Control: Treat grubs with nematodes (*Steinernema* and *Heterorhabditis* spp.) if soil temperatures are above 20° C and there is adequate moisture.

Aphodius Beetles

A. granarius, A. pinguellus and others

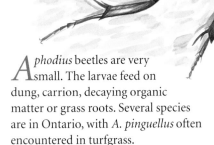

Aphodius Beetle

*A*phodius beetles are very small. The larvae feed on dung, carrion, decaying organic matter or grass roots. Several species are in Ontario, with *A. pinguellus* often encountered in turfgrass.

Adults emerge from overwintering from April through July, depending on the species and temperature. Females lay their eggs in dung, thatch or soil. Larvae go through three instars and pupate in the soil. The beetles typically overwinter in the adult stage. There can be one or more generations per year, depending on the temperature.

Now that more people incorporate compost into their gardens and top-dress their lawns, and with the widespread use of manure on agricultural fields, we should expect to see more Aphodius beetles visiting our yards and gardens.

Also Known As: Dung Beetle

ID: *Adult:* stout with broad head equal in width to pronotum and abdomen; legs sport backward-projecting spines to aid in digging; most are black or black with reddish or brown elytra. *Larva:* small, whitish, C-shaped grub with well-developed thoracic legs.

Size: *Adult:* 3–7 mm. *Larva:* 1–5 mm.

Habitat and Range: Province-wide in open pastures; many are specific to one kind of dung, whether cow or deer, while others prefer decaying vegetable matter, including thatch in lawns.

Scouting: Adults can be seen crawling through turfgrass from early April until autumn. The most common species, *A. pinguellus*, emerges in late June through July. Adults prefer turf warmed by the sun and are especially prevalent on sun-drenched golf course greens. Larvae feed on decaying organic matter in the thatch layer of lawns. Rarely do these insects become a pest. In cases where populations are very high, crows may tear up the turf in search of the tasty little grubs. *A. granarius* has been reported feeding on roots of turfgrass in Ontario.

Cultural/Physical Control: Maintain a healthy lawn and de-thatch to reduce available food sources and keep beetle numbers low.

Biological Control: Soil-dwelling predators such as ground beetles and rove beetles feed upon the larvae.

Japanese Beetle
Popillia japonica

The Japanese Beetle is an abundant and serious pest and is highly damaging in both the adult and larval stages. The adult feeds on the foliage of more than 300 different species of plants including rose, mountain ash, willow, linden, elm, grape, Virginia creeper, bean, Japanese and Norway maples, birch, pin oak, horse chestnut, rose of Sharon, sycamore, ornamental apple, plum and cherry. Larvae feed on the roots of many turfgrasses, causing extensive damage. The Japanese Beetle is widely dispersed throughout parts of southern Canada.

Nearly full-grown grubs overwinter in the soil below the frost line. As the soil warms in spring, the grubs begin to feed again on grass roots. They pupate 30 to 100 centimetres below the surface. Adults emerge during the end of June through to July and begin to feed on plant foliage, returning to the ground each evening. Adults that emerge earliest release an aggregation pheromone that attracts other adults.

ID: *Adult:* oval shaped; brilliant metallic green with coppery wing covers; abdomen has a row of 5 tufts of white hairs on each side. *Larva:* white overall; C-shaped when disturbed.

Size: *Adult:* 9–11 mm. *Larva:* 1.5–32 mm.

Habitat and Range: Occurs throughout Ontario; can be found in large numbers in some areas but be absent in nearby areas.

Scouting: The larvae inhabit the soil or sub-surface layer of turf beneath the thatch in open fields, meadows, lawns, grasslands, pastures, tree and shrub nurseries and cultivated fields. Larval damage, consisting of irregularly shaped patches of dead turf, occurs in late summer and autumn. The larvae cut the roots, loosening the sod. Adults can be found in large aggregations feeding on host leaves during the day.

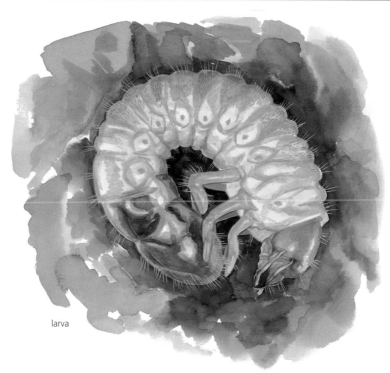

larva

In early August through to September, females breed and mate for several days. They then burrow three to five centimetres deep into the soil and lay their eggs. Most grubs are large by October and begin to dig deeper into the soil to overwinter. Over most of its range, the Japanese beetle has a one-year life cycle, though it can be two years in northern areas.

The Japanese Beetle was accidentally introduced to North America in the 1920s. It is now a serious pest throughout eastern North America.

Cultural/Physical Control: Pick off adults and destroy them by dropping them into a container of soapy water before they attract additional pests. Several commercially available traps can reduce damage and populations only when they are isolated from other breeding areas. In most urban areas, traps may actually attract more beetles into the area than would normally be present.

Biological Control: Ground beetles, birds and small mammals feed on the grubs. Manage the white grubs, and you should not have any problems with the vertebrates. Nematodes (*Steinernema* and *Heterorhabditis* spp.) can be used to treat the grubs if soil temperatures are above 20° C and there is adequate moisture.

Lady Beetles

Adalia bipunctata, Coccinella spp., *Hippodamia* spp. and others

Seven-spot Lady Beetle

Lady beetles are coloured so distinctively as a warning to predators that they taste bad. Some lady beetles contain alkaloids that they can excrete in a behaviour called "reflex bleeding," hence the smelly liquid on your fingers after handling a lady beetle.

Most lady beetles are predators, feeding on soft-bodied insects and insect eggs. There are 200 different species of lady beetle in North America. The most commonly encountered species are the Seven-spot Lady Beetle (*C. septempunctata*), an introduced species from Europe, and the Convergent Lady Beetle (*H. convergens*). Other commonly encountered lady beetles include the Twice-stabbed Lady Beetle (*Chilocorus*

Also Known As: Ladybugs, Lady Bird Beetles

ID: *Adult:* round body; variously coloured, but predominantly black head and thorax (some have white markings on pronotum), orange-red elytra and 1 or more black spots or stripes. *Seven-spot Lady Beetle:* has 7 black spots. *Convergent Lady Beetle:* has 13 black spots and 2 converging white steaks on pronotum. *Larva:* looks like a rough little alligator, usually black with white, orange or pale markings and tapering toward rear.

Size: *Adult:* 4–8 mm. *Larva:* 3–10 mm.

Habitat and Range: Virtually everywhere in Ontario; some species are herb, forb or shrub specialists, whereas others are better adapted to hunting in trees such as birch, spruce, Manitoba maple, mountain ash, wolf willow, caragana and alder.

Scouting: Eggs are laid singly on the leaf surface. Larvae can be readily seen on the upper and lower surface of the leaf, particularly in the vicinity of aphids. Adult lady

Spotted Lady Beetle larva

Convergent Lady Beetle

stigma), Thirteen-spot Lady Beetle *(H. tredecimpunctata)*, Five-spot Lady Beetle *(H. quinquesignata)*, Parenthesis Lady Beetle *(H. parenthesis)*, Two-spot Lady Beetle *(A. bipunctata)* and Transverse Lady Beetle *(C. transversoguttata)*.

Adults lay up to several hundred eggs in spring and throughout summer. Not all eggs are destined to hatch; some, called trophic eggs, serve as the first meal for the newly emerged larvae. There are four larval instars and one pupal stage. Development from egg to adult can be as quick as two weeks or as long as seven weeks. There may be more than one generation per year. Adults may live from a few months up to two or three years. Some species aggregate in dense masses under leaf litter or in homes when overwintering.

beetles roam the leaves and stems in search of suitable prey. They are also capable fliers and can be seen "on the wing."

How to Attract: The lady beetle has long been considered the "gardener's friend" because of its penchant for feasting on aphids. This reputation is largely undeserved. Most aphid populations will be reduced more or less by lady beetles, but some aphids, such as foxglove and potato aphids, can become more of a problem if lady beetles are about. Also, lady beetles are not the best or the most effective aphid predators. Store-bought lady beetles disperse away from your yard shortly after release. You would do better to encourage natural colonization by lady beetles by providing many different plants in your yard (lady beetles feed on nectar and pollen in the absence of aphid prey).

Multicoloured Asian Lady Bird Beetle

Harmonia axyridis

Ladybugs eat aphids, and because aphids eat crops and garden plants, ladybugs are usually considered good bugs. However, Multicoloured Asian Lady Bird Beetles do not have such a good reputation. These beetles have an annoying habit of invading buildings in autumn by the hundreds or thousands as they prepare for hibernation. Also,

when populations get very high, as they did in Ontario in 2001, they damage fruit and bite people. In the 1920s, a few hundred of these insects were introduced in the eastern United States for aphid control. They quickly established themselves across most of the U.S. and Canada, and during the mid-1990s, the population exploded. This Asian import is now the most common species of lady bird beetle in North America and is rapidly displacing native lady bird species.

Adults overwinter in great masses, often inside buildings including houses. In spring, females lay eggs on host plants. Eggs hatch in about three to five days, and larvae begin searching plants for aphids and other soft-bodied arthropods to feed on. After four moults, the larvae pupate and adults emerge after several days. Development from egg to adult takes two to seven weeks, and there may be more than one generation per year. Adults may live from a few months up to two or three years.

ID: *Adult:* round body; occur in a wide variety of colour forms and various spotting patterns; recognized by white, M-shaped mark on pronotum. *Larva:* looks like a rough little alligator; usually bright orange with black and white; tapers toward rear.

Size: *Adult:* 5–8 mm. *Larva:* 3–10 mm.

Habitat and Range: Widespread in Ontario on a variety of plants.

Scouting: Eggs are laid singly on the leaf surface. Look for larvae on upper and lower leaf surfaces, particularly in the vicinity of aphids. Adult lady beetles roam the leaves

and stems in search of suitable prey. Lady beetle adults are also capable fliers.

How to Attract: Although it can be a nuisance, the Multicoloured Asian Lady Beetle does help to control aphids. Try to encourage a wide variety of lady beetles to your yard, including rapidly disappearing native species, by providing many different plants in your yard (lady beetles will feed on nectar and pollen in the absence of aphid prey). To prevent them from entering your home, ensure all exterior cracks and crevices are caulked before the beetles seek overwintering sites.

Bark Beetles

Dendroctonus spp., *Ips pini*

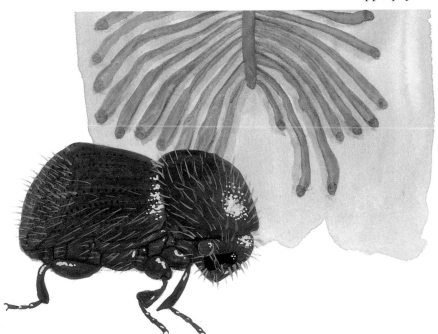

These beetles are the miners of the beetle world. Their primary hosts are conifers, where they live in galleries under the bark. They attack stressed trees and can lead to the trees' demise. Unfortunately, the beetles are quite difficult to control or eliminate. If you happen to encounter an unhealthy tree or an old tree that is infested, consider removing it.

Bark beetles often seen in our region are the Spruce Beetle (*D. rufipennis*), Eastern Larch Beetle (*D. simplex*), Lodgepole Pine Beetle (*D. murrayanae*), Red Turpentine Beetle (*D. valens*) and Pine Engraver (*I. pini*).

ID: *Adult:* dark, ovate body. *Larva:* legless, white grub.

Size: *Adult:* 4–7 mm. *Larva:* similar to adult, but earlier stages are smaller.

Habitat and Range: Found throughout Ontario in stressed and decaying conifers such as spruce, pine and larch.

Scouting: Watch for tiny holes ("pitch tubes") on the trunk or branches, sawdust at the base of tree and signs of beetle galleries underneath bark. A sappy paste containing wood particles oozing out of pitch tubes is a common sign. In later stages of infestation, bark easily peels away to reveal beetle galleries.

Cultural/Physical Control: Keep trees healthy and stress free and prune off dead or dying branches in early spring before beetles start looking for new homes. Remove and dispose of infested trees. If there are only a few beetles, about 10 or less, dig them out with a knife so that only a small wound is created on the trunk. Larger wounds can be treated with a dressing such as pine tar or pruning paint.

Biological Control: Hang synthetic, anti-aggregation hormones from trees to deter some beetles from attacking.

Elm Bark Beetles

Hylurgopinus rufipes, Scolytus multistriatus

Elm Bark Beetles are the vectors of one of the most destructive diseases in North America, Dutch Elm Disease (DED). The beetles themselves are relatively harmless to elms and can live in trees without killing them, but they are deadly when combined with the DED fungus. When DED arrived in North America and began infecting and weakening elms, it created the perfect conditions for these opportunistic beetles.

Bark beetles and their larvae spend most of their lives feeding on plant tissues under the bark, creating a series of tunnels known as galleries. Adults emerge in early to mid-spring and move to the crowns of healthy elms to feed. Healthy trees often make life difficult for bark beetles, which bore through the bark and are flushed out by sap. In early to midsummer, the beetles seek unhealthy, weakened or dead trees or firewood, where they lay eggs and build galleries under the bark.

Almost every elm infected with DED dies within two years.

ID: *Adult:* dark, ovate body. *Native Elm Bark Beetle (H. rufipes):* dark brown to black. *European Elm Bark Beetle (S. multistriatus):* dark red to brown; smaller overall. *Larva:* white, legless grub.

Size: *Adult:* 2–3 mm. *Larva:* similar to adult.

Habitat and Range: Throughout Ontario where elm trees are found.

Scouting: Trees infected with DED have wilting, yellowing foliage on some branches (called "flagging") and a brown ring in the infected area underneath the bark. Contact your municipality if you suspect a tree has this disease or if you want to know more about the status of the disease in the region. Do not

transport firewood into Ontario from other provinces and report anyone who does.

Cultural/Physical Control: Keep elms healthy and vigorous and water them in years of drought. Prune off any dead or dying branches annually in late winter. Remove and destroy infected trees. Replace with another species or with a DED-resistant elm variety such as *Ulmus davidiana* var. *japonica* 'Jacan' or the 'Liberty' elms. Purchase a variety that is hardy for your area.

Biological Control: Bark beetles spend most of their lives feeding under bark and are therefore protected from predators.

Eastern Ash Bark Beetle

Hylesinus aculeatus

This pest bark beetle from the family Scolytidae damages and kills branches and twigs of ash trees. Wilting or yellowish foliage on branches is one of the key symptoms of trees that may be under attack. To confirm whether a tree has beetles, check under the bark of ash branches for adults, grubs or galleries.

The adults emerge in spring and form a gallery under the bark of branches and twigs, where they court, mate and lay eggs. Larvae hatch in June and feed into July, when they pupate. Adults re-emerge in August and overwinter at the base of the tree in surrounding soil.

Many Scolytidae beetles have a symbiotic relationship with fungi. The fungus relies on the beetles for transport to new trees, and the beetle relies on the fungus to weaken its host.

Hylesinus spp.

ID: *Adult:* dark, ovate body with dorsal "herring bone" pattern. *Larva:* white, legless grub.

Size: *Adult:* 2–3 mm. *Larva:* 3–4 mm.

Habitat and Range: Throughout Ontario where ash trees are found; prefers green ash.

Scouting: Watch for dead or dying branches and look in tree crevices for boring holes, boring dust and copious sap flow. Use binoculars to check for signs in tree crown. Dust is most obvious at the base of trees in September and August.

Cultural/Physical Control: Prevention is the best control. Keep ash trees healthy and vigorous and water in years of drought. Prune off dead or dying branches and remove old, decaying trees that have many dead branches. Apply a band of adhesive around the trunk at the base of trees in early April to catch adults wandering up from their overwintering sites.

Biological Control: In a few areas, a hymenoptera parasite and mite infest larvae, resulting in high mortality. Also, a braconid wasp in some areas can provide control of larvae.

Strawberry Root Weevil

Otiorhynchus ovatus

The Strawberry Root Weevil bites and chews in the larval and adult stages. This weevil was introduced from Europe and is found across Ontario.

Adults and larvae overwinter in debris or soil beneath host plants. Adults also have the annoying habit of entering homes to overwinter and can be found trundling about in autumn and late spring, looking for a host plant on which to lay eggs. Eggs are laid near food hosts. Larvae from spring-laid eggs burrow down to feed on roots and pupate in the soil. Larvae from autumn-laid eggs will overwinter. Adults are incapable of flight, instead relying on determination to walk everywhere, and they certainly can walk!

There are no male Strawberry Root Weevils, only females. All eggs laid hatch into females. With no time wasted looking for a mate, females just plug along, business as usual, which is possibly one key to their success.

ID: *Adult:* stout, black body with rounded sides; mouthparts positioned at end of broad muzzle. *Larva:* C-shaped, legless, white grub with light brown head.

Size: *Adult:* 6 mm. *Larva:* 3–12 mm.

Habitat and Range: Thrives throughout Ontario.

Scouting: Adults feed at night on the foliage of strawberry, clover, grasses and various weeds, notching the edge of leaves. They puncture strawberry fruit, but this feeding does not cause unsightly damage. Larvae feed on the roots of strawberry, raspberry, containerized evergreens, grasses and weeds. Larval feeding on roots stunts plants, and severe infestations can result in death of the plant.

Cultural/Physical Control: Move your strawberry plants to different patches or rotate them with another plant species each year. The adult weevils in your home are harmless and only need be vacuumed up. Ensure your house is sealed at the windows and entryways.

Biological Control: Ground beetles and rove beetles, among others, will eat the larvae.

White Pine Weevil

Pissodes strobi

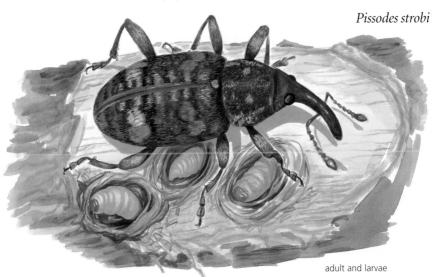

adult and larvae

The White Pine Weevil infects both pine and spruce. It is easy to tell if a spruce or pine has the White Pine Weevil attacking it because the top growth of the tree (leader) is either dead or swollen and wilting. These pests cause disfigurement when they kill the top growth of the tree.

Adults overwinter in the duff beneath infested trees. They emerge in early spring and either walk or fly to a nearby host to begin feeding and laying eggs in last year's leader. Young trees in full sun are most susceptible. The larvae feed and pupate inside the stem, emerging as adults in late summer.

Damage is often observed in late spring and early summer and can be diagnosed by a wilting leader that has a series of tiny holes at its base. Pitch (conifer sap) may flow from the holes. If you dig into this area, you will often observe white grubs as well. Don't panic if you have to remove the tree's leader; a new leader can be easily trained, and the tree will be back to normal after a couple of years.

There are 26 fly and wasp parasites of Pissodes *weevils in Canada.*

ID: *Adult:* small, dark, elephant-like beetle. *Larva:* white, legless grub.

Size: *Adult:* 4–7 mm. *Larva:* similar to adult, but earlier stages are smaller.

Habitat and Range: In forests and parklands throughout Ontario; in conifer trees such as young white, Colorado and Norway spruce as well as lodgepole pine and Jack pine in open, sunny locations.

Scouting: Look for dead or wilting leaders on conifers. Adults may be present near the trees' terminal buds in early spring.

Cultural/Physical Control: Prune off the infested area, and bag and dispose of it. Keep the ground under infested trees free of duff.

Biological Control: Provide plenty of habitat for natural predators such as parasitic wasps and flies.

Poplar and Willow Borer

Cryptorhynchus lapathi

The Poplar and Willow Borer is an introduced weevil from Europe, and it is probably the most prevalent species encountered in landscape willows and poplars. The damage it causes can set back, weaken, disfigure and kill trees.

The life cycle takes two years to complete. Adult beetles emerge from late June until late July, depending on the year, and feed heavily on new shoots. After mating, the female lays eggs in small holes chewed in the lower part of the stem. Once the eggs hatch, the first instar larvae burrow under bark and hibernate over winter. In spring, the larvae become active and bore into the wood, forming tunnels that meander around and into the stem. Larval feeding causes quite extensive damage. The larvae continue to feed and grow, eventually pupating at the end of the tunnel. Adults then mine their way back through the tunnel, making their way outside.

A number of shoot and stem boring insects attack poplars and willows in our region. The Cottonwood Twig Borer (Gypsonoma haimbachiana) larvae feed on the young shoots of hybrid poplar.

ID: *Adult:* black, elephant-shaped beetle with dark, erect hairs and light-coloured rump patch. *Larva:* white, legless grub with brown head.

Size: *Adult:* 8–10 mm. *Larva:* 13 mm, but other stages may be smaller.

Habitat and Range: Throughout Ontario.

Scouting: Look for dead, wilting or discoloured stems and branches, irregular splits and holes in the tree bark that exude sawdust-laden sap, and sawdust at the bottom of the stem. Tunnels may be seen in split stems.

Cultural/Physical Control: Remove infested branches and burn or bury them deep in the ground. Slide a piece of wire into tunnels and jam it into the larvae.

Biological Control: Chickadees and nuthatches pick larvae off leaves and out of bark crevices. Other predators include predacious beetles and parasitic wasps and flies. Letting nature take its course is often the cheapest, easiest and simplest control.

Rose Curculio

Merhynchites bicolor

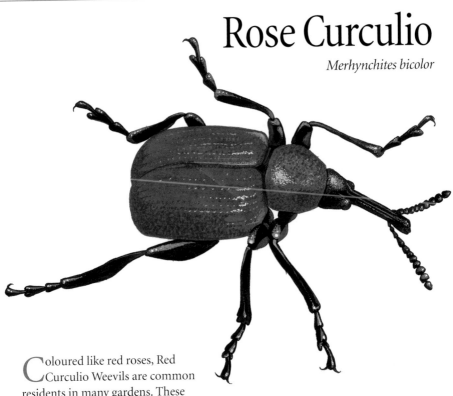

Coloured like red roses, Red Curculio Weevils are common residents in many gardens. These weevils look like miniature, red-backed elephants with a black head and belly. Unfortunately, they are often nuisances and can kill rose buds or riddle flowers with unsightly holes.

Adults feed on rose buds, petals and pollen in June. The females lay eggs in the developing rose hip, where the white, legless grubs feed throughout summer on developing seeds. In September, these mature grubs fall to the ground, where they pupate in the soil. The damage these weevils cause is mostly cosmetic, meaning fewer flowers, and can be managed. If you make the necessary precautions an annual routine, these weevils can be easily controlled.

There are more species of weevils of the superfamily Curculionoidea than there are known vertebrates. There are approximately 43,000 species of vertebrates and 60,000 weevils.

ID: *Adult:* small, red, elephant-like beetle. *Larva:* white, legless grub.

Size: *Adult:* 8 mm. *Larva:* similar to adult, but earlier stages are smaller.

Habitat and Range: Rose gardens across the province.

Scouting: Watch for weevils on buds in June and July, and deformed rosebuds and defoliation on petals.

Cultural/Physical Control: In spring, pick off and dispose of adult weevils and deformed rose hips.

Biological Control: To provide plenty of habitat for natural predators such as ground beetles, parasitic wasps and flies, leave some wild areas in your garden and minimize or eliminate insecticide use. No insecticides are currently registered for this species.

Asian Long-horned Beetle

Anoplophora glabripennis

The Asian Long-horned Beetle is a serious forest pest in Asia and has been introduced to Canada through infested wooden crates and pallets used to ship items overseas. It was first detected in the early 1990s. In 2003, beetle-infested trees were discovered in the Toronto-Vaughn area. It is a great threat to hardwood trees including elm, maple, poplar, chestnut, butternut, beech and ash. Now all non-manufactured wood from Hong Kong and China must undergo kiln drying, fumigation or treatment with preservatives prior to shipping. The beetle has either a one- or two-year life cycle. It overwinters as an egg, larva or pupa under the bark of the tree. Eggs are deposited in the inner bark. The eggs develop in one to two weeks in summer, or over several months if laid in autumn. Young larvae feed for 20 days in the sappy, green inner bark. This causes a reduced flow of nutrient and water transport within the tree. Older larvae bore into the sapwood and heartwood, chewing tunnels through the trunk and branches, compromising the structure of the tree. Mature larvae pupate inside the wood in early spring. Adults emerge and chew exit holes in the bark in late June. Females disperse, feed and chew egg pits through the bark of the host trees, in which they deposit a single egg within the cambium and plug the pit. Adult populations peak in July and August.

ID: *Adult:* bullet-shaped; glossy black, with up to 20 white dorsal spots; antennae are 1–2.5 times longer than body length, with 11 black segments with whitish blue bases. *Larva:* creamy white overall.

Size: *Adult:* 1.7–3.5 cm. *Larva:* 1–5 cm.

Habitat and Range: Isolated to Toronto-Vaughn border hardwood trees.

Scouting: Look for adults on street and backyard trees, isolated or open grown trees, hedgerows and edges of woodlots or ravines.

Egg pits are oval or round and are 10–15 mm in diameter; they can be found on the trunk, branches or exposed roots of trees greater than 5 cm in diameter. Sap may be seen leaking at egg pits and may attract other insects. Exit holes are 10–15 mm in diameter.

Cultural/Physical Control: Movement of firewood, nursery stock and any other potential sources of infected wood, such as wood chips, is prohibited from infested areas.

Biological Control: No known natural predators in North America.

Poplar Borer

Saperda calcarata

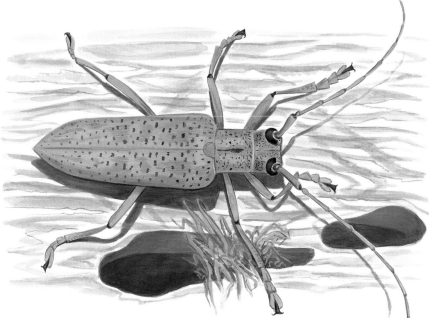

This species is one of our longest-living beetles and can take up to five years to fully develop. It is in the family Cerambycidae, which is commonly known as the long-horned beetles.

Adults emerge in late June, when they feed on foliage for about a week. Females mate and seek out a stressed tree in which to lay their eggs. One or two eggs are laid in crescent shaped notches that the females chew into the trunk in the upper crown and exposed areas. Once the eggs hatch, the larvae bore into the inner bark. Larvae feed, grow and hibernate each autumn until maturity. Mature larvae hibernate one last time in a prepupal stage and pupate the following spring.

ID: *Adult:* pale with colourful flecking; antennae are same length as body. *Larva:* white, legless grub with brown head and thoracic shield.

Size: *Adult:* 20–30 mm. *Larva:* 20–35 mm, but other stages may be smaller.

Habitat and Range: Primary hosts are native aspen and black poplar, but sometimes attacks ornamental species such as hybrid poplar; occurs throughout forest regions.

Scouting: Watch for copious, bark-staining, amber-coloured sap flow and emergence holes. Sawdust is present at the base of the trunk and in sap. In young trees, borers are found either at the trunk base or in the root collar region.

Cultural/Physical Control: Keep trees healthy and vigorous to reduce tree susceptibility. You can mimic a woodpecker by thrusting a piece of wire into gallery entrances on the trunk to injure and kill larvae.

Biological Control: Natural predators include woodpeckers, which can reduce populations by up to 75%, and parasitic insects such as wasps.

White-spotted Sawyer

Monochamus scutellatus and others

Long-horned beetles such as the White-spotted Sawyer are beneficial forest insects that help speed up the breakdown of dying, fallen and dead trees. Adults are easily recognized by their long antennae (hence the common name), which give them a "demonic" appearance. These harmless guys rarely bite people; they are actually boring beetles that attack conifers. If they do land on you, just flick them off.

White-Spotted Sawyers have a two-year life cycle. Adults emerge in early June and fly until the end of July. For the first 10 days, adults forage on dead and dying conifers. They especially love firewood and fallen trees. Later they mate, and females find a suitable tree, chewing a small notch at the base of a branch, where they deposit one or more white, elongate eggs. About two weeks later, the larvae hatch and begin feeding, at first just under the bark, and later, into the deeper sapwood where they overwinter as larvae. In spring, they continue mining into the tree, eventually reaching the heartwood, at which point they begin to head outward again, forming a U-shaped tunnel in the tree. In late summer or autumn, they

White-spotted
Sawyer

ID: *Adult:* black overall; long, dark antennae are much longer than body; thorax has 2 lateral spines; white spot at base of elytra. *Larva:* whitish, legless grub with yellowish thorax and brown head; head region often appears slightly swollen, giving larva a club-like appearance.
Size: *Adult:* 20–25 mm. *Larva:* 35–50 mm.

Habitat and Range: On spruce, pine, fir and sometimes larch trees across Ontario.
Scouting: Watch for signs of wood chips and frass at the base of dead or dying conifer trees or around freshly cut firewood. If you hear a chewing sound coming from a tree trunk, you are likely listening to a feeding sawyer beetle.

Male White-Spotted Sawyers have antennae that are twice their body length, whereas females have antennae that are half the length of the males.'

Northeastern Sawyer

form a pupal chamber under the bark and hibernate in a prepupal stage until spring, when they pupate.

A similar species, the Northeastern Sawyer *(M. notatus)*, is larger and much less common. Adult size ranges from 25 to 35 millimetres. This species has a mottled grey body and lacks the distinct elytra spot present on the White-Spotted Sawyer. Its biology and life cycle are pretty much the same as the White-Spotted Sawyer's, though the Northeastern Sawyer also attacks white pine in eastern Canada. There are a few much smaller sawyers in the genus *Tetropium* that are sometimes encountered. These sawyers have a one-year life cycle. They are easily identified because they are basically miniature forms of the above two *Monochamus* species, but their antennae are only half the length of their body.

Cultural/Physical Control: Keep trees healthy. If you are a woodlot owner and suspect that sawyers are attacking your standing or fallen trees, process the logs within one year, if not sooner. Beetle larvae tunnelling through logs will reduce their value as lumber.

Biological Control: Predators include woodpeckers and parasitic wasps, so having some native forest or wilderness as habitat is of great benefit.

Bronze Birch Borer

Agrilus anxius

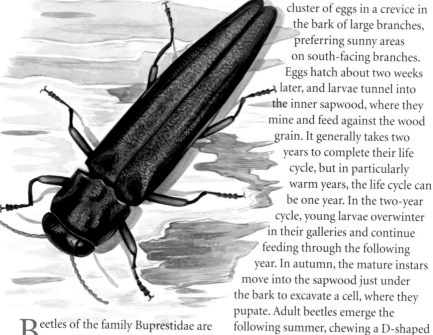

Beetles of the family Buprestidae are some of the world's most attractive beetles and have earned the title of "jewel beetle." Unfortunately, they also have a destructive side, as is the case with the Bronze Birch Borer.

In August, adult females seek out stressed trees and lay an egg or small cluster of eggs in a crevice in the bark of large branches, preferring sunny areas on south-facing branches. Eggs hatch about two weeks later, and larvae tunnel into the inner sapwood, where they mine and feed against the wood grain. It generally takes two years to complete their life cycle, but in particularly warm years, the life cycle can be one year. In the two-year cycle, young larvae overwinter in their galleries and continue feeding through the following year. In autumn, the mature instars move into the sapwood just under the bark to excavate a cell, where they pupate. Adult beetles emerge the following summer, chewing a D-shaped emergence hole through the bark and feeding on the foliage.

Agrilus is one of the world's biggest beetle genera and has nearly 3000 species described.

ID: *Adult:* slender, cylindrical body, olive green to black with metallic bronze sheen. *Larva:* white, distinctly segmented, legless grub with deeply embedded brown head in a slightly swollen prothorax.

Size: *Adult:* 6–11 mm. *Larva:* similar to adult, but earlier stages are smaller.

Habitat and Range: Occurs in weakened birch trees, including native species such as paper, yellow and grey birch as well as ornamental species.

Scouting: Look for dead or dying treetops, wilting and flagging branches and D-shaped holes in the bark of trunks and branches.

Larval galleries in fast-growing trees are filled with new tissue and create a bumpy ridge in the bark.

Cultural/Physical Control: Prevention is the best control. Plant resistant species, and do not plant trees in full sun. Keep trees healthy and vigorous. Water well, especially during droughts. Remove dead and dying branches annually. Cut off and burn infested branches before adults emerge.

Biological Control: Woodpeckers and wasp parasitoids are natural controls for the Bronze Birch Borer.

Emerald Ash Borer

Agrilus planipennis

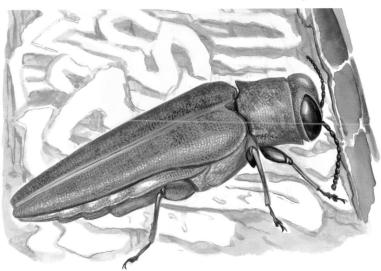

The Emerald Ash Borer is a recently introduced species from China. It was first discovered in North America in southeastern Michigan in 2002 and has since spread to Ohio, Indiana, Maryland and near Windsor, and most recently, in London, Ontario. It is considered a very serious pest because it kills ash trees. The adults feed on the foliage of ash trees but cause little damage. The larvae cause severe damage as they feed on the inner bark of live ash trees, disrupting the transport of water and nutrients within the tree and resulting in the tree's death.

Adults emerge in spring. Females lay 75 eggs from early May to mid-July. The larvae feed on the inner bark of the trees, creating snake-shaped galleries under the bark. After several moults, they pupae and emerge as adults. Research is ongoing to help fully understand the timing of the life cycle in Ontario. There is probably one generation per year.

Black ash is important to many Native American cultures because it is the only wood used to make black ash baskets.

ID: *Adult:* metallic green overall. *Larva:* whitish overall.

Size: *Adult:* 20 mm; *Larva:* 15 mm.

Habitat and Range: Forests containing ash trees in and around Windsor and London.

Scouting: Adults leave a D-shaped exit hole in the bark when they emerge in spring. Look under the bark for characteristic snake-shaped burrows filled with fine sawdust. Heavy woodpecker damage may indicate the presence of larvae.

Cultural/Physical Control: Remove and destroy infected ash trees. The CFIA has been establishing ash-free zones in areas where the pest is present to provide a barrier to slow its spread. Moving any ash forest products, including nursery stock, logs, debris and firewood, from regulated areas is banned.

Biological Control: A parasitic wasp, *Tetrastichus planipennisi*, lays eggs into larvae under the bark and may control the beetles; woodpeckers search out and eat the larvae.

Tiger Swallowtails

Papilio spp.

Canadian Tiger
Swallowtail

If Canadian Tiger Swallowtail larvae are gently squeezed or disturbed by a predator, they evert (expand from inside) a brightly coloured, two-pronged, glandular organ known as an osmeterium, which is tucked away behind the head and has a horned appearance when fully everted. This organ produces foul-smelling, terpene-based defensive compounds that often deter attackers.

Every spring, our region comes alive with large, attractive Canadian Tiger Swallowtails (*P. canadensis*) and the much larger Eastern Tiger Swallowtail (*P. glaucus*). They dart swiftly through gardens and yards. Adults are valuable pollinators and can often be observed feeding on nectar from flowers in gardens or along lilac shelterbelts. Large groups can be seen drinking at puddles after a rain shower or feeding on fresh scat. There have

ID: *Adult:* dark body; yellow wings striped with black; hindwings have black tails. *Eastern Tiger Swallowtail:* some females are dark and mimic the toxic Pipevine Swallowtail. *Larva:* dark green, resembling snake; thin, yellow stripe separates thorax and abdomen; swollen head region has 2 black, yellow and blue eyespots; immature larva resembles bird droppings and is brown and white.

Size: *Adult:* wingspan 53–90 mm. *Larva:* body length up to 50 mm.

Habitat and Range: Common throughout Ontario; host plants include aspen, poplar and willow.

Scouting: Watch for adults in May and June cruising through openings in wooded areas, and for larvae in curled leaves of host trees.

Tiger Swallowtails feed on nectar of lilacs and other flowers

been a number of sightings of groups feeding on coyote dung.

Adults fly from spring to early summer, eventually mating. Females lay eggs on host plant leaves and may mate more than once. The eggs hatch in a week or so, and larvae spend the summer feeding. In late summer, mature larvae seek out a suitable pupation site, often in the duff beneath the host tree, and can sometimes be found crawling through the garden. They pupate and overwinter as chrysalises, emerging as adults the following spring.

Canadian Tiger Swallowtail

How to Attract: These butterflies are attracted to a few garden flowers, but their favourite ornamental seems to be lilacs. Leave some natural bluffs of swallowtails' host trees, such as aspen, poplar and willow, undisturbed.

Cabbage Butterfly

Pieris rapae

The Cabbage Butterfly can be one of the most unwanted garden pests and is a common sight in gardens. It was introduced to Quebec in 1860 from Europe and is now all over the continent. This average-sized butterfly is sometimes referred to as a Cabbage Moth or Cabbage Worm.

This species can have up to three generations per year in our region, with adults emerging from overwintering chrysalises in spring. A female lays eggs on the host. Larvae hatch, feed and mature within three or four weeks.

Cabbage Butterfly larvae have very successful defensive capabilities. Glandular hairs arranged in rows on their back flanks excrete oil that repels insect predators such as ants. During experiments in which ants were allowed to interact with larvae, the ants immediately became irritated upon contact with the larvae and began cleaning themselves, eventually leaving the larvae alone. In other experiments, birds were given an opportunity to feed on a mixture of different edible caterpillars. After they'd picked through the mass, all that was left were Cabbage Butterfly larvae.

ID: *Adult:* white with black forewing tips; female has 2 black forewing spots. *Larva:* velvety, green caterpillar with faint yellow dorsal line.

Size: *Adult:* wingspan 30–50 mm. *Larva:* body length up to 30 mm.

Habitat and Range: Throughout Ontario, especially in gardens; host plants include cabbage, cauliflower, broccoli, canola and other domestic and wild mustard family plants.

Scouting: Check leaves for feeding damage such as holes, and for the presence of frass.

Cultural/Physical Control: Hand pick larvae off plants. Deter ovipositing females by covering plants with a floating row cover (spun polyester fabric that allows light and water to penetrate) or lightweight netting as a barrier. Interplant repellent plants such as mint, sage, rosemary, catnip, nasturtium, tomato and celery.

Biological Control: Many beneficial insects parasitize and feed on the larvae, including an array of parasitoid wasps, and predators such as ground beetles, hornets and birds. Leave or develop some natural areas in the yard to encourage these beneficial animals.

Clouded Sulphur

Colias philodice

The Clouded Sulphur is common from spring to autumn in our yards and gardens. A few similar-looking species also appear in our gardens. The Alfalfa Butterfly (*C. eurytheme*) tends to have orange forewings. The two species hybridize, and the resulting adults have characteristics of both species.

This species has two to three generations. Eggs are laid in spring on herbaceous legumes. Larvae later hatch and feed on legume foliage and, once mature, pupate. The first big adult population appears in June, the second occurs in July and a third small population appears in autumn. Adults of this final generation can survive into October and are able to withstand a few frosty days. There is some debate as to which stage overwinters; some literature suggests it is the pupae and other literature suggests it is the third instar larvae, which then start feeding on emerging host plants in April and May. The latter seems to make the most sense here, though it is possible that pupae may also overwinter. More research is needed to clarify this matter.

ID: *Adult:* forewing has somewhat centrally placed black dot; dorsal hindwing has central orange spot; ventral hindwing has row of spots behind single larger white dot lined with red; male is yellow with broad, black marginal forewing bands; female is either yellow or white, with yellow spots within black borders. *Larva:* green with white stripe along side; stripe is lined with dark green and has faint orange to red line within.

Size: *Adult:* wingspan 32–54 mm. *Larva:* body length 35 mm.

Habitat and Range: Throughout Ontario wherever alfalfa, clover, and many other legumes are found.

Scouting: A yellow butterfly flitting in your garden is likely a Clouded Sulphur.

How to Attract: This species is easy to attract because host plants are quite common here, especially in rural areas. Plant a butterfly garden with various nectar-producing flowers that bloom from spring to autumn.

Spring Azure & Eastern Tailed Blue

Celastrina ladon, Everes comyntas

Spring Azure

Spring Azure
"lucia" form (male)

These butterflies are the gems of gardens as they flutter from flower to flower. Spring Azures (*C. ladon*) emerge in late April and flutter among the flushing trees. Once the leaves flush, the Eastern Tailed Blues (*E. comyntas*) arrive. Blues are nectar feeders, so they love having a garden full of nectar-producing flowers. On hot, dry days, large groups of blues can be observed drinking at puddles.

ID: *Adult:* male is more colourful than female. *Spring Azure:* purplish blue dorsal wings; grey ventrally with black spotting. *Eastern Tailed Blue:* easily separated from all others by its hindwing tails. *Larva:* slug-shaped caterpillar. *Spring Azure:* green overall. *Eastern Tailed Blue:* can be green to purplish, with darker dorsal stripe and lighter diagonal stripes.

Size: *Adult:* wingspan 20–32 mm. *Larva:* body length 15–20 mm.

Habitat and Range: Throughout Ontario, especially in areas near native bush, ravines or riparian areas. *Spring Azure:* prefers sheltered woodland; host plants for larvae include dogwoods, cranberries, bunchberries, blueberries and other low shrubs. *Eastern Tailed Blue:* prefers fields, gardens and wildflower meadows, and legumes such as vetch, clover, pea vines, locoweed and lupine as hosts.

Eastern Tailed Blue (male)

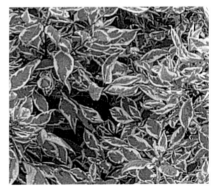

Eastern Tailed Blue (female)

Spring Azure adults emerge in spring, mate and lay eggs. Small, slug-like larvae produce a sticky secretion that attracts ants. In return, the ants protect them. Larvae feed on flowers and flower buds throughout summer and overwinter as pupae. The other species' life cycles are similar, occurring slightly later. The larvae eat the flowers, leaves and seeds of their hosts.

Planting small shrubs such as dogwood (above) will help attract Spring Azures to your garden.

Scouting: From early spring to early summer, look for adults feeding at flowers and for males perched on plants, especially in gardens bordering woodlands.

How to Attract: All species thrive where natural and wild areas have been maintained, so the preservation of these habitats, especially those with host plants, is essential. To attract these butterflies, plant flowers that produce nectar and flower early in the year.

Mourning Cloak Butterfly
Nymphalis antiopa

The appearance of Mourning Cloaks is often a sign that seasons are changing. Adults emerge in August, indicating that autumn is just around the corner. On a warm day in March, they are one of the first out of hibernation, signalling that spring is coming. Adults feed on sap, decaying fruit, nectar and scat into autumn. They hibernate in nest boxes, woodpiles and a number of other spots in the yard. If you are burning wood in the house and bringing logs in from outside, watch for these guys—there may be a few sitting on a log you intend to burn. These amazing butterflies increase the levels of antifreeze chemicals in their bodies in autumn so that they don't freeze in winter.

Once spring settles in, adult females lay clusters of eggs on tree branches. Larvae hatch and feed colonially, often defoliating an entire branch before moving to another. Mature larvae then pupate, emerging as adults in late July or early August.

Also Known As: Spiny Elm Caterpillar

ID: *Adult:* brown with yellow to white banding on rims of wings; forewings have row of blue spots along inside of band; resembles dead leaf when sitting. *Larva:* black caterpillar covered in branchy spines and tiny, white dots; distinct row of red spots along dorsal area.

Size: *Adult:* wingspan 60–80 mm. *Larva:* body length 50 mm.

Habitat and Range: Widespread in forested areas; larvae feed on willow, white elm and aspen.

Scouting: Adults lay clusters of eggs, so the branch they hatch on is usually defoliated. Watch for defoliation on host plants and for the presence of dark, spiny caterpillars.

Cultural/Physical Control: These caterpillars really aren't much of a pest but can have years in which they are quite common. Hand pick colonies of larvae.

Biological Control: Many parasitic wasps and other predators such as birds attack this species.

Painted Lady
Vanessa cardui

When Painted Ladies arrive in Ontario, they capture everyone's attention because they are virtually everywhere. It all starts in the United States, where populations slowly build up until the butterflies eat themselves out of house and home and then migrate north looking for food. This happens once every 10 years or so, and our last big migration was in 2005. This species doesn't migrate annually like the Monarch, and larvae are not hardy enough to survive our winters, so the huge populations virtually disappear in autumn. However, there are usually a few of these butterflies around every year because the invasion can last two to three years.

Larvae appear in spring shortly after the migrants have arrived and laid eggs.

ID: *Adult:* brown with hairy thorax and abdomen; orange wings with white-spotted, black wing tips. *Larva:* dark-coloured head; pale body has yellowish dorsal and lateral stripes and is covered with light-coloured hairs; each body segment has 6 unbranched spines known as scoli.

Size: *Adult:* wingspan 50–60 mm. *Larva:* body length 45 mm.

Habitat and Range: migrant, found throughout Ontario during northern migrations; feeds on a variety of plants, especially thistles such as Canada thistle.

Painted Lady (continued)

Painted Lady butterflies like nectar-producing flowers such as asters.

These spiny larvae are nest builders that build silken structures on the leaves of their host plants. In years of heavy infestation, their host plants can be entirely defoliated.

This species is wonderful for learning about butterfly life cycles. If you notice a thistle with these caterpillars, stick the thistle and caterpillars in a jar. By midsummer, the larvae will form golden, jewel-like chrysalises to pupate. After about one week, watch the chrysalises closely because they become transparent one day or so before the adults emerge. Be alert so you can watch the adults' shrivelled wings and swollen body emerge. It is amazing to watch them pump fluid from their body into their wings, slowly enlarging them to full size. If the chrysalis turns whitish and appears dried or dead, sometimes an Icnemonidae wasp will emerge instead.

In years of massive migrations, this species continues as far north as Ellesmere Island and Greenland, and can even travel to Iceland.

Scouting: Everyone knows when Painted Ladies are in town because they often arrive in huge numbers. They love nectaring at flowers, so look for them if you have some good producers in your garden.

How to Attract: Have plenty of nectar-producing flowers in the garden.

White Admiral

Limenitis arthemis

This graceful black and white butterfly often glides or swoops through our gardens and marks the start of the summer season. It feeds on nectar but is more attracted to rotting fruit, mud puddles and fresh scat.

Adults emerge in late June and early July and mate shortly thereafter.

Females then lay eggs on host plants, and larvae hatch in late July and feed on the host's foliage until autumn. Partially grown larvae then overwinter and resume feeding in spring. Mature larvae pupate in spring. There is usually one generation per year, but there may be a second generation near the end of summer.

ID: *Adult:* black with wide, white wing bands and a row of red spots along outside of white band on hindwing. *Larva:* resembles bird droppings and is black with yellowish and purplish white markings; head has pair of spiny, globe-like horns.

Size: *Adult:* wingspan 65–75 mm. *Larva:* body length 40 mm.

Habitat and Range: forests, clearings, gardens and parks; host plants include birch, aspen, poplar and willow.

Scouting: Watch for this species gliding gracefully through forest openings, ravines and river valleys.

How to Attract: White Admirals are much more excited about fermenting fruit than nectar, so put out a tray of overly ripe bananas, apples or both. These butterflies are also secondary feeders on trees that are bleeding sap, especially birch trees that are being attacked by yellow-bellied sapsuckers.

Monarch

Danaus plexippus

The Monarch is probably the most recognized butterfly. This amazing butterfly is one of our region's largest and showiest species. It is a huge orange and black butterfly and is unmistakable when you see it. This spectacular migrant travels up to 2000 kilometres, from its summer grounds in Ontario to its overwintering sites near Mexico City. To attract this butterfly to your garden, it is best to have a thriving patch of milkweed.

ID: *Adult:* bright orange with heavy, black wing veins and white spots on wing margins and tips. *Larva:* has black, white and yellow bands; 2 pairs of fleshy filaments, 1 pair just behind head and 1 near rear.

Size: *Adult:* wingspan 90–105 mm. *Larva:* body length 50 mm.

Habitat and Range: Throughout Ontario where milkweed grows; prefers open habitats including fields, wildflower meadows and ditches.

Scouting: Look for adults in gardens and yards, often gliding but sometimes feeding at host plants.

How to Attract: One of the Monarch's favourite nectar sources is a species of milkweed called butterfly weed, but all plants in the *Asclepias* genus attract these butterflies. If you often see Monarchs, plant a few of these plants in your garden.

Adults mate in spring before they migrate. Eggs are laid on milkweed in the southern United States. The caterpillars hatch, feed on the milkweed, form a chrysalis and emerge as adult Monarchs. This and subsequent generations of Monarchs continue the migration northward. Monarchs that arrive in Ontario in early summer are the third or fourth generation. Adults emerging in summer live for three weeks; Monarch adults emerging in late summer migrate south to overwinter in Mexico.

Plants in the genus *Asclepias*, the primary food of Monarchs, contain cardiac glycosides that the Monarch larvae and adults retain in their bodies, making them toxic and distasteful to predators. Birds have learned to avoid them, and another species of butterfly, the Viceroy (*Limenitis archippus*), even mimics them. The Viceroy is almost identical in appearance, but it has a black line through its hindwing and is much smaller.

Monarch butterfly larva

Try planting butterfly weed (*Asclepias tuberosa*) in your garden to help attract Monarch butterflies.

European Skipper

Thymelicus lineola

unwelcome guest is an excellent example of how quickly something can spread if conditions are favourable. The European Skipper is not considered a serious pest, but it can cause significant defoliation of hay crops. Some places in eastern Canada and British Columbia are treating fields for it. Areas with populations of 20 to 25 larvae per square metre could suffer significant crop damage.

Adults emerge and plague fields from July into mid-August. Females lay up to 30 eggs on the leaf sheath or grass seedheads. The eggs overwinter, and larvae hatch in spring.

Because it lays its eggs on seedheads of grasses such as Timothy, this species is easily transported to other countries. Even after thorough seed cleaning, eggs are still present. The eggs are quite hard and can withstand freezing temperatures.

In late summer, this intruder can be the most abundant butterfly on the wing and is often observed in gardens, farmyards and fields. It arrived in North America from Europe in 1910. This

ID: *Adult:* orange wings with dark border and dark wing veins. *Larva:* green with dark green dorsal stripe and 2 lateral and subdorsal stripes; head is pale green and has pair of black and white stripes on either side.

Size: *Adult:* wingspan 26 mm. *Larva:* body length 25 mm.

Habitat and Range: Throughout Ontario, especially in urban and surrounding areas; larvae feed on Timothy, cock's-foot, quackgrass, bentgrass and velvet grass.

Scouting: In mid- to late summer, watch for orange skippers flitting among grassy fields or nectaring at garden flowers.

Cultural/Physical Control: Purchase hay locally; confirm with the growers that this insect is not present in their field.

Biological Control: Predators include parasitic flies and wasps, predatory beetles and birds. Ensuring habitat for these beneficial predators will help reduce European Skipper populations.

Lilac Leaf Miner

Caloptilia syringella

The Lilac Leaf Miner, also known as the Lilac Slender-moth, is a common pest of lilac and was introduced from Europe. It now can be found across Canada anywhere lilac is grown. A browning or shrivelling leaf on a lilac may indicate that there are Lilac Leaf Miner larvae inside. This miniscule moth is so small that its larvae can live inside a leaf. The damage the larvae cause is cosmetic and does not kill the plant.

This moth often has two generations per year. Adults emerge in late May and early June. Eggs are laid in groups of 5 to 10 on the underside of a leaf near a vein. The eggs hatch and the larvae enter the leaf, creating a series of mines. As they grow, the mine begins to appear blister-like. Older larvae leave the mine, roll the leaf and continue feeding. Once mature, these little guys drop to the ground on silken threads and pupate in the duff. The second generation emerges in August, and the cycle repeats with their pupae overwintering. The first generation tends to attack the shrub's lower foliage, but the next generation moves up to higher leaves.

ID: *Adult:* narrow, brown-mottled wings; forewings have black and silver markings. *Larva:* yellowish worm with brownish head.

Size: *Adult:* wingspan 10 mm. *Larva:* body length 7–8 mm.

Habitat and Range: Throughout Ontario; larvae feed mainly on lilac, but also on ash.

Scouting: Trees or shrubs will look unhealthy. Foliage may appear scorched, having reddish, dried patches, especially in late summer. Early in the year, leaves appear discoloured,

sometimes yellowish. Look closely at blister-like tunnels on the leaf, or unroll a rolled leaf to see if there are larvae within.

Cultural/Physical Control: Keep trees healthy during an outbreak by watering them during dry conditions and fertilizing them every spring. You should be able to control reasonable sized infestations by picking infected leaves off by hand.

Biological Control: Natural predators for this species include parasites, diseases and birds such as warblers.

Peach Twig Borer

Anarsia lineatella

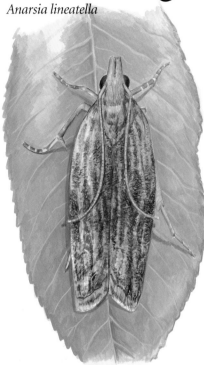

The Peach Twig Borer is a moth whose larvae attack peach, plum, apricot and nectarine trees. Larvae bore into buds and developing shoots, causing them to wilt and die. Wilted shoots are often called "shoot strikes" or "flags." Larval feeding on fruit creates oozing holes and cavities at the stem end.

Caterpillars overwinter on host trees in a tiny cell (called a hibernaculum) in branch or twig crotches, pruning wounds or deep cracks in bark. A small, cylindrical, reddish brown tube of frass sticks out from the bark at each site. In early spring, the larvae emerge and crawl up to new shoots, blooms and developing fruit, where they burrow and feed. They then pupate, giving rise to the first adult generation, called "brood moths," which lay eggs on leaves, twigs and young, green fruit in May and June. From June to August, the summer caterpillars burrow into ripening fruit, pupate and a second generation of adults emerges in late summer. These adults produce the next generation of caterpillars, which feed for a short time in September before burrowing into the wood for winter.

ID: *Adult:* dark grey overall; mottled forewings; pale grey underwings; palps extend out from head and look like a snout. *Larva:* young larva is white with dark brown head; later instar is reddish brown to chocolate brown with narrow, white, ring-like bands between dark segments and dark brown or grey head.

Size: *Adult:* wingspan 8–11 mm. *Larva:* body length up to 12 mm.

Habitat and Range: Throughout fruit-growing regions of Ontario.

Scouting: Look for frass tubes in the crotches of twigs and branches in winter. Check developing buds, shoots and fruit at bloom for young larvae. The ring-like bands distinguish Peach Twig Borer larvae from other caterpillars that attack stone fruit.

Cultural/Physical Control: Cut off wilted shoots and infested branches and destroy larvae. Seal infested fruit in a plastic bag to dispose of it or freeze it solid before composting. Remove frass tubes in late autumn and winter.

Biological Control: At bloom, apply sprays with B.t.k. to kill larvae before they tunnel into twigs or fruit. A dormant or delayed dormant (pre-bloom) spray with horticultural oil can help to control this insect. Mating disruption pheromones are effective in commercial orchards but are less effective in small plantings or backyard trees where mated females can fly in from outside. This borer has several natural enemies including parasitic wasps and some species of ants.

Peach Tree Borer

Synanthedon exitiosa

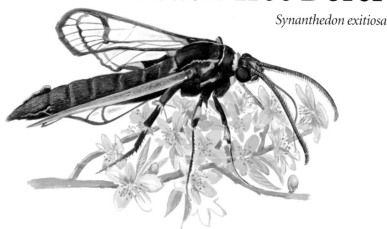

The Peach Tree Borer, sometimes called the Peach Crown Borer, is a clear-winged moth that attacks peaches, plums, cherries, apricots and other wild and cultivated stone fruit trees. It is native to North America and occurs across the continent. The larvae bore into the trunk, which results in girdling and causes young trees to wilt, yellow and die back. Older trees usually survive but are weakened because the tunnels provide entry for bacterial and fungal diseases. The Lesser Peach Tree Borer (*S. pictipes*) is a related species found in eastern North America; it is also very damaging to peach and plum trees. The larvae develop throughout the trunk and large branches.

Adults are active from July to September. Females lay eggs on the base of the tree trunk and larvae crawl down to soil level, where they burrow into the inner bark and cambium at the base of the tree and roots. The larvae feed and tunnel under the bark, where they overwinter. In spring, they pupate for 18 to 30 days in a silken cocoon that they cover with bits of chewed wood.

ID: *Adult:* dark, steel blue, clear-winged moth resembling a hornet. Male: narrow, yellow bands around abdomen. Female: 2 broad, orange bands. *Larva:* cream-coloured with brown head.

Size: *Adult:* wingspan 2.5–3 cm. *Larva:* body length 1.5–3 cm.

Habitat and Range: Throughout Ontario wherever stone fruit trees grow.

Scouting: Trees yellow and wilt. Look for a reddish brown gum containing bits of sawdust oozing from holes at the base of the trunk. You may find empty, brown pupal cases at the base of the tree.

Cultural/Physical Control: In autumn, cut out the larvae with a sharp knife or push a piece of stiff wire into their tunnels. Carefully remove the soil about 10–15 cm deep around the tree base to find all larvae, without cutting or damaging the tree. Wrap the bottom 45 cm of the trunk with a cone-shaped collar, and seal as tightly as possible at the top without damaging the bark. Starting shortly after petal-fall, put up sticky traps containing a pheromone to trap male moths.

Biological Control: Several natural predators and parasites attack borer eggs and larvae, but do not control the pest. In early June before the moths fly, commercial orchard owners can hang dispensers that release a mating-disruption pheromone called Isomate-P. This control is less successful where mated females can fly in from outside.

Raspberry Crown Borer

Pennisetia marginata

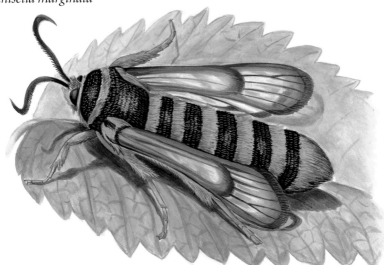

This member of the Sesiidae family is one of the most interesting masters of mimicry in Ontario. The adult mimics the feared yellow jacket wasp, a crafty adaptation that protects it from predators, but this species can be a pest.

Complete development takes two years. Adults fly from mid-August into September and will feed at flowers such as asters. Within a few days, females start depositing single eggs, usually two to three per plant, on the undersides of leaves. They can lay 130 to 150 eggs during their short lives. In late September and early October, the larvae hatch and crawl to the hosts' root crown, burrowing under the bark to form a blister-like hibernation chamber just below the soil's surface. In spring, the larvae bore into new and old canes, feeding into autumn and hibernating in the feeding chambers. They continue to feed and grow the following spring. In July, mature larvae burrow upward and outward, forming a pupal chamber near the surface of the cane. In August, the pupae works its way through the bark, and the adults emerge.

ID: *Adult:* black body with yellow banding on abdomen; clear wings have brown borders. *Larva:* white, grub-like worm with dark head and thoracic shield; 3 pairs of thoracic legs; series of 8 small, hooked appendages on abdominal segments 3–6.

Size: *Adult:* wingspan 25–30 mm. *Larva:* body length 25 mm.

Habitat and Range: Throughout Ontario; larvae feed on *Rubus* species.

Scouting: Watch for weak or spindly canes, and signs of boring and girdling, such as boring dust and galls. Prune out suspect canes. Adults are elusive.

Cultural/Physical Control: Remove infected canes from the ground up. Burn or thoroughly smash or squish cane bases.

Biological Control: Predators include parasitic wasps, predatory beetles and birds. A biological spray containing the predatory nematode *Steinernema carpocapsae* can be sprayed around the bases of the canes in infested areas. Spray at night on moist soils to prevent nematode dessication.

Ash Borer

Podosesia syringae

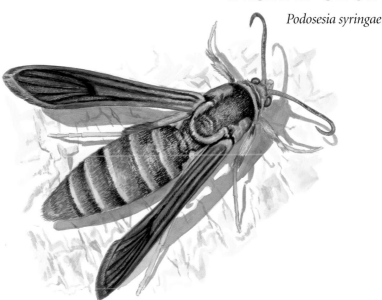

This day-flying, clearwing moth of the family Sesiidae mimics wasps. This species is a common pest, though it rarely does serious damage to trees.

Adults appear in June and July, and females lay eggs in cracks or near wounds on trunks or tree branches. Larvae hatch about 10 days later and bore into the bark, feeding until late summer, when they bore into the wood. Most larvae hibernate in the sapwood.

In the second year, larvae feed primarily in the sapwood all summer, moving into the tree's heartwood in autumn to hibernate. In spring of the third year, larvae tunnel up alongside the bark, where they pupate. In June, the pupae push through the thin bark, and the adults emerge. Exit holes are often found with a partially protruding brown pupae days after emergence. Similar damage is caused by Carpenter Worms.

Also Known As: Lilac Borer

ID: *Adult:* dark body with yellow-banded abdomen; yellow and black legs; clear hindwings; opaque forewings. *Larva:* white, grub-like worm with brown head and thoracic shield; 3 pairs of thoracic legs; series of 8 small, hooked appendages on abdominal segments 3–6.

Size: *Adult:* wingspan 25–35 mm. *Larva:* body length 18–24 mm.

Habitat and Range: Throughout Ontario; larvae are pests of ash and lilac.

Scouting: Watch for scarring and swelling on branches and trunks and for frass and sawdust near bore holes approximately 6 mm in width. Branches may wilt on hot days.

Cultural/Physical Control: Keep trees healthy. Remove and destroy dead and dying branches. Poke a piece of wire into the hole and down the gallery to kill larvae. Wrap trunks and the bases of branches with burlap to trap and kill emerging adults. Use a sticky trap with a pheromone attractant to capture and confuse males before they mate. Place traps out just before adults emerge and leave them until end of the flight season in July.

Biological Control: Natural predators include parasites, diseases and birds.

Boxelder Twig Borer
Proteoteras willingana

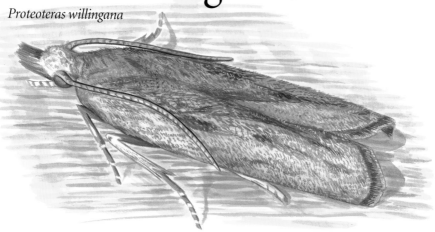

This moth in the family Tortricidae is a common Manitoba maple (boxelder) pest. Damage done by the larvae never kills the tree but affects development of new growth. Infested areas often have some dieback, which acts like pruning, and trees that have been fed on for many years tend to be quite shrubby. Two species with similar life cycles also bore into the twigs of Manitoba maples—the Black-crescent Proteoteras Moth *(P. crescentana)* and the Maple Twig Borer *(P. aesculana)*.

Adults emerge in late June and early July. Females lay eggs on the undersides of leaves, and larvae appear shortly after. Larvae spin a silken hideout and feed on the leaf's underside. From late July into early August, larvae bore into a shoot or bud. Not much more feeding occurs as they hunker down to hibernate. In spring, larvae hollow out soft new buds. Mature larvae continue to burrow and feed, plugging the bore holes with silk and frass. The holes are quite noticeable, and boring often causes the shoot to swell. By mid-June, mature larvae drop to the ground and pupate in a cocoon among leaf litter.

ID: *Adult:* mottled grey forewings; smoky grey hindwings. *Larva:* cream-coloured body with tiny setae that have dark bases; dark head and thoracic shield are virtually black in mature larvae.

Size: *Adult:* wingspan 15–20 mm. *Larva:* body length 10–11 mm.

Habitat and Range: Throughout Ontario; most common in areas with native stands; larvae bore into and feed on new shoots of Manitoba Maple.

Scouting: Watch new twig growth for dieback or swelling and for signs of boring. Break open suspected shoots or buds to look for larvae or larval activity such as silk and frass deposits. The best time of year to find larvae is in spring or in late summer and autumn.

Cultural/Physical Control: Prune infected shoots to disrupt the life cycle. Prune suckers at tree base every year to remove potential habitats. Burn clippings or bury in a deep hole.

Biological Control: Natural parasites exist for this species and other maple twig borers. Many parasitoid wasps prey on them, with the wasp *Campoplex crassatus* being reported as one of the best. Altogether, parasites can wipe out 30% of the population.

Aspen Twoleaf Tier & Aspen Leafroller

Enargia decolor, Pseudexentera oregonana

Aspen Leafroller

Leaf-rolling behaviour is a strategy that both camouflages and shields caterpillars from predators. Ontario has a wide variety of leaf-rolling Lepidoptera. The Aspen Twoleaf Tier (*E. decolor*) and Aspen Leafroller (*P. oregonana*) are two common species, neither a severe defoliator.

The Aspen Twoleaf Tier is a Noctuidae moth that in some years can appear in huge numbers. Adults fly, mate and lay eggs in late summer and autumn. Eggs overwinter with larvae hatching the following spring. Larvae feed from within two leaves that they have tied together.

The Aspen Leafroller is a Totricidae moth that flies in early spring, often April, and lays eggs on its host during this period. Larvae hatch and construct feeding chambers by rolling a leaf and using silk to fasten it in position. Once mature, in mid- to late summer, larvae drop to the ground and overwinter as pupae in the duff.

ID: *Adult: Aspen Twoleaf Tier:* yellow to orange wings. *Aspen Leafroller:* brown wings; forewings have black and white marking. *Larva: Aspen Twoleaf Tier:* pale green with dorsal, subdorsal and lateral white lines. *Aspen Leafroller:* creamy white with dark brown head and thoracic shield.

Size: *Adult: Aspen Twoleaf Tier:* wingspan 30–40 mm. *Aspen Leafroller:* wingspan 15 mm. *Larva: Aspen Twoleaf Tier:* body length 25–35 mm. *Aspen Leafroller:* body length 12–15 mm.

Habitat and Range: Throughout Ontario, especially in forests; larvae of both species feed primarily on aspen and also on ornamental poplar, birch and willow.

Scouting: Look for defoliation and rolled leaves, which may have larvae inside.

Cultural/Physical Control: Keep yard and shelterbelt trees healthy and well watered, especially in dry weather.

Biological Control: Predators include predacious and parasitic wasps, parasitic tachinid flies and other predatory insects. Predacious ground beetles are often observed pulling larvae out of their protective nests. Many birds such as vireos, woodpeckers and warblers also feed on leaf rollers.

Northern Pitch Twig Moth

Petrova albicapitana

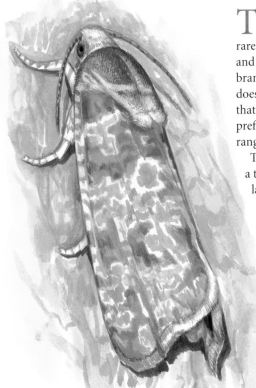

This moth gets its name from the sappy nodule its larva forms. It rarely does extensive damage to trees and often does not girdle or kill branches. The most common damage it does is to weaken twigs and branches so that they break in the wind. This moth prefers young trees aged 8 to 12 that range in height from 0.5 to 5 metres.

The Northern Pitch Twig Moth has a two-year life cycle. Adults appear in late June to July, and females lay their eggs at the base of needle buds. Larvae later hatch and burrow into tissue to begin feeding. Over time, a protective nodule is constructed from frass, silk and sap. Young larvae overwinter within the nodule, continuing to feed the following spring. Once June arrives, the larvae migrate to new feeding sites, forming nodules up to 30 millimetres in diameter. Mature larvae overwinter in the new nodules and pupate the following spring.

ID: *Adult:* reddish wings with dark speckling and black banding. *Larva:* variable body colour, from yellow to orangey brown; reddish brown head.

Size: *Adult:* wingspan 16–23 mm. *Larva:* body length 15–17 mm.

Habitat and Range: In regions that border forests with wild pines; larvae feed on lodgepole, Jack and ornamental pines, such as Scots pine.

Scouting: Look for red needles, needles losing colour, broken twigs and branches and blister-like growths at the nodes of branches and twigs. Fresh nodules appear red, whereas older ones are encrusted with white. Active nodules are often a combination of these colours and possess a larva.

Cultural/Physical Control: Dig out and dispose of larvae. Prune off broken twigs and branches. Catch the larvae early—older larvae weaken braches more extensively. Grow resistant pines or conifers such as spruce in areas that encounter repeated outbreaks. Develop a natural style of garden and limit insecticide use.

Biological Control: Many parasites and natural predators, including chickadees, keep pitch moth populations low. Parasitoid wasps can control up to 10% of the population.

Codling Moth

Cydia pomonella

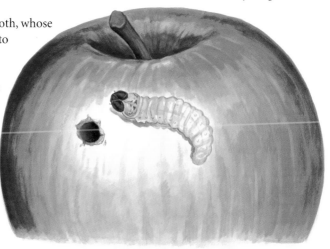

The Codling Moth, whose larvae bore into apple, crab apple, quince and pear fruit, is a common pest in Ontario. This little moth from Eurasia was introduced to North America in the 1800s by European settlers and quickly spread across the continent.

Caterpillars overwinter in cocoons in main tree crotches or bark crevices, usually at the base of the tree, as well as in grass, weeds and litter under the tree. They pupate in spring, and adults emerge at bud-break and bloom. Females lay their eggs on leaves and young fruit, often at the top of the tree. Larvae burrow into fruit at the calyx end, moving down into the core, where they feed on seeds. Feeding holes are typically surrounded by a large amount of frass. Circular, reddish spots called "stings" are often seen on the fruit. The second generation adults appear in early August. There are two generations per year throughout most of Ontario; in the Georgian Bay area, there is one generation per year.

The Codling Moth was first described in 371 BCE by the Greek horticulturist, botanist and philosopher Theophrastus. It is believed to have originated in Central Asia, where apples were first domesticated.

ID: *Adult:* brownish grey body and forewings; forewings have lighter, net-like markings; hindwings are brown with a pale fringe. *Larva:* white to pinkish, grub-like caterpillar with black or dark brown head.

Size: *Adult:* wingspan 15–22 mm. *Larva:* Young: 2–3 mm. Mature: 12–20 mm.

Habitat and Range: Apple, crab apple, quince and pear trees throughout Ontario.

Scouting: Check fruit for frass, stings, small holes or feeding damage at the calyx end in June and July.

Cultural/Physical Control: Prune trees to open and lower the canopy, allowing them to produce fruit on lower branches; more vigorous, productive trees will result. Wrap corrugated cardboard bands, 10–15 cm wide and corrugated side next to the tree, around the base of trees and main branches in mid-June. Larvae will collect in and under the band. Remove and replace the first band in mid-July and the second band in autumn or winter. Destroy old bands and kill the larvae.

Biological Control: B.t.k. kills young caterpillars, but because it stays on the surface of the leaves and fruit, and the caterpillars bore into the fruit, it does not provide sufficient control. Several natural predators and parasites attack larvae but also don't provide sufficient control.

Uglynest Caterpillar

Archips cerasivoranus

It is when a garden shrub is draped with a silky tent that we come to know the Uglynest Caterpillar. In severe cases, the nest appears so abruptly that it is enough to induce panic. As the name suggests, this caterpillar's nest is an ugly sight, though the adult moth is rather attractive. This species rarely causes significant damage.

The adults emerge from late July into September. Egg masses are laid on the host plant and do not hatch until late spring. The gregarious larvae climb to the top of the plant to build a silken nest that engulfs branches and leaves. Nests become quite unsightly, often growing larger and larger and accumulating frass. The nest protects the larvae, and if the larvae are disturbed, they wiggle backward deeper into it. Larvae pupate randomly starting in June and lasting into September, building silken pupal cells around the edge of the nest.

This species is unique in the moth world in that it is considered to be a social insect. Larvae work together to form an elaborate silken nest that protects them from predators and the elements. The nests also absorb and trap heat. By living together, this species can be quite successful and is therefore considered a pest at times.

ID: *Adult:* reddish head and body; red wings have touch of yellow and iridescent sheen. *Larva:* dark head and green to yellow body with dark spots.

Size: *Adult:* wingspan 20–24 mm. *Larva:* body length 20–23 mm.

Habitat and Range: Throughout Ontario on pin, choke and ornamental cherries.

Scouting: Watch for silken tents in spring and for egg bands in late autumn and winter.

Cultural/Physical Control: Deal with hatchlings early in spring before they form huge nests. Pull apart the nests, squish the larvae and leave the stragglers for the birds. Remove eggs bands in autumn and winter.

Biological Control: Predators include predacious and parasitic wasps, parasitic tachinid flies and other predatory insects. One researcher observed a hornet that would chew a hole in the nest and ambush the larvae that came to repair the hole. Birds also zero in on these nests and pull out larvae. Cool days and rainy weather can lead to a build-up of diseases.

Eastern Tent Caterpillar

Malacosoma americanum

moth

Tent caterpillars are a group of relatively large caterpillars. They nest in groups in silk tents and are defoliators of shade trees and shrubs. Tent caterpillars are always present throughout Ontario.

The life cycles of the different tent caterpillar species are very similar. The short-lived adults emerge and take flight in July. Adult females lay between 150 and 200 eggs in a silvery grey mass that wraps around a small twig or branch. They cover the egg masses with a frothy, silvery substance known as spumaline, which turns dark and shiny as it hardens. The spumaline acts as an adhesive for the egg mass, as a protective coating that prevents eggs

ID: *Adult:* robust, furry body; reddish brown wings. *Larva:* dark overall with distinct light dorsal stripe and series of blue markings on sides.

Size: *Adult:* wingspan 35–45 mm. *Larva:* body length 45–55 mm.

Habitat and Range: throughout Ontario in forested areas.

Scouting: Watch trees for severe defoliation, silky webbing or masses of caterpillars. Look for egg bands beginning in late July.

Cultural/Physical Control: Pick or gently scrape egg bands off twigs and branches. In early spring, squish the larval colonies.

Eastern Tent Caterpillar (continued)

caterpillars with tent

from drying out and as a shield against egg parasites. Tent caterpillars overwinter as eggs.

Larvae hatch the following spring right around bud break. The larvae are gregarious and feed together, and silken lines appear everywhere. When resting, these caterpillars bunch together on a silken pad on a branch. The tent expands as the caterpillars get bigger. Feeding primarily at night, the caterpillars return to the nest to rest during the day. Late instar caterpillars disperse and produce white cocoons on nearby plants and rocks. Adults emerge in early summer. One generation is produced each year.

Some trees being eaten by tent caterpillars fight back. During an infestation, hybrid poplars produce volatile chemicals that attract tent caterpillar parasites.

Biological Control: Certain birds and insects flourish during tent caterpillar outbreaks. There are over 40 species of parasites and predatory insects that feed on tent caterpillars. These range from predacious ground beetles to parasitoid tachinid flies (*Sarcophaga* spp.) . Tachinid flies are sometimes called the "friendly fly." They thrive during outbreaks and can suppress tent caterpillar populations by 80%. The female drops a newly hatched maggot onto the caterpillar cocoon, and the maggot burrows in and feeds on the pupae. Birds love outbreak years, too, and their young may be raised almost entirely on tent caterpillars. During outbreaks, diseases caused by viruses, bacteria and fungi build up. In the year after an outbreak, tent caterpillars that survive are being hunted by hundreds of creatures. A combination of all these factors leads to the extreme population crashes of tent caterpillars. It is tough to find a single caterpillar the year following a population collapse.

Common Plume Moth & Many Plumed Moths

Amblyptilia pica, Alucita spp.

Alucita spp.

These elegant moths are rarely observed but are always present around our homes, gardens and yards. Once you learn how to find them, you will likely see them everywhere.

Common Plume Moths (*Amblyptilia pica*) flit about in spring, summer and autumn. They are micro-moths of the family Pterophoridae. This species has two generations per year, the first in early summer and the second in autumn and early spring. Their larvae mine leaves, flowers and seeds. Adults of the second generation overwinter and are often observed nectaring at pussy willows or coltsfoot in April.

Many Plumed Moths (*Alucita* spp.) are most often observed on the walls of houses in autumn and even into winter. They are members of the family Alucitidae and are easily separated from the Pterophoridae by their multi-lobed forewings. Adults overwinter and lay eggs in spring. Their larvae are fruit, flower, bud and stem borers. Three species occur in our region, *Alucita montana*, *A. adriendenisi* and *A. lalannei*, and you need to be an expert to separate them.

ID: *Adult: Common Plume Moth:* dark grey overall; non-lobed, grey-brown mottled forewings have dark, central, triangle-shaped patch; 3-lobed hindwings are smoky grey, and 3rd lobe has distinct dark, triangle-shaped spot called "scale tooth." *Many Plumed Moths:* wings are feather-like plumes that spread apart fan-like when moth is at rest; 6 plumes on each wing. *Larva:* pale and tapered at both ends; has tiny hairs with swollen tips; prolegs slender and stalk-like.

Size: *Adult:* wingspan 10–18 mm. *Larva:* body length 8–10 mm.

Habitat and Range: Throughout Ontario.

Common Plume Moth: host plants include Indian paintbrush, snapdragon and geranium. *Many Plumed Moths:* host plants include honeysuckle and snowberry.

Scouting: Both species are sometimes seen around porch lights. The Common Plume Moth is often observed flitting among snapdragons in summer or nectaring at pussy willows in spring. Many Plumed Moths are often seen in autumn in our gardens and at our windows.

How to Attract: Plant larval hosts or adult nectar sources in the garden.

Luna Moth

Actias luna

The Luna Moth is one of North America's most distinctive and spectacular moths. The adult's wings are pale green with elongated hindwings that resemble those of a swallowtail. This moth belongs to the Giant Silkworm family (Saturniidae spp.), which includes the Cecropia and Polyphemus moths. In Ontario, the Luna Moth larva feeds primarily on the leaves of white birch but will also feed on sweetgum, walnut and persimmon. The Luna Moth does not feed as an adult, so that stage of its life is very short. The larva grows quite large because it must store enough energy to sustain itself as an adult through mating and egg laying.

The adult emerges in late spring and mates. The female lays her eggs on leaves. The larva develops over two to three months. It overwinters as a pupa inside an oval, silken cocoon on the forest floor and emerges in spring. As the adult emerges, it pushes itself out through a weakening in the silk created by its saliva. There is one generation per year.

ID: *Adult:* pale green wings with small eyespot on each wing; long, curved hindwings; furry, white body; male's antennae appear more feathery. *Larva:* translucent pale green overall; pale yellow line along lower side.

Size: *Adult:* wingspan 95 mm. *Larva:* body length 120 mm.

Habitat and Range: Deciduous forests in southern Ontario.

Scouting: Saturniidae spp. moths are attracted to lights and will occasionally be seen at night near porch lights.

How to Attract: This species has declined in numbers in recent years and it is a rare treat to see one. To attract Luna Moths, plant their favourite larval host plants, especially white birch.

Polyphemus Moth

Anthera polyphemus

This moth is one of the biggest and showiest moths in Ontario. It is a nocturnal species and is a member of the Giant Silkworm Moth family, Saturniidae. Other silk moths that you may encounter are the Columbia Silkmoth (*Hyalophora columbia*) and the Cecropia Moth (*H. cecropia*). These two moths have large, dark to reddish wings with a central white band. The wings each have a centrally placed, kidney-shaped eyespot. The Cecropia is generally larger and has a red band alongside the white band.

Adults emerge from cocoons in late May into early July. Pregnant females cruise at night and lay eggs on hosts. Large caterpillars emerge in early summer and mature by late August. They spin elaborate silken cocoons among the leaves or on the ground. The cocoons are quite tough and protect the caterpillars from predators and the elements during winter. Adults have no mouthparts and basically hatch and breed.

ID: *Adult:* light brown wings with transparent eyespot; hindwing eyespot is rimmed with dark scaling; outer edges of wings are lined with purple and white bands. *Larva:* florescent green with faint, vertical lines on central part of body; segments have 8 central, reddish spots and a series of red and silvery "warts" with a few clear hairs sticking out; often retracts orange-brown head into thorax slightly when resting.

Size: *Adult:* wingspan 110–125 mm. *Larva:* body length 75 mm.

Habitat and Range: Throughout Ontario; larvae feed on trees and shrubs including birch, oak, elm, dogwood, apple, ash, hazel, hickory, maple, rose and willow.

Scouting: Adults and larvae are both tricky to find, but the larvae are more often seen. Watch branches of host plants for half-eaten leaves or small areas of defoliation. Scan for a large green lump sitting on a branch among the leaves. This search may take a while, but once you find one, you may be surprised at how many others you will see.

How to Attract: This species is seldom a pest, but the caterpillars are large and have big appetites. If you wish to attract them to the garden, plant a variety of potential host trees and shrubs.

Twin-spotted Sphinx

Smerinthus jamaicesis

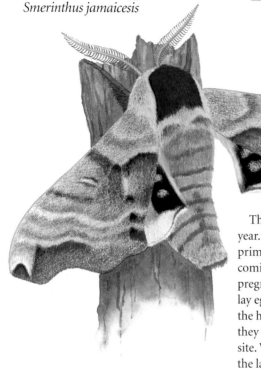

If you see a hornworm, you are likely looking at the larva of a sphinx or hawk moth from the Sphingidae family. The Twin-Spotted Sphinx is likely our most widespread species of sphinx moth. Unlike many other sphinx moths, it does not nectar at flowers. In fact, it does not feed at all and has no mouthparts.

This species has one generation per year. Adults appear in June and are primarily nocturnal, often observed coming to lights at night. After mating, pregnant females cruise around and lay eggs on host plants. Larvae feed on the hosts and mature in August, when they begin a march to find a pupation site. When they find a suitable location, the larvae submerge themselves in the soil and pupate in an underground pupation chamber.

Two other similar species may be encountered, the Big Poplar Sphinx (*Pachysphinx occidentalis*) and the Waved Sphinx (*Ceratomia undulosa*). The Big Poplar Sphinx is much less common and is larger than the Twin-spotted Sphinx. The Waved Sphinx is very well camouflaged on tree trunks.

ID: *Adult:* brown to black forewings have wide, light stripe; dark hindwings have central pink to red band. *Larva:* variable, from green to brown or black, with red horn on posterior; body lined with light spots.

Size: *Adult:* wingspan 60–90 mm. *Larva:* body length 70 mm.

Habitat and Range: Throughout Ontario; larvae feed on poplar and willow species.

Scouting: In summer, watch for larvae on poplar and willow or on open ground looking for a pupation site.

How to Attract: Plant a variety of nectar-producing plants such as lilacs. Also leave some wild areas intact—especially those that possess host plants such as fireweed and bedstraw.

Snowberry Clearwing

Hemaris diffinis

"Is it a bumble bee, a hummingbird or a moth?" This question often occurs to a gardener who sees a Snowberry Clearwing for the first time. This moth is swift and agile, as are all members of the Sphingidae family. The adult is a day flier and hovers at flowers such as lilacs. It often looks like a miniature hummingbird as it zips from flower to flower. If you watch closely, you will see it hovering as it extends its long proboscis into a flower.

The adult emerges in spring and is on the wing starting in late May and continuing into early June. Larvae hatch and feed throughout summer, pupating in the soil. There are two other species of clearwing moths. The Hummingbird Moth *(H. thysbe)* and the much less common Slender Clearwing *(H. gracilis)* are found in Ontario and also may be observed nectaring in gardens.

Sphingidae moths have a long proboscis that is an adaptation for reaching nectar deep inside trumpet-shaped flowers such as honeysuckle.

ID: *Adult:* resembles bumble bee; yellow with dark abdominal band covered in hairs; wings have brown edges and dark veins. *Larva:* blue-green or brown with dark lateral spots along abdomen; horn at end of abdomen is black with yellow base.

Size: *Adult:* wingspan 40–50 mm. *Larva:* body length 45 mm.

Habitat and Range: Open areas throughout Ontario; larvae feed on snowberry, honeysuckle and dogbane.

Scouting: The best way to find these guys is to grab a lawn chair and a cold drink on a sunny day and sit in front of your lilacs. These moths seem to enjoy purple lilacs the best. It may take a while, but if your weather and timing are right, the moths will be there.

How to Attract: These moths prefer brightly coloured flowers such as honeysuckle, phlox and lilac. Flowering cherry, saskatoon and hawthorn trees as well as wild snowberry and dogbane also attract this species.

Garden Tiger Moth

Arctia caja

The name Garden Tiger Moth suggests that this species is a common sight in gardens. However, it is this species' larval stage—the woolly bear caterpillar—that is most frequently encountered. The Garden Tiger Moth is holarctic and ranges from Canada to Great Britain and into other regions in Europe and Asia. It is sometimes called the Great Tiger Moth and is the largest and most attractive species of the tiger moth family, Arctiidae, in our region.

The adults appear in August, and females lay their eggs shortly after. Eggs hatch in late August and caterpillars overwinter. In spring, the polyphagus caterpillars begin looking for food. In late June to early July, they spin a cocoon made of silk and their own body hair. The naked caterpillars pupate inside, and adults emerge about four weeks later.

When the Garden Tiger Moth flies at night, it can detect a bat's ultrasonic calls from 40 m away with its specialized tympanal organs. The moth starts making a series of clicking noises that jam the bat's ability to detect the moth's exact location.

ID: *Adult:* chocolate brown forewings have white patches and banding; orange hindwings have large, black to blue spots; orange abdomen. *Larva:* woolly caterpillar covered with short, dense, black hair, with orange hair around head and long, whitish hair on abdomen.

Size: *Adult:* wingspan 55 mm. *Larva:* body length 60 mm.

Habitat and Range: Forested and suburban areas; larvae feed on a variety of forbs and shrubs, including dandelion, common plantain and willow.

Scouting: Watch for the caterpillars as they march through the garden or across a sidewalk.

How to Attract: Leave some untouched and naturalized patches that contain this species' host plants.

Gypsy Moth
Lymantria dispar

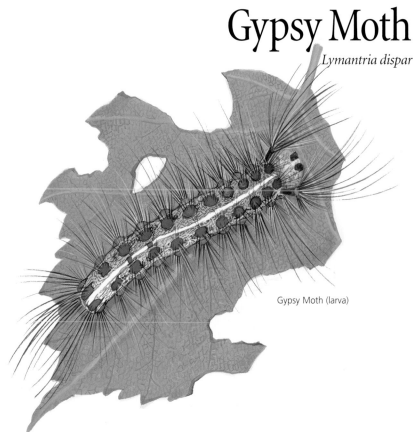

Gypsy Moth (larva)

Gypsy Moth caterpillars feed on at least 200 species of deciduous and evergreen trees and shrubs; estimates indicate that just one eats about a square metre of foliage during its life.

The Gypsy Moth is native to Europe (where it has European and Asian strains) and North Africa. The European strain became established in the northeastern U.S. in the 1870s, in Ontario and Quebec in the 1960s and in Nova Scotia, New Brunswick and British Colombia in the 1980s. In 1991, the Asian version was introduced to British Colombia from Russia, but it has been successfully controlled and has not yet reached Ontario. Federal, provincial and municipal agencies have worked hard to eradicate this moth.

European females don't fly. They lay eggs close to the ground at the base of trees. The Gypsy Moth overwinters as

ID: *Adult:* Male: brown overall. Female: white with dark brown zigzag band across midwings. *Larva:* tan (young) to dark grey (older) with double row of 5 blue and 6 red dorsal spots; tufts of short spines.

Size: *Adult:* wingspan 3 cm. *Mature Larva:* length 6-7.5 cm. *Pupa:* length from 2 cm (male) to 3.5 cm (female).

Habitat and Range: Throughout Ontario in deciduous and coniferous trees and shrubs; prefers oak and aspen; eradication efforts underway.

Scouting: Watch for tan, chamois-like egg masses on tree trunks, leaves and even on fences, sheds, decks, vehicles and lawn furniture. Look for the caterpillars on tree

Gypsy Moth (continued)

Oak trees are favoured by Gypsy Moths

an egg on bark or in a sheltered area. Egg masses are chamois-like and are cream to tan in colour. They can range in diameter from the size of a dime to a loonie and contain 100 to 1000 eggs each. European caterpillars must crawl up the tree trunk before they begin to feed. Caterpillars feed for about seven weeks and then pupate for 10 to 14 days in late June and July in protected areas on the tree. Pupae are brown, tear-drop shaped and covered with tiny hairs. Moths fly in July and August. There is one generation per year.

In 1869, a French scientist introduced the Gypsy Moth to Massachusetts, hoping to breed it with the Asian silk moth and create a silk industry in the U.S. Although he was unsuccessful, the Gypsy Moths escaped and soon became established in the New World.

trunks at bud break, and later feeding on leaves. Destroy egg masses and caterpillars before they develop into adults in July and August. Notify authorities in your area if you find Gypsy Moth eggs or caterpillars.

Cultural/Physical Control: Kill egg masses with dormant oil in winter or with a spray of soap, bleach, household ammonia or vegetable oil and water. In early spring, trap caterpillars by wrapping tree trunks with burlap tied with string and folded over. Pick off and destroy pupae and caterpillars. Handle caterpillars with gloves because the hairs can cause allergic reactions. Cut, crush or freeze pupae solid before disposal.

Biological Control: Use home garden insecticides containing B.t.k., a crystal produced by the naturally occurring bacterium *Bacillus thuringiensis kurstaki*, to kill young caterpillars. Spray it on leaves when you first see the caterpillars.

Underwing Moths

Catocala spp.

Underwing moths detect predators by using specialized tympanal organs that act as ears. Some of their main predators are bats. The underwing tunes into the bats' ultrasonic calls, and when a bat gets too close, the underwing stops flying and drops to the ground.

White Underwing

"Cats," as many lepidopterists refer to them, are some of the most attractive moths we have and rival the giant silk, tiger and sphinx moths in popularity. They are elusive, nocturnal species but are common in our gardens. Three commonly encountered species are the White Underwing (*C. relicta*), Briseis Underwing (*C. briseis*) and Once-married Underwing (*C. unijuga*).

Larvae hatch from eggs in spring and move up the tree to feed. Mature larvae descend to the ground to pupate. The adults emerge in August, mate and lay eggs on the bark of host trees.

ID: *Adult: White Underwing:* white birch bark-patterned forewings; black and white hindwings. *Briseis Underwing:* greyish black forewings with a few central whitish patches; red-orange hindwings with broad outer black bands and central black bands. *Once-married Underwing:* similar to the Briseis but larger with lighter grey forewings that lack whitish patches. *Larva:* grey overall; resembles a stick or lump on tree bark.

Size: *Adult:* wingspan 59–80 mm. *Larva:* body length 55–75 mm.

Habitat and Range: Forested areas; host plants include poplar, birch, oak and willow.

Scouting: Larvae and adults are well camouflaged and nocturnal.

How to Attract: Heat beer, molasses and rotten fruit in a pot and mix until smooth. At dusk, paint your brew onto a few tree trunks or fence posts. Wait until dark, and with flashlight in hand, go check out the sugary masses. On a good night, there will be a flurry of moths. The mixture will attract a variety of moth species, but look for large moths with brilliant red hindwings. If you find one, approach it quietly, maintaining a comfortable distance. Active yellow-bellied sapsucker galleries on birch are also an excellent attractant for these moths, especially on warm August nights.

Linden Looper
Erannis tiliaria

It is not uncommon for folks who have gone for a hike in the woods to return home with an inchworm or two on their shoulders.

These distinctive caterpillars are often called inchworms and belong to the Geometriidae moth family. Larvae cause mild to severe defoliation of yard and shelterbelt trees, never actually killing the trees but certainly slowing their growth. Outbreaks occur occasionally and can last for a couple of years.

Adults appear in large numbers in autumn, especially in early October. In Ontario, it is not uncommon to see these truly Canadian moths flying even after a fresh snowfall. Males appear at night on lighted walls of buildings. In autumn, wingless adult females crawl up tree trunks to lay eggs in cracks and crevices on host trees. The eggs overwinter, with larvae emerging in spring. Larvae are defoliators and begin feeding on foliage after hatching. Early instars chew holes in leaves, and older larvae eat the entire leaf right to the leaf stalk. Larvae mature in about a month and drop to the ground on silken threads. They burrow up to 25 centimetres deep in the soil, construct an earthen cell and pupate.

ID: *Adult:* male has light brown wings with wavy, dark line on forewings; female is white with black spots. *Larva:* long, yellow body with dark dorsal stripes; red to orange head.

Size: *Adult:* wingspan 42 mm. *Larva:* body length 35–37 mm.

Habitat and Range: Throughout Ontario; larvae feed on linden, Manitoba maple and elm, as well as poplar, birch, other maples and other hardwoods.

Scouting: Infested trees have numerous larvae on the leaves.

Cultural/Physical Control: Keep trees healthy, especially during outbreaks. In areas where there is an outbreak, wrap the base of host trees with a wide, sticky wrap to prevent females from laying eggs high up in the tree. This strategy is best initiated in late summer before adults emerge.

Biological Control: Predators include birds such as warblers, vireos and chickadees, parasitic wasps and flies as well as other predatory insects.

Speckled Green Fruitworm

Orthosia hibisci

These guys, despite their common name, rarely damage fruit and are primarily defoliators. The adults are among the first moths to emerge and are an indication that spring truly has arrived.

Adults appear in April and fly into early May. Females lay their eggs during this period, and the eggs hatch just after the host's leaves begin to flush. Larvae are primarily defoliators but get their name from the damage they do during an outbreak. They do not bore into fruit but eat flower petals, developing fruit and stems. Larvae mature in early summer, often the first week or two of July. They drop to the ground and burrow 5 to 10 centimetres into the soil, where they hibernate as pupae.

ID: *Adult:* brown wings; robust. *Larva:* green to bluish green overall with dorsal, mid-dorsal and lateral white stripe; body is covered in white speckles; some caterpillars are smoky green with similar markings and more distinct white striping.

Size: *Adult:* wingspan 40 mm. *Larva:* body length 30–40 mm.

Habitat and Range: Throughout Ontario; larvae are generalists, feeding on aspen, willow, poplar, cherry, gooseberry, elm, maple, oak and even spruce, larch and fir.

Scouting: Watch for patchy, localized defoliation on host trees.

Cultural/Physical Control: Tree mortality is rare during an outbreak because many trees are adapted to defoliation by insects. If there are only a few larvae, you can let them be.

Biological Control: Predacious and parasitic wasps, parasitic tachinid flies and other predatory insects feed on these larvae, as well as many birds including vireos, woodpeckers and warblers. Leave the appropriate habitat for these beneficial animals so they can control outbreaks. Plant wildflowers and shelterbelts, and leave areas of naturalized woodlands intact.

Armyworm Moth & Army Cutworm

Pseudaletia unipuncta, Euxoa auxiliaris

Armyworm Moth

The literature refers to two species when it says "army worm." The Armyworm Moth *(P. unipuncta)* has an old genus name of *Mythimna*, and some literature refers to it as *M. unipuncta*. Armyworm adults emerge in late May to June. The female lays up to 1400 eggs in rows along the underside of leaf blades. Larvae hatch in two weeks and feed nocturnally in groups. Larvae mature in one month, pupating in the soil. The next generation hatches in midsummer. There are usually two generations, with the second generation overwintering as larvae and pupating in spring.

ID: *Adult: Armyworm:* pale brown forewings with central, white spot that is often highlighted by orange patch; smoky grey hindwing. *Army Cutworm:* variably coloured forewing can be patchwork of yellow and brown or sometimes solid yellow-brown; smoky grey hindwing. *Larva: Armyworm:* pale green to brown with orange, brown and white, lateral, dorsal and subdorsal stripes. *Army Cutworm:* pale brown with pale and dark, lateral, dorsal and subdorsal stripes.

Size: *Adult: Armyworm:* wingspan 35–45 mm. *Army Cutworm:* wingspan 40–45 mm. *Larva:* body length 40 mm.

Habitat and Range: Throughout Ontario. *Armyworm:* feeds on corn, grasses such as oats, wheat, barley, and other forages. *Army Cutworm:* feeds on corn, sunflowers and a variety of vegetables and grasses.

Scouting: In early spring, emerging garden plants may be broken or snipped off. Foliage will also be slightly or heavily eaten.

Perennial sunflower (*Helianthus salicifolius*)

Army Cutworm (*E. auxiliaris*) adults emerge in summer and feed briefly before seeking shelter in higher elevations and cooler locations until autumn. They return in September and mate, with pregnant females bearing 1000 to 3000 eggs, which are laid in late autumn on open ground and disturbed soil among host plants. Eggs hatch shortly after, and larvae feed briefly and then overwinter in the soil, emerging the following spring to feed on new shoots. Larvae mature in May and pupate in the soil at a depth of seven centimetres. They remain there for approximately one month.

The larvae of these moths in the family Noctuidae march in groups in search of food once they have eaten everything at their original site.

With each pregnant Army Cutworm female laying thousands of eggs, the resulting larvae can quickly deplete their food source. When this happens the larvae can then move, armylike, in huge masses to find new food. Such "migrations" are uncommon, but they have been recorded moving a distance of as much as five kilometres.

Cultural/Physical Control: Dig your garden in spring and autumn to expose hibernating larvae and pupae to predators and the elements.

Biological Control: Natural controls include parasitic wasps, tachinid flies and other predatory insects.

Carpenterworms & Carpentermoths

Acossus spp., Prionoxystus robiniae

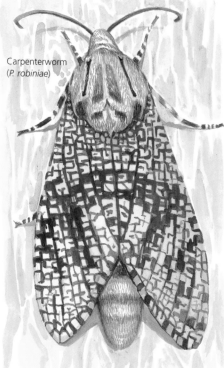

Carpenterworm
(*P. robiniae*)

Carpenterworms have an up to four-year life cycle and often do not kill their hosts, though heavily infested trees riddled with tunnelling become weak and may break off in windstorms. The three main species in our region, the Carpenterworm (*P. robiniae*), the Poplar Carpentermoth (*A. centerensis*) and the Aspen Carpentermoth (*A. populi*) have similar life cycles.

Adults emerge in June, and females lay eggs in crevices and wounds on branches and trunks. Up to 800 eggs are laid, but only a couple in each location. Larvae hatch in about 10 days and burrow through the bark into the cambial layer of the tree, constructing numerous tunnels that extend into the heartwood. Larvae push sawdust and frass out of tunnel openings. After a few years, larvae mature and pupate in May. The pupae wriggle to the surface and adults emerge from the tree.

ID: *Adult: Carpenterworm:* male has grey-mottled forewings and yellow-orange hindwings; female is larger than male and has grey hindwings. *Poplar Carpentermoth:* smoky black forewings; grey hindwings. *Aspen Carpentermoth:* light grey forewings with black markings; light grey body. *Larva:* white to green body sparsely covered with short, stout hairs; brown head and thoracic shield.

Size: *Adult: Carpenterworm:* wingspan 50–75 mm. *Poplar Carpentermoth:* wingspan 40–50 mm. *Aspen Carpentermoth:* wingspan 50–70 mm. *Larva: Carpenterworm* and *Aspen Carpentermoth:* body length 50–75 mm. *Poplar Carpentermoth:* body length 40–50 mm.

Habitat and Range: *Carpenterworm:* throughout the region; feeds on poplar, green ash, mountain ash, elm and oak. *Poplar*

Carpentermoth and *Aspen Carpentermoth:* feed on poplar and aspen.

Scouting: Watch trunks, especially at their base, for holes with sap, sawdust and frass extruding from them. Look for sunken areas on the trunks.

Cultural/Physical Control: Keep trees healthy and watered. Remove dead or damaged branches and trees. Wrap bases of trees with burlap to prevent adults from emerging and laying eggs. Wraps should be left on for up to 4 years. Use a knife to dig out larvae that are near the surface. Poke wire into tunnels to kill larvae.

Biological Control: Natural controls include parasitic wasps and nematodes, diseases and predatory birds. Hairy woodpeckers will spend days working over an infested tree.

Sod Webworms

Pediasia trisecta and others

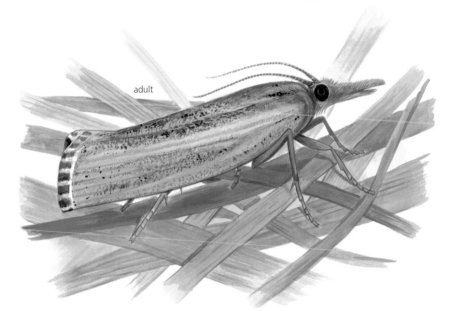

adult

Ever wonder what those little white moths are that fly up whenever you walk across the lawn? They are known as lawn/grass moths or sod webworms and include species from the moth family Crambidae. In Ontario, species that are considered lawn pests include the Larger or Great Sod Webworm (*P. trisecta*) and the Cranberry Girdler (*Chrysoteuchia topiaria*).

Both species have one generation per year, with the Great Sod Webworm adults being most active in August. Although Cranberry Girdlers seem to have multiple broods, they have overlapping generations, with adults appearing from mid-June to early September. Adults are active in mid- to late summer and are busy flying over lawns at night. Females drop and

Also Known As: Lawn Moths

ID: *Adult: Crambidae moths:* slender, brown and white body; resembles grass seed when sitting with wings folded around body; mouthparts protrude, resembling a snout. *Great Sod Webworm:* yellowish body; yellow and brown forewings have brown marks (usually 2); smoky grey hindwings. *Cranberry Girdler:* whitish body with pale, golden-tipped forewings that have arching white line; smoky grey hindwings. *Larva:* pale to dark overall with dark spots and coarse hairs; head tends to be brown.

Size: *Adult:* wingspan 15–20 mm. *Larva:* body length 20 mm.

Habitat and Range: Throughout Ontario wherever grasses grow; larvae feed on many species of grass including common lawn and pasture grasses; most sod webworm larvae feed only on the blades of grass plants. *Cranberry Girdler:* larvae feed in the soil, where they eat crowns and roots of grasses, cranberries and even conifer seedlings such as Douglas-fir and true fir.

Sod Webworms (continued)

larva

scatter eggs or place them at the base of a grass stem. Larvae emerge from the eggs in approximately a week and begin feeding. They could be called "mini loggers" because they cut down individual blades of grass like loggers in a forest. They haul the blade into a silken nest they have constructed and begin feeding. The silken nests for most sod webworm species are built in the thatch layer and are usually flush with the ground. Larvae hibernate within the nests and resume feeding in spring. In summer, once they are mature, larvae build a silken cocoon in the soil to pupate.

Other sod webworms in our region that are less frequently encountered or are not recorded as pests are the Bluegrass Sod Webworm (*Parapediasia teterrella*), Striped Sod Webworm (*Fissicrambus mutabilis*) and Vagabond Sod Webworm (*Agriphila vulgivagella*).

Scouting: Webworm damage may resemble damage from other lawn insect pests or diseases, so proper identification is critical. Damage to lawns becomes most apparent when hot weather is combined with drought. Watch for dead or brown patches; active feeding occurs at the edge of the patch. Look for the larvae themselves or the presence of silken threads or feeding chambers in the thatch. Watch for large flocks of moths flying up when you walk across the lawn. A large number of birds congregating and picking at the lawn may indicate the presence of webworms.

Cultural/Physical Control: Keep your lawn healthy. Healthy lawns are better able to withstand and recover from sod webworm damage. Switch to a different variety of grass or groundcover if outbreaks are frequent.

Biological Control: A number of predators and parasites attack webworms. Ground beetles often scamper through grasses and munch on any webworm they encounter. Birds such as American robins and sparrows spend the entire spring and summer hunting for webworms and other insects in our lawns. Steinernema nematodes exist naturally in soils and will kill a few larvae. These nematodes are available commercially. For the best results, spray them on a moist lawn in the evening or at night.

Root Maggots

Delia spp.

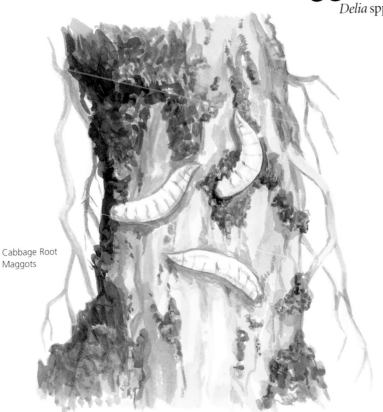

Cabbage Root
Maggots

Adult root maggots feed on nectar of wild flowers. Cabbage Root Maggot (*D. radicum*) larvae feed by shredding roots of crucifers, whereas Onion Maggot (*D. antigua*) larvae prefer the roots of onions.

Root maggots overwinter as pupae in the soil. Adults emerge in early spring to feed on nectar of wild flowers. They live for five to six weeks, and females lay up to 200 eggs singly or in small batches at the base of host plants.

ID: *Adult:* resembles a house fly but slightly smaller; grey with dark stripe down abdomen. *Larva:* whitish maggot that tapers toward head; no legs or distinct head capsule.

Size: *Adult:* 7 mm. *Larva:* 10 mm.

Habitat and Range: Widespread throughout Ontario.

Scouting: Onion Maggot females tend to lay eggs in bunches; the larvae move from plant to plant, so damage in the garden is often patchy. Onion Maggots also attack garlic,

leek and chives. Larvae begin feeding on root hairs, eventually moving into the taproot. Damage to seedlings is most destructive, often resulting in death of the plant. Second generation feeding rarely results in plant death but does reduce yield and marketability of produce. Damage can be recognized aboveground by wilting and yellowing of the leaves. Cabbage Root Maggot larvae tunnel or burrow into tubers of radish, turnip and rutabaga, exposing the tuber to increased risk of disease infection.

Root Maggots (continued)

Root Maggot adult

The Cabbage Root Maggot has been studied to better understand its egg-laying behaviour. The female does a spiral descent to a host plant, senses if it is acceptable as a host and then takes off. She repeats this three more times before laying her eggs. If at any time she lands on a non-host plant, she will fly away to start the process all over again. Therefore, planting susceptible crops in a monoculture will increase root maggot pressure, whereas planting in mixed rows or randomly with other crops will greatly reduce root maggot pressure.

Females prefer cool, moist soil for egg laying. Larvae hatch and develop in three to four weeks. Pupation during summer lasts two to three weeks, and second generation adults emerge to lay eggs again. This second generation overwinters in the pupal stage. Onion Maggots may have up to three generations per year, whereas Cabbage Root Maggots have only two generations.

Cultural/Physical Control: Onion Maggots prefer damaged or diseased plants as egg-laying sites, so remove these plants to reduce the number of adults visiting your garden. Remove all culls in autumn. Rotating crops will reduce but not eliminate the problem because root maggot adults are good fliers.

Biological Control: Many predators, parasitoids and pathogens suppress root maggots. You may have seen flies at the tops of grasses, clinging to the seedhead in a death grip. These flies are infected with the fungus *Entomophthora muscae*. The fungus causes the fly to move to a high point, ensuring the spores will disperse over a wider area to increase the chance of infecting other flies. A rove beetle, *Aleochara bilineata*, is a parasitoid of the pupae.

Crane Flies

Tipula spp.

Larval crane flies, known as leather jackets, feed on roots and crowns of turfgrass, vegetables and tree seedlings. There are more than 1500 species of crane fly in North America, most of which are benign decomposers in soil and wetlands.

Crane fly larvae overwinter in the soil, resume feeding in spring for a short time and then pupate. Adults emerge throughout the summer to mate and lay eggs in soil and turf. Moist soil conditions are essential for egg survival. Adults are very short lived and are non-feeding. Larvae feed throughout summer and autumn and move down in the soil to overwinter. There is one generation per year.

Although adult crane flies (often called mosquito hawks) are large and imposing, they are completely harmless because the adults of many species do not feed.

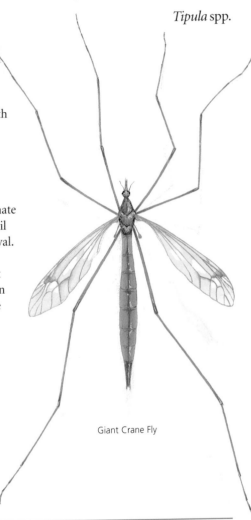

Giant Crane Fly

ID: *Adult:* slender; long-legged; looks remarkably like enormous mosquito. *Larva:* long, cylindrical, rough-skinned and legless; has thick, tentacle-like appendages on posterior end for breathing.

Size: *Adult:* 15–25 mm. *Larva:* 5–20 mm.

Habitat and Range: Mostly in moist soils or wetland habitats throughout Ontario.

Scouting: Adults are clumsy fliers that will come to lights and are often encountered indoors. The larvae remain below sod level during the day, feeding on the roots and crown at night. They are also known to feed on crucifers and tree seedlings. Look for shredding of the crown. Crane flies prefer soils with persistent surface moisture as egg-laying sites.

Cultural/Physical Control: Allow the soil to dry between watering. De-thatch the lawn on a regular basis to prevent the accumulation of decaying organic matter.

Biological Control: Generalist predators such as ground beetles and rove beetles routinely control crane flies.

Fruit Flies

Euphranta canadensis, Rhagoletis spp.

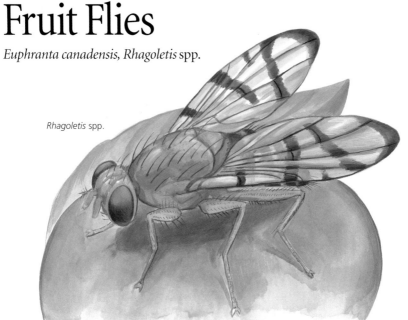

Rhagoletis spp.

Fruit fly larvae tunnel into fruit, consuming the pulp and then the seeds. Fruit flies are more or less host specific, with the Cherry Fruit Fly *(R. cingulata)* and the Black Cherry Fruit Fly *(R. fausta)* attacking sour cherry and pin cherry. The Currant Fruit Fly *(E. canadensis)* attacks black, red and white currant and gooseberry. The Apple Maggot *(R. pomonella)* attacks apple, crab apple and hawthorn.

Fruit flies overwinter as pupae in soil at the base of the host plant. Adults emerge in early summer, usually coinciding with flowering. Adults will feed for 7 to 10 days before laying eggs in developing fruit. Eggs hatch shortly afterward, and larvae tunnel into the fruit. Prior to harvest, larvae drop out of the fruit to pupate in the soil. There is only one generation per year.

ID: *Adult:* dark overall; distinctive dark pattern on wings is used to distinguish species. *Currant Fruit Fly:* light brown body and wing markings. *Larva:* legless maggot that tapers from rear to front.

Size: *Adult:* 3–5 mm. *Larva:* 1–4 mm.

Habitat and Range: *Currant, Cherry, Black Cherry* and *Apple Maggot fruit flies:* province-wide distribution; wild hosts such as hawthorn and pin cherry serve as reservoirs for fruit flies.

Scouting: Females pierce green fruit to feed on fluid, and these punctures appear as small holes ringed in dead brown tissue. Some of these puncture wounds will have eggs deposited in them. The eggs are elongate, rice-grain shaped and lie just under the outer skin. Larval feeding under the skin appears as meandering tunnels. The larvae usually dive straight for the core and seeds. Affected fruit ripen more rapidly and often fall prematurely.

Cultural/Physical Control: Pick up fallen fruit daily to prevent larvae from emerging to pupate in the soil. Shallow cultivation below the plant in autumn will expose pupae to harsh winter conditions. Remove wild hosts such as pin cherry and hawthorn.

Biological Control: Robber flies and other aerial predators prey on adult fruit flies. Once they are inside fruit, this species has very few natural enemies. Most predation occurs on the pupae in the soil by ground beetles, rove beetles and the like.

Carrot Rust Fly

Psila rosae

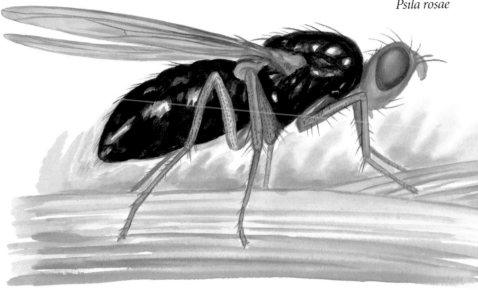

The Carrot Rust Fly is common across most of Canada. The larvae feed on the roots of carrot, celery, parsley, dill and parsnip.

Carrot Rust Flies overwinter as pupae in soil at depths as low as 10 centimetres. Adults emerge in May and June and move to sheltering plants to mate and feed. Females lay eggs at the base of carrot plants in the evening. Larvae hatch out and feed on the root hairs and roots, eventually leaving the root to pupate in the soil. A second generation of adults may emerge in late July and early August to lay eggs. There are two generations per year.

In the pursuit of an integrated control strategy, two parasitoids were released for protection of commercial carrot crops in BC and Ontario. Unfortunately, neither became established.

ID: *Adult:* reddish head; yellow legs. *Larva:* tiny, whitish maggot.

Size: *Adult:* 6 mm. *Larva:* 1–5 mm.

Habitat and Range: Throughout Ontario; female prefers moist soil to lay eggs; carrots near plantings that offer shelter are attacked more often.

Scouting: Infestations are difficult to detect by looking at the foliage. Often, the gardener detects disease that results from larvae feeding in the root. Early instar larvae feed on the root hairs, whereas later instar larvae move into the root itself, especially the basal third.

Cultural/Physical Control: Prevent the adults from laying eggs by using a floating row cover after seeding. Ensure the edges are securely sealed at the soil line and leave enough fabric to allow the plants to grow. The cover can be removed in July. You can also delay seeding until late June to escape the first generation of adults.

Biological Control: You will have to rely on egg predators such as rove beetles and ground beetles to suppress rust fly populations.

Tachinid Flies

Voria ruralis and others

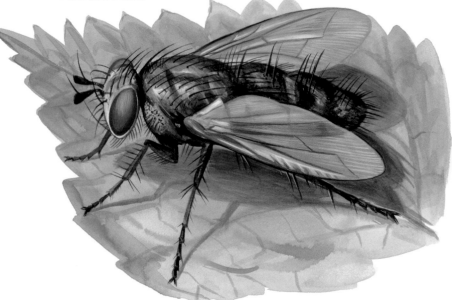

Larval tachinids feed on host insects from the inside out. Adult tachinids feed on nectar. There are upwards of 1300 species of tachinid in North America. *V. ruralis* is a parasitoid of the Cabbage Looper.

Tachinid adults lay their eggs in the host, on the host near the head, or on plant material. If laid on the plant, the eggs either hatch and the larvae seek out a host insect, or the eggs are meant to be eaten by the host insect and then hatch inside the host. Larvae will kill the host as a result of their feeding. Some species pupate inside the host insect, while other species drop to the ground and pupate in the soil. Most tachinids overwinter as pupae.

Nearly half of all known insect species are parasitoids of one kind or another.

ID: *Adult:* resembles a house fly but has stout spines at tip of abdomen (for defence when laying eggs on an uncooperative victim). *Larva:* whitish, legless grub; no distinct head capsule.

Size: *Adult:* 2–20 mm. *Larva:* 1–10 mm.

Habitat and Range: Widespread throughout Ontario; preferred hosts include immature moths, sawflies and beetles, and adult beetles and true bugs.

Scouting: You may be able to see a small egg, appearing much a like a tiny grain of rice, attached near the head of a caterpillar.

Parasitized insects tend to be sluggish, cease feeding and then simply die. You might find wrinkled caterpillars with a gaping hole where the larva or adult emerged.

How to Attract: No measures should be taken to limit these beneficial insects. Tachinids are likely the most unsung heroes of your garden. They are highly host specific, meaning that they are finicky about who they attack, usually restricting themselves to only one species of host. Therefore, they are considered to be specialists and are quite capable of devastating a host population.

Hover Flies

Syrphus ribesii and others

Adult hover flies do not harm plants. Immature hover flies feed on a range of foodstuffs including putrefying manure and old, rotten trees, but they are best known for eating aphids and other insects. These flies are referred to as hover flies or flower flies because of the adults' hovering flight and their preference for flowers as a source of nectar. There are over 800 species of hover fly in North America, many of which, such as *S. ribesii*, are found in Ontario.

Syrphus spp.

Hover flies overwinter as larvae, pupae or adults, depending on the species. Eggs are laid, in the case of predatory hover flies, near the prey. There are usually four larval instars, followed by pupation on the plant or in the soil. There is usually only one generation per year.

The hover fly's striking colour, resembling a bee, is a form of mimicry to fool potential predators into thinking they will get a sting, when, in fact, the hover fly adult is harmless.

ID: *Adult:* black and yellow overall; hovers in flight; some species are very hairy, often mistaken for bees, whereas others are hairless and could pass for wasps or yellow jackets. *Larva:* whitish, legless grub.

Size: *Adult:* 5–40 mm. *Larva:* 2–12 mm.

Habitat and Range: Some hover fly larvae prefer decaying or even putrid matter; many species are found on plants across Ontario.

Scouting: Adults are often observed hovering in front of flowers, where they collect pollen and drink nectar. Larvae of predator species are often found wherever aphids are, such as on undersides of leaves. Do not be alarmed to find maggots on your leaves; they are likely hover flies and will not harm your plants.

How to Attract: A yard or garden with many flowering plants will attract hover flies, and you will experience all the benefits of this pollinator and predator. They are the first "bees" to visit in spring and the last to leave in autumn. If pollination were not enough of a reason to adore these flies, the immatures are voracious predators of aphids and other soft-bodied insects. You may be fortunate enough to observe a larva hoist an aphid high in the air in what appears to be a show of triumph.

Robber Flies

Laphria spp., *Promachus* spp. and others

Beeish Robber Fly
(*Laphria spp.*)

Adult and larval robber flies are predators of other insects. Adult robber flies feed on anything up to their own size, including beetles, other flies, bees and wasps. The larvae feed on other insect larvae in the soil. Robber flies can be found across Ontario but are particularly abundant in dry, sandy areas (*Promachus* spp.) and open woodland areas (*Laphria* spp.).

Adult robber flies may lay their eggs in soil, on foliage or in cracks and crevices in bark, or they may drop them randomly during flight, depending on the species. Larvae inhabit soil and leaf litter, burrowing down to overwinter. The larvae resume feeding in spring and then pupate. Adults emerge in early summer.

A feature unique to robber flies is a stout group of hairs on the front of the face, called a mystax. The hairs protect the face from thrashing limbs and wings of captured prey. Mystax—funny name for a moustache...

ID: *Adult:* can be robust, bee-like fly or have elongate abdomen and stout thorax; eyes and pointed mouthparts are very well developed. *Larva:* legless and cylindrical with dark head capsule.

Size: *Adult:* 5–50 mm. *Larva:* 3–25 mm.

Habitat and Range: Widespread throughout Ontario. *Laphria* spp.: prefer open woodland habitats, perching on foliage to scan for prey. *Promachus* spp.: often observed in sandy areas.

Scouting: Adults take their prey on the wing during the sunniest part of the day. You might see an adult perched on a leaf with its hapless prey impaled on its mouthparts. The larvae search for prey in soil and leaf litter.

How to Attract: To entice robber flies into your yard, provide flowering plants as a nectar source and shrubs and trees for perches.

Chokecherry Gall Midge

Contarinia virginianae

The Chokecherry Gall Midge feeds within chokecherry fruit as a larva. The midge is present wherever chokecherry is found.

The Chokecherry Gall Midge overwinters as a pupa in the soil below chokecherry bushes. Adults emerge in late May to lay eggs in flowers. Larvae burrow into the developing fruit, causing the fruit to enlarge. Larvae will drop from the fruit in late July to pupate in the soil.

Formation of galls is not restricted to the Chokecherry Gall Midge. Many insects cause gall formation in plants, from wasps on roses to aphids on poplars. A gall is an ingenious way to make the plant do most of the work to protect the insect. Galls usually do not seriously harm the plant but are often unsightly.

ID: *Adult:* slight, delicate body. *Larva:* orange and legless with bulge in middle.

Size: *Adult:* 6 mm. *Larva:* 3–4 mm.

Habitat and Range: Wherever chokecherry is found.

Scouting: What at first appears to be pear-shaped, jumbo fruit is actually abnormal enlargement of fruit infested with 1–15 maggots. The fruit galls to accommodate the maggots growing and feeding inside, and it

will not ripen to a dark colour. Instead, it remains a pinkish red and usually drops before non-infested fruit ripens.

Cultural/Physical Control: Pick and destroy enlarged fruit. Immediately collect any unripened fruit from the ground before the maggots have a chance to leave.

Biological Control: Birds pick the large fruit. Nothing else can get into the fruit to kill the maggots.

Swede Midge

Contarinia nasturtii

I n Ontario, the Swede Midge is a serious pest of plants in the Cruciferae family. This tiny fly is native to Europe and was not recorded anywhere in North America until it was discovered in Ontario in 2000. In Europe, it feeds on such crops as broccoli, cabbage, cauliflower and Brussels sprouts. Weeds from the Cruciferae family include wild mustard, wild radish, shepherd's purse and stinkweed and may serve as alternate hosts for the pest. Larvae feeding on the growing tips induce the plant to undergo unusual tissue development. The plant produces a tumour-like growth that the larvae lives inside and feeds from, resulting in swollen, distorted and twisted leaf stalks and death of the main stem. This causes the development of several secondary stems, resulting in a multi-stemmed or multi-head plant.

Beginning in mid-May, adults emerge from overwintering pupae and mate. Females lay eggs in clusters of 2 to 50 eggs on the youngest growing tissues, usually near the growing tip. The eggs are very small and turn from transparent to creamy white. After three days, the larvae hatch and begin to feed. The larvae can complete their development in 7 to 21 days. When mature, they drop to the ground and tunnel in the soil to pupate. Adults emerge in two weeks. There are three to four generations each summer.

ID: *Adult:* tiny, light brown midge. *Larva:* yellow overall.

Size: *Adult:* 6 mm. *Larva:* 3–4 mm.

Habitat and Range: Currently only in pockets of infestation; prefers sheltered areas along field edges and buildings.

Scouting: Adults are not strong fliers and prefer areas with low wind, so look for damage in sheltered areas. Examine young shoots for unusual growth and side shoots. Brown scarring that can be seen with the naked eye indicates larval feeding. Infested fruit contains 1 to 15 maggots and will not ripen to a dark colour; instead, it remains a pinkish red and usually drops prior to the ripening of non-infested fruit.

Cultural/Physical Control: Remove and destroy infested plant material. When leaving an infested field, wash the soil from your boots because pupae may be transported. The Swede midge is a quarantine pest, and precautions must be taken to prevent its spread.

Biological Control: No predators can get into the galls to kill the maggots.

Fungus Gnats & Shore Flies

Bradysia spp., *Scatella* spp.

Fungus gnats (*Bradysia* spp.) and shore flies (*Scatella* spp.) are small, dark, gnat-like flies often seen in moist environments such as greenhouses, compost piles or wherever there is moist, rotting vegetation, algae or soil with a content of organic matter. They are generally a harmless nuisance, but the larvae chew on roots and can transmit pathogenic microorganisms that cause root rot. Fungus gnat larvae damage house plants and seedlings in cold frames and greenhouses. Shore fly larvae rarely chew on roots, but the adults leave undesirable fecal matter on leaves.

Fungus gnat eggs are tiny and are rarely seen. The larvae go through four instars and feed and pupate in the soil. There are many generations per year.

shore fly

fungus gnat

Midges and other small gnats often swarm in the air above rotting, wet vegetation, but their larvae feed only on rotted vegetation and algae and don't injure plants. Fungus gnats and shore flies are weak fliers and are more often found walking on the surface of soil or potting media. When disturbed, they will make short flights. Shore flies are better fliers than fungus gnats.

ID: *Adult: Fungus gnat:* fragile-looking, black fly; slender legs; antennae longer than body; clear to light grey wings with Y-shaped vein. *Shore fly:* stout, black fly; short legs; short, bristle-like antennae. *Larva: Fungus gnat:* small, white or transparent, legless maggot with shiny, black head. *Shore fly:* brownish yellow overall; no legs or distinct head; dark-tipped, forked breathing tube at hind end.

Size: *Adult:* 1–2 mm. *Larva:* 1–2 mm.

Habitat and Range: Throughout Ontario, especially in greenhouses and moist environments with abundant algae and high organic matter.

Scouting: Look for adults and larvae in moist, wet environments. Use yellow, sticky cards to monitor adult populations in greenhouses.

Cultural/Physical Control: Reduce watering, remove standing water and control algae in greenhouses and cold frames. Cut back house plants with high populations of fungus gnats and re-pot into clean pots with fresh growing media.

Biological Control: *Hypoaspis* predatory mites, *Atheta* rove beetles and predatory wasps are available commercially for control of fungus gnat larvae and pupae in the soil.

Mosquitoes

Aedes spp., *Culex piniens*

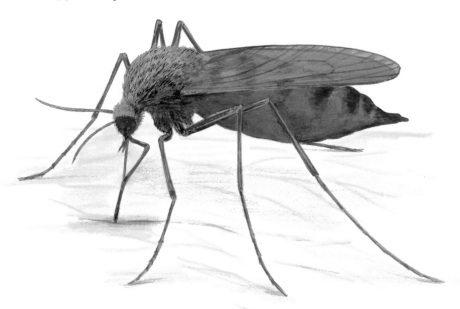

Most adult female mosquitoes require a blood meal. Some specialize on birds, some on mammals and some on amphibians, reptiles, birds and mammals. Larval mosquitoes dine on bacteria, decaying organic matter and even proteins dissolved in water. There are approximately 55 species of mosquito in Ontario. The most pestiferous is *A. vexans*, followed closely by *A. spencerii* and *A. dorsalis*. A major threat by virtue of its ability to transmit West Nile Virus is *C. piniens*. Mosquitoes can be found everywhere standing water is found.

There are three main life history strategies found among mosquitoes. Eggs are laid in permanent and semi-permanent ponds. The larvae go through four instars, filtering food out of the water. They pupate in the water and emerge as adults at

ID: *Adult:* slender, delicate fly with long antennae and long proboscis. *Larva:* bulging thorax; slender abdomen ends in forked structure for breathing and salt exchange.

Size: *Adult:* 5–10 mm. *Larva:* 2–3 mm.

Habitat and Range: Everywhere standing water is to be had, from snowmelt pools and sloughs to depressions in farm fields and even in discarded tires.

Scouting: Adults tend to stay out of hot sun, preferring to rest in vegetation and coming out at dusk to feed. Larvae can be observed

near the edge of shallow, still water bodies. *A. spencerii* is out early in spring and it is typically an ankle biter. *A vexans* and *A. dorsalis* are more common in June and July. *C. pipiens* is most abundant in July and August.

Cultural/Physical Control: The best way to manage mosquitoes is to eliminate the larvae by draining ponds and, especially for *C. pipiens*, containers such as plant pots and birdbaths. Reduce adult numbers by cutting the lawn low and by not having thick vegetation for them to use as resting sites.

the surface. There can be as many as three generations per year. Some species overwinter as adults, whereas others overwinter as eggs and hatch in snowmelt pools, typically having only one generation per year. *A. spencerii* overwinters as an egg and hatches in snowmelt pools but is also capable of hatching later in rain-fed pools; therefore, it has two or three generations per year. *A. vexans* overwinters as an egg but does not hatch until the warm rains of summer. This species can develop very quickly in sun-warmed roadside ditches. Eggs of *A. vexans* are very drought resistant and have been recorded to last up to seven years before hatching.

Mosquito on tulip

West Nile Virus (WNV) affects the brain and brain stem. Most cases have no symptoms, but a few infected people have contracted West Nile Neurological Syndrome (also known as West Nile Fever), which is akin to a bad flu but can persist for weeks or months and, in some cases, symptoms are similar to encephalitis and may result in paralysis or death. Many species of mosquito feed on birds throughout spring and early summer, amplifying the number of birds infected with the virus. In July, C. pipiens populations increase, and this species feeds on birds and humans, acting as a bridge for the virus. In Ontario, this period is when we are most at risk of contracting the disease. Why risk infection? Use repellent and avoid being outdoors at dusk. WNV is a serious disease that demands you to be serious about avoiding it.

Now, we have just described the ideal mosquito-free yard—a barren wasteland. Instead of this extreme, you could use repellent and long-sleeved clothing. We take for granted having screens on our windows and doors—why not go one step further and wear mosquito-netting clothing?

Biological Control: Larval and pupal mosquitoes have a host of aquatic predators, including dragonfly and damselfly nymphs, fish, frogs and predaceous diving beetles.

Birds, dragonflies and damselflies, empid flies—seemingly anything that flies and hunts—eat adult mosquitoes. Encourage birds and dragonflies to visit your yard by providing a birdbath or water feature (be sure to check it for mosquito larvae). Control larval mosquitoes by using a bacterial agent called *Bacillus thuringiensis* var. *israelensis* (B.t.i.). It is a stomach poison for flies and only flies.

Webspinning Sawflies

Cephalcia spp.

Members of the family Pamphiliidae are known as webspinning or nest-building sawflies for the homes they construct in their hosts. The Blue Spruce Sawfly *(C. fascipennis)* and the other webspinning sawfly, *C. provancheri*, are the most common species in Ontario. Despite its name, the Blue Spruce Sawfly actually feeds in the wild on white and Engelmann spruce.

Adults emerge in spring, and even before they mate, females start laying eggs in rows of two to four on needles.

Eggs that are fertilized produce females, whereas unfertilized eggs produce males. Larvae emerge about three weeks later and construct shelters out of silk and frass at the crotches of branches. They crawl out of their shelter, remove a needle and consume only the base, often leaving the tip to be incorporated into the silk of the shelter. Mature larvae drop to the ground and burrow into the soil. The larvae create earthen cocoons, where they overwinter in a prepupal stage, pupating in spring.

ID: *Adult:* typical winged sawfly with 2 sets of clear, veined wings. *Larva:* light-coloured with dark bands; characteristic short, segmented antennae; pair of prolegs at rear of abdomen (unique to Pamphiliids). *Blue Spruce Sawfly:* yellow with reddish banding and head. *C. provancheri:* tan with dark banding and head.

Size: *Adult:* wingspan unknown. *Larva:* body length approximately 20 mm.

Habitat and Range: Throughout Ontario, but primarily in river valleys and forested regions where native spruce occur; common on blue, white and Engelmann spruce.

Scouting: In spring, monitor trees for signs of needle defoliation and nests made of frass, needles and silk in the crotches of trees. If

you survey early, you may find nests possessing a rather reclusive larva. Later in the season and in following years, you will see larger nests and more defoliation.

Cultural/Physical Control: Severe damage to hosts has not been reported; however, the nests are unsightly. The most effective control is to pull inhabited nests and larvae out by hand in spring and early summer. Disturb the duff and soil at the base of infested trees in autumn to destroy larvae and their chambers.

Biological Control: Predators of these pesky sawflies include insectivorous birds, parasitic wasps, predatory spiders, beetles and other beneficial insects.

Dogwood Sawflies

Macremphytus spp.

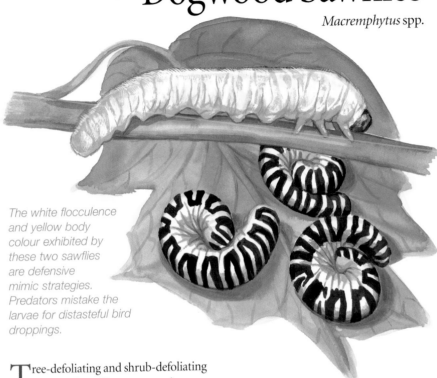

The white flocculence and yellow body colour exhibited by these two sawflies are defensive mimic strategies. Predators mistake the larvae for distasteful bird droppings.

Tree-defoliating and shrub-defoliating dogwood sawflies are sometimes a common sight in ornamental gardens or on wild dogwoods.

Adults emerge from late May to July. After mating, females deposit 100 or more eggs on the underside of a single dogwood leaf. These colonial larvae hatch and feed on the leaves. Young instars skeletonize leaves, and later instars defoliate the entire shrub from July into autumn. Mature larvae drop to the ground and overwinter in soil or debris in pupal chambers, pupating in spring. Some larvae will remain in these cells for a couple of years.

ID: *Adult:* typical winged sawfly with 2 sets of clear, veined wings. *Larva:* black head; often covered by white, waxy, wool-like covering that gives body overall white appearance. *M. tarsatus:* black body with dorsal, yellow transverse bars. *M. testaceus:* yellow body with rows of lateral and subdorsal spots.

Size: *Adult:* wingspan unknown. *Larva:* body length 22–35 mm.

Habitat and Range: Throughout Ontario where wild dogwood grows.

Scouting: In late June and early July, watch dogwood foliage for signs of leaf damage and for curled larvae on leaves, especially if defoliation has occurred in previous years.

Cultural/Physical Control: Hand picking and squashing larvae or dropping them into a pail of soapy water can save ornamental trees and shrubs from extensive defoliation. This method protects natural predators.

Biological Control: Many species prey on these pesky sawflies, including parasitic wasps, predatory spiders, beetles and other insects as well as many insectivorous birds. Plant a variety of nectar-producing flowers to attract parasitic wasps, and leave areas of native bush intact to attract predators.

Willow Redgall Sawfly

Pontania proxima

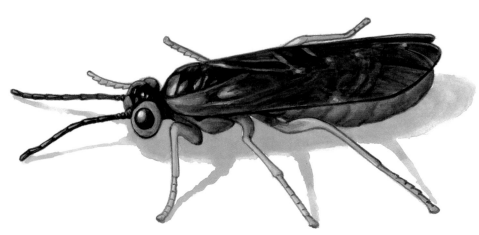

Gardeners often know summer has arrived when the unsightly little galls caused by these sawflies appear on willow leaves. The good news is that the galls do not harm our trees—they only make them look strange.

This species has one generation per year. Adults emerge in late spring and mate. Females insert an egg into a new leaf and, shortly after, a red, oval to bean-shaped gall forms on the leaf. There is usually only one gall per leaf, but there can be two or more. Eggs hatch after about a week, and the larvae begin feeding inside the galls. As the larvae grow, so too do the galls. In late summer, mature larvae drop to the ground, where they build a cocoon in the soil. They overwinter in a prepupal stage and pupate in spring.

There are two *Pontania* species that cause these galls in willows. The Willow Redgall Sawfly (*P. proxima*) is the most common species. It creates oval or bean-shaped galls. The other species is currently unnamed and creates apple-shaped galls. If you see similar galls on poplars, you are observing the *Pemphigus* genera of sawflies at work.

ID: *Adult:* dark body. *Larva:* light body with dark head; 3 sets of true legs on thorax and 1 set of prolegs on each abdominal segment.

Size: *Adult:* wingspan 3.5–5 mm. *Larva:* body length 10–12 mm.

Habitat and Range: Ornamental and wild willows throughout Ontario.

Scouting: Watch for galls forming on the leaves in late June and July.

Cultural/Physical Control: For minor infestations, you can pick off infected leaves and burn them, but this method lowers the tree's ability to photosynthesize and may do more harm to the tree than good. For heavy annual infestations, lightly rake the soil under the tree; this should harm some of the prepupal larvae.

Biological Control: Predators include parasitic wasps, ants and many insectivorous birds.

Raspberry Sawfly
Monophadnoides geniculatus

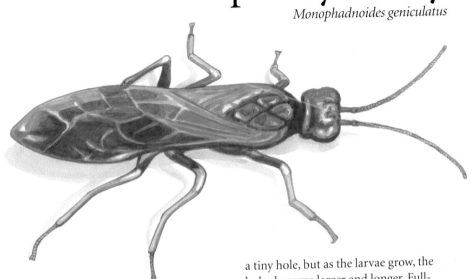

Gardeners and farmers with raspberry patches may encounter these interesting-looking sawflies from time to time. The larvae are skeletonizers and can sometimes defoliate an entire raspberry patch, leaving nothing but leaf stems and veins (sometimes called leaf skeletons).

Adults emerge and mate when raspberries are blooming. Females lay eggs in leaf tissue. Larvae hatch and feed on the underside of leaves, but during heavy infestations, they may also feed on flowers and newly formed raspberries. Leaf damage starts off as a tiny hole, but as the larvae grow, the holes become larger and longer. Full-grown larvae drop to the ground and build cocoons in the surrounding soil, where they hibernate in a prepupal stage and pupate the following spring. This species has only one generation per year.

Do you hate picking raspberries in autumn because of all the hornets cruising around? Well, you may feel better knowing that these hornets, in addition to feeding on juicy raspberries, are also hunting for Raspberry Sawfly larvae.

ID: *Adult:* winged, black and yellow body with red to orange markings on legs. *Larva:* light green body covered in white, spiny bristles; yellowish head.

Size: *Adult:* wingspan 6 mm. *Larva:* body length 12 mm.

Habitat and Range: Throughout Ontario, primarily in areas with wild raspberries.

Scouting: Look for small to large, ovate holes in leaves during spring and summer. Examine the underside of leaves for the small, spiny, white larvae.

Cultural/Physical Control: Pick larvae off leaves and squish them by hand.

Biological Control: Predators of these pesky sawflies range from parasitic wasps, predatory spiders, beetles and other insects to many insectivorous birds. Plant a variety of nectar-producing flowers to attract parasitic wasps, and keep some native bush intact to attract other predators.

Imported Currantworm

Nematus ribesii

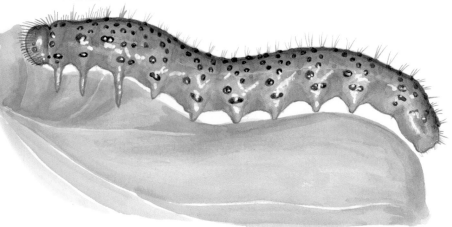

Another defoliator of ornamental shrubs is the Imported Currantworm, which feeds on currants and gooseberries. It is difficult to miss—its larvae can completely denude a shrub of its leaves.

This species has two generations per year, with the first adults emerging in late May or early June. Eggs are laid in rows on the underside of leaves and hatch one week or so later. The larval colonies feed on the foliage and grow very quickly, reaching maturity in another two to three weeks. A colony of these hungry little devils can severely defoliate the shrub during this period. Mature larvae then drop to the ground, where they pupate in surface debris. A second generation of adults then emerges, often in early July, and the cycle repeats, but this time, mature larvae or pupae drop to the ground to hibernate.

Have you ever wondered why plant-feeding sawflies look like ants with wings? It is because sawflies, hornets, wasps and ants are all members of the same order, Hymenoptera.

ID: *Adult:* dark body with yellowish abdomen and 2 sets of clear, veined wings. *Larva:* early instar larva has greenish body covered in black dots, with black head and legs; mature larva is uniform green with yellow head.

Size: *Adult:* wingspan 8–10 mm. *Larva:* body length 20 mm.

Habitat and Range: Primarily on currants and gooseberries throughout Ontario.

Scouting: Monitor currants and gooseberries in early spring for signs of defoliation or the presence of the defoliating worms.

Cultural/Physical Control: Controlling colonies early in the season, before the young larvae have a chance to do much defoliation, is the most effective option. Pick off and squish larval colonies. Organic farmers and gardeners effectively use floating row covers draped over the shrub before adults emerge, which deters them from laying eggs on leaves and can significantly reduce infestations. Use row covers with caution, though, because some may cause the shrubs to overheat, and covers prevent pollination of the shrubs' flowers by other insects.

Biological Control: Predators include parasitic wasps, ants and many insectivorous birds.

Birch Leaf Miners

Fenusa pusilla, Heterarthrus nemoratus, Profenusa thomsoni

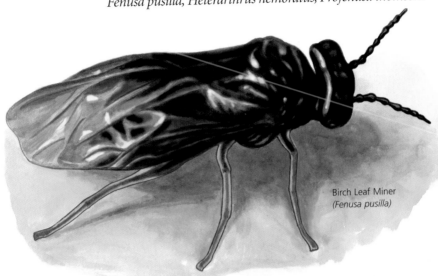

Birch Leaf Miner
(*Fenusa pusilla*)

Birch leaf miners arrived in North America from Europe and quickly spread. As their names suggest, the Birch Leaf Miner (*F. pusilla*), Birch Leaf Edgeminer (*H. nemoratus*) and Ambermarked Birch Leaf Miner (*P. thomsoni*) spend their lives within birch leaves, where they cause unsightly dead spots on the foliage and, in extreme cases, dead leaves. Although a heavily infested tree appears dead and has a rusty appearance, these three leaf miners damage the owner's ego more than the tree itself—the damage they cause is basically cosmetic and does not kill the tree. In extreme cases, however, damage may hinder tree growth.

The Birch Leaf Miner is the only one of these three species that has two generations in one year. The adult wasp emerges in late May. The female cuts slits with her ovipositor into the upper surface of leaves, where she deposits an egg. The larva hatches and feeds on the tissue between the leaf's epidermal layers. In some cases, there can be several larvae feeding within the same mine. The little worm continues to feed

ID: *Adult: Birch Leaf Miner:* black with yellow legs. *Birch Leaf Edgeminer:* black and white body. *Ambermarked Birch Leaf Miner:* black with white legs. *Larva: Birch Leaf Miner:* mature larva has white body with brown head and large, dark patch followed by 3 dark spots on ventral segments of thorax. *Birch Leaf Edgeminer:* dark head with 2 dark, round ventral spots on thorax. *Ambermarked Birch Leaf Miner:* light-coloured head with 2 ventral dashes on thorax.

Size: *Adult:* wingspan 2.5–3.5 mm. *Larva:* body length 5–8 mm.

Habitat and Range: Throughout Ontario, primarily on ornamental birches.

Scouting: Watch for larval mines and colour change in the foliage.

Birch Leaf Miners (continued)

leaf damage

A native species of parasitoid wasp (Lathrolestes luteolator), *in a great North American success story, has started to feed on the Ambermarked Birch Leaf Miner in Ontario and is significantly reducing the leaf miners' numbers.*

Birch Leaf Edgeminer females, which are believed to be parthenogenic, emerge in late May or early June and insert eggs into the edges of leaves. Larvae feed throughout spring and summer, forming clean mines that lack conspicuous frass deposits. Mature larvae hibernate in silken hibernation chambers in fallen leaves.

Ambermarked Birch Leaf Miner females are also parthenogenic. They emerge in July and lay eggs in central slits along leaf veins. This species has five feeding instars with a sixth non-feeding stage that hibernates in the soil in a prepupal stage and pupates in spring. Mines often have several larvae and contain obvious frass deposits.

into its fourth instar. The non-feeding fifth instar mines out of the leaf and drops to the ground, pupating in an earthen cell 2.5 to 5 centimetres deep in the soil. The second generation hatches two weeks later, and the cycle repeats. In warm years that have long growing seasons and late-season frosts, a third generation sometimes starts, but this species normally completes only two generations, overwintering as larvae in hibernation cells under fallen leaves.

Cultural/Physical Control: Keep your birch trees healthy and ensure your have healthy soil. Use organic fertilizers in spring to give the trees a boost so they can withstand a bit of defoliation and recover quickly.

Biological Control: Parasites and predators such as warblers, vireos, chickadees and parasitic wasps can substantially reduce the number of birch leaf miners.

Pear Slug

Caliroa cerasi

This glistening leaf skeletonizer resembles a slug. It is an introduced species from Europe and is often observed feeding on the leaves of fruit trees, creating brown patches.

Adults emerge in late spring after the host trees leaf out. Females insert an egg into the leaf, which creates a blister in response. About 10 to 15 days later, slug-like larvae hatch and begin feeding on the upper leaf surface. They continue to feed for two to three weeks, skeletonizing the leaves. Mature larvae drop to the ground and spin cocoons in the duff, where they pupate. A second generation of adults emerges in late July; this is when the most damage to tree leaves can occur. Mature larvae drop to the ground in autumn, pupate in the soil and remain there until spring.

Also Known As: Pear Sawfly

ID: *Adult:* black and yellow body. *Larva:* immature looks like dark, glossy slug with swollen head; mature is yellowish green.

Size: *Adult:* wingspan 10 mm. *Larva:* body length 10–12 mm.

Habitat and Range: Throughout Ontario on fruit trees, cotoneaster, hawthorn and mountain ash.

Scouting: Watch for signs of leaf skeletonizing in mid- to late June and again in late July and early August.

Cultural/Physical Control: Use a garden hose to blast the larvae off the leaves. Be careful to use a water stream that is strong enough to knock off the larvae but not the leaves. Larvae can also be picked off by hand and squished or dropped into soapy water.

Biological Control: There are many beneficial critters that help control these little pests, including birds and parasitoid wasps.

Ants

Formica spp., *Lasius niger, Tetramorium caespitum*

Wood Ant

Some species of wood and field ants practice slavery by stealing ant pupae of other species and raising them as their own. The emerging adults think they are at home and work for their captors with no complaints. This is why you may see black and red ants working together in the same mound.

Ants are scavengers and, in some cases, predators of other insects. Wood and field ants (*Formica* spp.) are common in both field and woodland habitats. Harvester ants (*Pogonomyrmex* spp.) are found in open grassland habitats. The Black Garden Ant *(L. niger)* is widespread in urban areas. The Pavement Ant *(T. caespitum)* builds nests under sidewalks and stepping stones.

ID: *Adult:* narrow waist between thorax and abdomen; long, elbowed antennae on head. *Wood* and *field ants:* can be all red, all black or have red head and thorax and black abdomen. *Harvester ant:* can be all red or all black. *Black Garden* and *Pavement ants:* all black. *Larva:* white, maggot-like grub.

Size: *Adult: Wood* and *field, Harvester* and *Black Garden ants:* 4–8 mm. *Pavement Ant:* 2–4 mm. *Larva:* 2–8 mm.

Habitat and Range: *Wood* and *field ants:* build nests in the ground, often creating large mounds. *Harvester ant:* seed-eater that builds

large mounds and covers them with plant material to act as a heat regulator. *Black Garden Ant:* nests in soil, creating small mounds. *Pavement Ant:* typically nests under paved walkways and stepping stones.

Scouting: Mounds are conspicuous because of the displacement of soil and possible disruption around roots of shrubs and flowers. Foragers use a chemical scent to mark the path to food sources, so you may often see lines of ants marching along. Wood, field and Pavement ants do not sting; instead, they bite and are capable of spraying formic acid from

Harvester Ant

Pavement Ant

Ants are social insects with one to many queens responsible for laying eggs in the heart of the nest. Larvae are cared for and fed by worker adults. The larvae pupate within the nest. Adult ants are sterile and serve many roles within the colony, ranging from nursery attendant and servant of the queen to housekeeper, guard and forager. Queens overwinter in the nest. New queens are produced in autumn and go on a nuptial flight; they then disperse, drop their wings and found a new colony or overwinter to start fresh in spring. Colonies may persist for years.

their rear. Harvester ants can inflict a painful sting. Wood and field ants will tend to aphids for their honeydew. The ants patrol the host plant, defending aphids from all attackers, which can exacerbate your aphid problems.

Cultural/Physical Control: Physically disturb the mound repeatedly, and you might convince the ants to move to another locality. Pouring boiling water into the mound will achieve the same result but will harm plant roots. Disrupt the march of ants into your home by observing the path they take and washing it with soap and water to eliminate the ants' chemical highway markers.

Biological Control: Birds, beetles, wasps and other insects feed on ants. However, ants are voracious predators in their own right. Having an ant colony nearby will reduce the pest problems you have in your garden. Ants are also good at mixing soil and removing plant debris. Overall, ants are beneficial and should be dealt with only if in direct conflict in your lawn or garden.

Carpenter Ants

Camponotus spp.

Carpenter ants are indicators that wood is rotting, and the ants basically remove, not eat, the decomposing wood. They prey on fungus, dead insects and aphid honeydew, and can be voracious predators of garden pests such as caterpillars and grasshoppers. If you locate a colony that is out of the way, you may just want to let it be. A colony consists of a single queen, workers and winged females and males.

The queen lays eggs throughout summer, and workers feed and maintain the larvae. Larvae develop throughout June and early July, and pupation occurs from July into August. Young adult males and females emerge a few weeks later. The following spring, these winged individuals leave the colony, mate and take flight. Do not panic if you see large numbers of winged ants—most will perish. Males die shortly after mating. Fertilized females drop their wings and seek out a suitable colony location. The surviving females lay 10 or more eggs that they rear using their stored reserves. These larvae pupate and emerge as workers. The new queen lays more eggs, and the colony begins to grow and forage. Individual colonies can exist for 15 years.

ID: *Adult: Carpenter Ant (C. herculeanus):* black body. *Red Carpenter Ant (C. noveboracensis):* red body. *Larva:* white, maggot-like grub.

Size: *Adult:* 15–20 mm (female or queen), 10 mm (male) or 6–10 mm (worker). *Larva:* a variety of sizes.

Habitat and Range: Throughout Ontario; prefers to feed on decaying spruce and pine.

Scouting: Watch for large, foraging ants in spring and summer and for sawdust at the base of dead, dying or old trees or beside stumps or logs.

Cultural/Physical Control: Locate the main colony. Follow foraging ants or seek out potential ant habitats for high ant traffic and wood dust. Bait ants with honey and follow those that come to feed back to the colony. Apply commercial ant trap bait. Carpenter ants are most active at night, so you may need a flashlight.

Biological Control: Birds such as woodpeckers love ants. Naturally occurring nematodes, which can be purchased commercially, live in soil and debris.

Honey Bee

Apis mellifera

European Honey Bee

Karl von Frisch received one of only two Nobel Prizes that have been awarded for discoveries involving insects. His award-winning research studied how bees communicate with each other. In 1923, he described the honey bees' "waggle dance," which allows worker bees to exchange information about the whereabouts of good foraging sites. The bees learn where the site is located and what kind of flowers are present and how productive the site is.

Honey bees forage for nectar and pollen. They do no damage to plants; instead, they serve a vital role in pollinating flowers, especially tree fruits, which have heavy, sticky pollen. Honey bees are raised for honey production as well as their pollinating services. The European Honey Bee was introduced to North America by European colonists.

Honey bees are social insects that live in a hive. A single, fertile queen establishes the colony and cares for the early brood of larvae, collecting pollen

ID: *Adult:* fuzzy, black and yellow body; elbowed antennae. *Larva:* plump, whitish, legless grub without noticeable head capsule.
Size: *Adult:* 15–20 mm. *Larva:* 5–10 mm.
Habitat and Range: Widespread throughout Ontario, though most are domesticated by beekeepers.

Scouting: Honey bees are most active on warm, sunny days, rarely venturing out in cloud and never in cold or drizzle. You can measure how industrious a honey bee has been by the size of the pollen load it carries on its hind legs.

Honey Bee (continued)

Honey bees are essential for fruit pollination and have a place in all gardens, ornamental or producing; healthy espaliered apple tree, *Malus* (above).

to mix with honey into "bee bread" to feed the young. Once sterile workers emerge, the queen is relegated to strictly egg-laying duty. Young adult bees care for the larvae and pupae and maintain the hive, while older bees defend the hive and forage for food. In time, some larvae are fed "royal jelly" from birth until pupation and become new queens who go on a nuptial flight to mate with males, or drones. If the colony is big enough, the old queen will take some drones and workers with her in a swarm to found a new hive; otherwise, she is ousted by the new queen. Hives are perennial provided there is enough stored honey and the hive is adequately sheltered to survive winter.

How to Attract: Honey bees require nectar and pollen all summer long, so a diverse garden is their best friend. If you can ensure a steady supply of blooms throughout summer, you will be able to enjoy honey bees' determined pollinating activities for a long time. These bees are not aggressive unless you threaten their nest. Workers will be dispatched to defend the nest and die in the process. Their stinger is barbed and, when inserted, it stays along with the venom sack, so that the victim continues to get a dose even after the bee is gone. Honey bees suffer many stresses, including disease, robber flies, hive-attacking beetles and mites, and lack of blooms. Recent problems with colony decline are being vigorously investigated; however, similar declines have occurred several times over the last century.

Solitary Bees

Megachile spp., *Osmia* spp.

Although we often think of bees, such as Honey Bees (*Apis mellifera*) as social insects, most bees are solitary insects. Leafcutter bees in the genus *Megachile* are solitary bees. They saw semicircular disks out of leaves for use in building their nests. A recently introduced leafcutter bee is the Giant Resin Bee (*Megachile sculpturalis*) which lines its nest with tree resin. The Alfalfa Leafcutter Bee (*M. rotunda*) was introduced from Europe for alfalfa pollination. Another group of solitary bees are mason bees in the genus *Osmia*. These bees do not cut leaves but instead use mud to fashion their nests. The Blue Orchard Mason Bee (*Osmia lignaria*) is an important pollinator of apple and cherry trees. Leafcutter and mason bees are widespread throughout Ontario.

Solitary bees are not social; instead, fertile females bear the responsibility of rearing their young. Adult leafcutter bees emerge from the overwintering pupa in spring to construct cells out of leaf material in natural voids, or they excavate holes in rotten wood. The cells

Alfalfa Leafcutter Bee

The sting of a solitary bee is very mild, and the bees are not at all aggressive.

ID: *Adult: Leafcutter:* similar to honey bee but slightly flattened and black and white or black and grey. *Blue Orchard Mason:* smaller than honey bee, shiny dark blue. *Larva:* both: plump, whitish, legless grub without noticeable head capsule.
Size: *Adult: Leafcutter:* 12–18 mm. *Blue Orchard Mason:* 12–14 mm. *Larva: Leafcutter:* 3–10 mm. *Blue Orchard Mason:* 2–8 mm.

Habitat and Range: Province-wide; females like to nest in natural voids in standing trees or in plants with pithy stems, such as roses. You can entice leafcutter bees into your yard by placing on a stand a 5 cm x 20 cm block of wood with 3–5 mm holes drilled to a depth of 15 cm.

Solitary Bees (continued)

Blue Orchard Mason Bee

are lined with leaf material and provisioned with nectar and pollen. Females can produce 30 to 40 eggs and require a cell for each one. Nests tend to contain six to eight cells each. The larvae hatch to feed for the remainder of summer and pupate before winter comes. There is only one generation per year. The Blue Orchard Mason Bee nests in holes in the ground in sheltered areas and overwinters as an adult inside the cocoon. The bees emerge in spring or early summer when flowers are in bloom. After mating, females forage for pollen and nectar. Females have a pollen brush on the underside of their abdomen called a scopa, which the males lack. Each female finds a preexisting hole suitable for nesting and deposits her eggs in cells, sealed with mud. Mason bees are so called because they build a separate cell for each egg. There is one generation per year.

Scouting: You can distinguish between honey bees and leafcutter bees by their colour, and also by the way they carry their pollen. Leafcutter bees carry their pollen on the underside of their abdomen, whereas honey bees carry it on their legs. Leafcutter bees collect leaf disks from rose, lilac, ash and Virginia creeper. The damage is not harmful to the plant. Female mason bees carry pollen on the undersides of their abdomen.

How to Attract: You should encourage these bees into your yard because they are important pollinators and they will fly in cloudy and cool weather when honey bees are nowhere to be seen. Solitary bees are active early in spring, just when many of our native bush fruit are flowering and are in dire need of their services.

Cultural/Physical Control: If numbers are so high that they cause substantial damage, cover the plant with a floating row cover to protect it. Prevent bees from nesting in rose stems by plugging the end of cut stems with glue or wax.

Biological Control: Solitary bees are rarely so numerous that you would need to entertain thoughts of controlling them. However, there are parasitoids and blister beetles that will go after the nests.

Bumble Bees

Bombus spp.

B. terricola

Bumble bees are excellent native pollinators that do no harm to plants. They can be found throughout Ontario. Most are in the genus *Bombus,* but members of the genus *Psithyrus* invade *Bombus* nests and lay eggs for the *Bombus* workers to raise for them.

A mated female bumble bee overwinters in a sheltered space, emerging in spring to begin colony establishment. She will find an abandoned rodent burrow or similar cavity and construct a wax pot to provision with honey, then lay her eggs nearby on a bed of pollen. A wax sheet is laid overtop for protection. Once the first brood has emerged, the founding female remains in the nest to lay more eggs near additional honey pots constructed by her offspring. Egg laying continues all summer, and in autumn, the queen will produce unfertilized eggs that yield males to mate with new daughters that were allowed to turn into queens. It is these late-emerging queens that overwinter to found new colonies in spring. The old queen and her sterile daughters die off with the coming of winter. Unlike honey bees, bumble bee colonies last only one season.

Some bumble bees practise what is called buzz pollination, essentially shaking the pollen off the flower.

ID: *Adult:* very hairy black and yellow body; elbowed antennae. *Larva:* plump, whitish, legless grub without noticeable head capsule.
Size: *Adult:* up to 25 mm. *Larva:* 5–20 mm.
Habitat and Range: Widespread throughout Ontario.
Scouting: New queens establish nests in abandoned rodent burrows. Bumble bees are good natured, allowing us to get quite close to them when they are foraging or coming and going from the nest. They are active very early in spring and late into autumn.

How to Attract: Bees are beneficial and should not be considered for control. Although their sting is very painful, the stinger is not left in the victim, and bumble bees are usually very docile and approachable. Keep a variety of pollen-producing flowers in the garden to ensure bumble bees will visit.

Parasitoid Wasps

Families Braconidae and *Ichneumonidae*

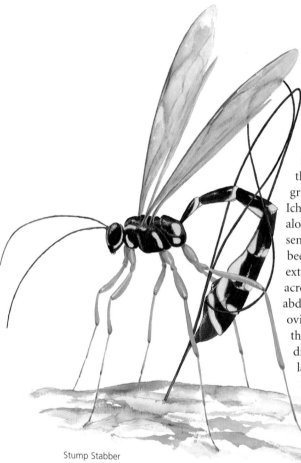

Stump Stabber

The life cycle of parasitoid wasps could have come straight out of a sci-fi movie. These amazing creatures are one of the most beneficial species that inhabit our gardens, but their life cycle is rather gruesome. Some Ichneumonid females walk along tree trunks until they sense a vibration of a boring beetle within. Then, with extreme precision, the females acrobatically curl their abdomen, coil their long ovipositor and drive it through the bark and the inner wood, directly into the unsuspecting larva. After laying an egg, the females pull out their ovipositor and continue hunting. An immunity-suppressing virus often accompanies the egg. The weakened

ID: *Adult:* varied body, but ant-like with 2 sets of wings; some adult females have abnormally long ovipositor projecting from tip of abdomen. *Larva:* whitish, maggot-like worm.

Size: variable in both adult and larva.

Habitat and Range: Throughout Ontario, in all habitats and gardens.

Scouting: Watch for wasps feeding on nectar or buzzing in garden vegetation. They are most often observed during pest outbreaks. Also watch for wasps sitting on plant leaves. They are easily spotted wiggling their antennae as they smell for prey.

How to Attract: Adults are attracted to nectar-producing flowers. Minimize or eliminate the use of harmful insecticides to keep wasp populations healthy.

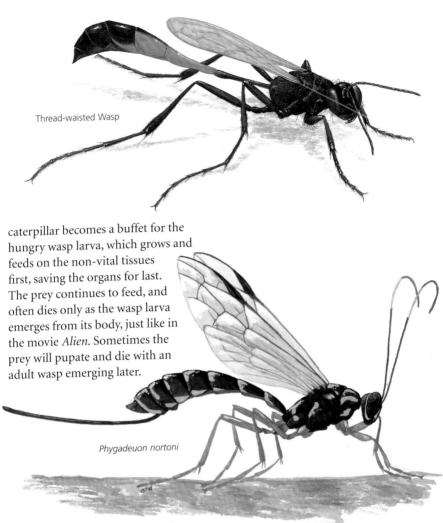

Thread-waisted Wasp

Phygadeuon nortoni

caterpillar becomes a buffet for the hungry wasp larva, which grows and feeds on the non-vital tissues first, saving the organs for last. The prey continues to feed, and often dies only as the wasp larva emerges from its body, just like in the movie *Alien*. Sometimes the prey will pupate and die with an adult wasp emerging later.

Some wasps, such as Braconids, complete their life cycles within an egg. They can suppress a pest's population by as much as 30 percent! A combination of parasitoid wasps and other predators and disease can virtually eliminate the pest. This combination is observed in species such as tent caterpillars, which build up huge populations that vanish the next year.

Amazingly, some wasps parasitize other wasps, which is known as hyperparasitism. A parasitoid's larva feeding inside a caterpillar isn't always safe. There are smaller wasps that seek them out, insert their ovipositors through the caterpillar and into the wasp larva.

Yellow Jackets

Dolichovespula spp., *Vespula* spp.

Bald-faced Hornet

Some queens are "pirates" that invade other yellow jacket colonies. This behaviour is called "obligate social parasitism." Queens of D. arctica and V. austriaca are unable to build their own colonies. They instead invade another species' nest and kill its queen, effectively taking charge. They lay their own eggs, and the previous queen's workers become their slaves and raise their young.

Yellow jackets are known by a number of names, including wasps and hornets. The name "yellow jacket" comes from the yellow or white striping on the wasps' black bodies. The two main genera in our region are *Dolichovespula* and *Vespula*. In our gardens, we often encounter both genera, but the yellow jackets (*Vespula* spp.), with their distinctive yellow and black banding, are the most common.

ID: *Adult: Yellow Jacket:* black with yellow bands. *Bald-faced Hornet:* black with white bands. *Larva:* white grub.

Size: *Adult:* wingspan 12–20 mm. *Larva:* body length variable.

Habitat and Range: Gardens and landscapes throughout Ontario.

Scouting: It is not difficult to find these guys; they are in most yards and gardens.

Cultural/Physical Control: Prevention is often the best method to deal with these dangerous insects. Keep your yard free of rotting fruit, decaying garbage, food and empty pop or beer cans. You can trap famished queens before they build nests in spring. Lure traps can be purchased from gardening stores, or you can make your own. For a water trap, use a 20-litre pail filled with soapy water, with a small piece of meat (liver,

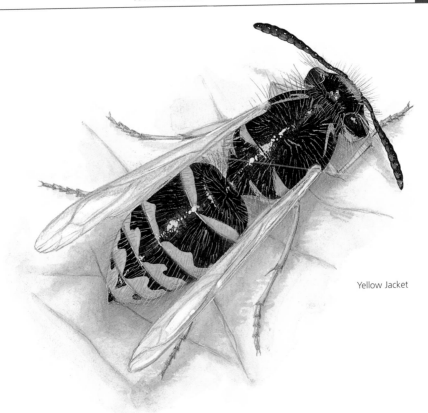

Yellow Jacket

The Bald-faced Hornet (*D. maculata*) is the other commonly encountered species in Ontario and is the big, black and white hornet that is often seen in our yards or garden.

We don't have to look hard to find these nerve-racking wasps in the garden. They tend to be attracted to sweet substances and can be found feeding on aphid honeydew or flowers, or crashing our garden parties in late summer and autumn. Yes, they are frustrating and have a nasty sting, but they are beneficial as insect predators.

The pregnant female queen overwinters as the only survivor from the previous year's colony. When she comes out of dormancy in spring, she seeks a suitable nest site, which can range from a rodent burrow or

fish, etc.) suspended by a string 2.5–5 cm above the water. When a wasp comes to grab a piece of food, it falls into the water and drowns. To prevent other critters from stealing your bait, place a piece of screen over the bucket so only wasps can get in.

Small, early-spring nests are the easiest to deal with. If you have a bee allergy or sensitivity, hire a professional. Take action after dark when colonies are relatively inactive. Wear a long-sleeved shirt, pants and any other attire that can reduce the risk of being stung. Small, external nests can be removed by hand. Approach the nest quietly and cautiously, and slip a bag over it from below. Detach the top of the nest using a knife or paint scraper and immediately seal and dispose of the bag. Large nests should not be controlled using this method—hire a professional. Do not knock a nest down because the queen will only build a new one

Yellow Jackets (continued)

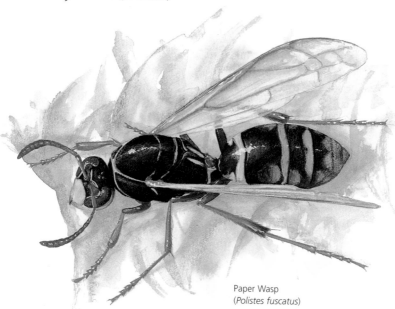

Paper Wasp
(*Polistes fuscatus*)

a crack in a wall to an exposed paper nest under a tree branch or the eaves trough. The yellow jacket makes a nest out of a paper-like material composed of plant fibres and saliva. This new queen builds a small nest that encases a series of up to 45 larval cells where eggs are laid. Larvae hatch and develop in the cells, maturing into sterile female workers. The queen and her new workers begin expanding the colony, which can become quite large and may have hundreds of workers toward the end of summer. The workers take over all tasks except laying eggs. Adults feed on nectar, pollen and smaller insects, while larvae are fed chewed insects. Late in summer, the queen lays eggs that develop into new queens and reproductive males, which leave the colony to mate. The males die and the new queens search out suitable hibernation sites, while the rest of the colony perishes after the first hard frost.

or join another local colony. Do not seal entrances of underground nests or nests in walls; the yellow jackets will chew themselves a new entrance and may end up emerging on the opposite side of the wall.

Remember that yellow jackets are beneficial predators. If the nest is in an area where it is not a hazard to people, leaving it alone is the easiest solution. Remind everyone of its presence and perhaps mark the nest's location.

Biological Control: Because of their aggressive nature, hornets have few predators. Robber flies have been seen feeding on hornets, and some of our larger spiders most likely do so as well. Other animals such as shrews and voles may tackle an injured or sick wasp that is crawling on the ground. In winter, bees, mice and other insectivores often ravage nests. Chickadees, for example, are often seen hanging from old hornets' nest in autumn, looking for abandoned larvae and pupae.

Other Bugs
of
Garden Interest

Spruce Spider Mite

Oligonychus ununguis

Spider Mite webbing

The Spruce Spider Mite feeds on chloroplasts in spruce needle cells. It is common across Ontario.

The Spruce Spider Mite overwinters in the egg stage on branches of spruce. The eggs hatch in May and June, yielding six-legged larvae that feed on new foliage and shoots. The larvae moult into eight-legged proto- and then deutonymphs, and then into eight-legged adults. From egg to adult can take as little as nine days in warm weather. Adults live for up to a month and can lay up to 50 eggs. There may be as many as six generations per year, with feeding pressure greatest in August and September.

A male spider mite will find a female deutonymph, tie her down with silk and patiently wait until she moults to adulthood to ensure he has a mate.

ID: *Adult:* 8 legs; moderately hairy with pale front and dark rear. *Larva* and *nymph:* resemble adult, only smaller; larva has only 3 pairs of legs.

Size: *Adult:* 0.5 mm. *Larva:* 0.1–0.2 mm. *Nymph:* 0.2–0.4 mm.

Habitat and Range: Across Ontario on host plants such as spruce, Douglas-fir, balsam fir and juniper.

Scouting: Look for webbing among the branches and needles. Tap a branch over a white piece of paper to better see the mites. Needles will appear yellow and have black flecks on them (mite waste). Mites are most abundant on drought-stressed, open trees in hot summers. Feeding can result in needle loss, death of twigs and limbs and, in extreme cases, death of the tree.

Cultural/Physical Control: Open, dry trees are most susceptible; closing in the canopy with multiple plantings will help raise the humidity within the branches. Dislodge mites with a strong pressure jet of water.

Biological Control: Many insects feed on tasty spider mite eggs; they are the caviar of the insect world. Predator mites are very effective in suppressing spider mite populations, so don't use pesticides to conserve their numbers.

Eriophyid Gall Mites

Aceria fraxiniflora, Trisetacus gemmavitians, Vasates quadripedes and others

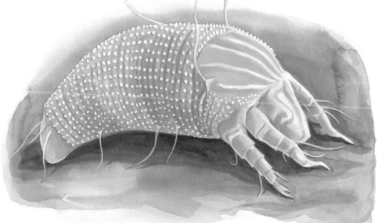

Eriophyid mites cause galls to form on conifers and deciduous trees and shrubs. The Ash Flower Gall Mite (*A. fraxiniflora*) causes unsightly galls on male ash flowers. *Aceria* nr. *dispar* induces galls in trembling aspen. There are many *Eriophyes* species, each inducing galls on a particular host, ranging from elm, maple and birch to poplar, boxelder, mountain ash and cherry. The Maple Bladder Gall Mite (*V. quadripedes*) induces galls on leaves, in this case, maple. The Pine Rosette Mite (*T. gemmavitians*) causes large, round galls on the twigs of jack pine.

In general, gall mites overwinter as fertilized adult females in bark crevices or leaf and flower buds. They emerge in spring and move to leaves or flowers. There are two nymphal stages and then the adult, which lives for up to a month. There can be several generations per year. A special case arises for species of gall mites on plum and chokecherry. No summer females are produced; instead, males and overwintering females emerge from spring eggs. Therefore, although the overwintering female produces a gall, there is only one generation per year.

ID: *Adult:* extremely tiny, elongate mite with 2 pairs of legs near head; pale to white overall. *Nymph:* identical to adult, only smaller.

Size: *Adult:* 0.2 mm. *Nymph:* 0.1 mm.

Habitat and Range: Widespread throughout Ontario; most species are very host specific, infesting only 1 or a few tree species; hosts include hardwood trees and shrubs.

Scouting: Gall mites can be free-living vagrants, and the damage they cause resembles that of spider mites; they can form erinea on upper or lower leaf surfaces; they can produce bladder galls—small pouch-like growths on the upper surface of a leaf; or they can form larger, woody galls out of flowers and on limbs. Whatever the type of damage, it usually does not seriously harm the plant.

Cultural/Physical Control: Once the gall has formed, prune off the affected limb, flower or leaf. Apply horticultural oil in early March to help reduce the number of overwintering females.

Biological Control: Mites are well protected once the erinea or gall has formed. Generalist predators such as predatory mites, thrips and pirate bugs prey on free-living mites.

Spider Mites

Panonychus ulmi, Tetranychus urticae

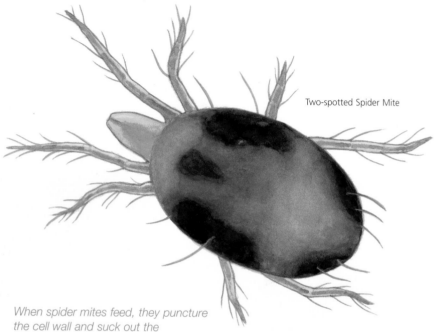

Two-spotted Spider Mite

When spider mites feed, they puncture the cell wall and suck out the chloroplast, the organelle responsible for photosynthesis. The remainder of the cell's contents bleeds out. Surrounding cells detect the leaking fluid and respond by committing suicide (technically called apoptosis) to remain intact, which hopefully will stop whatever ruptured their neighbour. This results in a larger feeding wound than the spider mite originally made, hence the characteristic stippled appearance from such a small mite.

Spider mites suck the chloroplasts out of plant cells on the undersides of leaves. The Two-spotted Spider Mite (*T. urticae*) is the most common spider mite you will encounter in Ontario. It infests many different plants including flowers, shrubs and trees. The European Red Mite (*P. ulmi*) damages orchard trees and many rosaceous plants.

ID: *Adult: Two-spotted Spider Mite:* roughly parallel-sided; mildly hairy; 2 large, dark, lateral spots. *European Red Mite:* brick red. *Nymph:* 8 legs; resembles adult, only smaller. **Size:** *Adult:* 0.3–0.5 mm. *Nymph:* 0.1–0.3 mm. **Habitat and Range:** Throughout Ontario on many flowering, shrub and tree hosts. *Two-spotted Spider Mite:* has been recorded from over 1200 different plant species; prefers arid

conditions. *European Red Mite:* especially in orchards.

Scouting: Spider mites spin silk to tie food together, ensnare potential predators, make a nice microhabitat, disperse pheromones and tie down potential mates. This silk is not formed into a spider-like web; rather, it is more dispersed. Look for moving dots that seem to float in the air, when actually they are

In autumn, when the weather cools, food quality declines and day length shortens, spider mite adults go into diapause, a form of hibernation. The mite turns a reddish colour, its shell becomes thicker and its metabolism slows down, allowing the mite to survive even severe winters. In spring, the mite reverts back to the active form, laying up to 100 eggs over its two-week lifespan. The eggs hatch into six-legged larvae, then moult into proto- and then deutonymphs before becoming

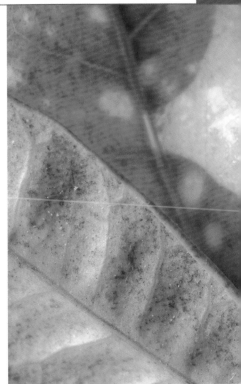

Spider Mite damage

adults. The period from egg to adult can be as short as five days or as long as 25 days, depending on how warm or cool the summer is. There can be many generations per year. Spider mites disperse by walking, catching a ride on insects and other animals and by ballooning, whereby they secrete a line of silk that gets caught up in the wind to carry them away.

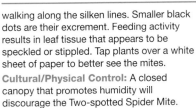

walking along the silken lines. Smaller black dots are their excrement. Feeding activity results in leaf tissue that appears to be speckled or stippled. Tap plants over a white sheet of paper to better see the mites.
Cultural/Physical Control: A closed canopy that promotes humidity will discourage the Two-spotted Spider Mite.

Alternatively, you can easily dislodge the mites with a strong jet of water.
Biological Control: Predatory mites, thrips, pirate bugs, lacewings and lady beetles are all prey on spider mites.

Blacklegged Tick

Ixodes scapularis

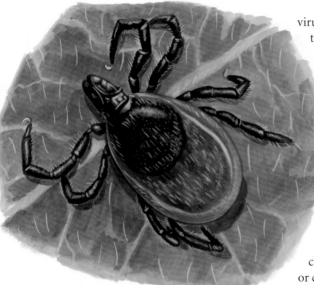

viruses and bacteria. This tick is a known vector for three diseases: human granulocyic ehrlichiosis, human babesiosis and Lyme disease. Signs and symptoms of Lyme disease appear within 3 to 30 days after an infected bite. A bulls-eye rash usually appears along with flu-like symptoms that can progress to chronic joint, neurological or cardiac problems. The key to avoiding infection is to remove the tick during the first 24 hours of attachment.

Ticks are wingless, have two body regions, and can have either six or eight pairs of legs, depending on their life stage. When ticks bite, special mouthpart structures called stylets penetrate and anchor into the skin during feeding. The host blood is taken and held in the idiosoma body region.

The Blacklegged Tick, also called the Deer Tick, is a threat to human health because it can transmit diseases caused by organisms such as protozoa,

There are four stages of tick development: egg, larva, nymph and adult. Ticks feed once during each stage and require a blood meal to moult. Each feeding usually takes several days. Ticks do not jump or fly and must come into contact with a host, including small mammals, birds and deer. All stages will bite and attach to humans, with the smaller stages often going unnoticed.

ID: *Adult:* female is dark brown; male is lighter. *Nymph:* similar to adult.

Size: *Adult:* female 3 mm, male 2 mm. *Nymph:* 0.25–0.5m.

Habitat and Range: Although not native here, this tick is widespread in southern Ontario in leaf litter and tall grasses; migrating birds are thought to be a primary source of migrant ticks.

Cultural/Physical Control: It is important to remove ticks immediately. Grasp the tick with tweezers close to the skin and pull gently. Once the tick has been removed, apply antibiotic cream to the site. Save the tick in a vial for identification. To avoid being bitten, stay out of areas of tick infestation; walk on cleared trails and avoid touching grasses; wear light clothing and closed-toed shoes, tuck your pants into your socks, and apply an insect repellent that contains DEET.

Crab Spiders

Coriarachne spp., *Misumena* spp. and others

Goldenrod Crab Spider

Crab spiders are best described as deadly assassins. They do not spin webs to capture or wrap their prey; they are ambush spiders. They are quite common in Ontario, but because of their ability to camouflage themselves, they are not often observed. If you carefully check out your flowerheads, you may come across a small, camouflaged spider patiently waiting for a meal. These amazing spiders sit for hours on a flower waiting for unsuspecting prey. Then, with lightening speed, they lunge forth, grab their victim and give it a deadly, venomous bite. The digestive enzymes in the venom break down the insect's innards into a soupy liquid that is sucked out by the spider. These little guys are harmless to humans—their tiny fangs can't penetrate our skin.

Females lay fertilized eggs in a nest made of a folded-over leaf woven in silk. They defend the nest from predators and often die before the eggs hatch. The young spiderlings emerge from the nest in about two to three weeks.

Crab spiders can change colour like chameleons. For example, the common Goldenrod Crab Spider changes its body colour from white to yellow to match the flower it is sitting on.

ID: *Adult:* body colour often matches surroundings; bellybutton-like dot on underside of abdomen marks where spinerettes are; front 2 sets of legs are longer than back 2 sets and are held out to side in crab-like posture. *Goldenrod Crab Spider (M. vatia):* female is white to yellow with 2 reddish streaks on abdomen; male tends to be darker, in shades of grey, brown and red. Other species and genera resemble male *M. vatia* but vary in colour, size and pattern. *Immature:* same as adult.

Size: *Adult:* body length up to 1 cm; legs spread much wider; males are smaller than females. *Immature:* body length 0.25 mm–1 cm.

Habitat and Range: Throughout Ontario in gardens and wild areas.

Scouting: Look in newly opened flowers, such as yarrow and goldenrod, with plenty of insect activity. An awkwardly positioned insect hanging or sitting on a flower may indicate a spider's presence. Some species hunt in the leaf litter or on trees or logs.

How to Attract: Plant flowers that attract insects, especially white, yellow or nectar-producing flowers. Do not use harmful insecticides.

Wolf Spiders

Pardosa spp.

which loves open areas such as gardens and farm fields.

Adult males and females breed in spring, with males dying shortly after. Females later appear with egg sacs, which they carry until the eggs are ready to hatch in summer. Hatching times vary and often depend on the weather—warm summers lead to earlier emergences of spiderlings. Egg sacs hold 45 to 50 eggs, and this mass of spiderlings, exact replicas of the adults, immediately disperses after emergence. They start helping gardeners and farmers right away by feeding on insects. As they grow, the spiderlings moult, shedding their skin a few times before they reach maturity, which takes about two years. They overwinter the first winter as spiderlings and the second winter as adults or smaller, immature sub-adults. Gardeners can often tell that spring isn't far away when they observe sexually maturing sub-adults running over the melting patches of snow in March and April.

This group of spiders is the one that often makes folks jump by darting unexpectedly through gardens. They move fast and basically outrun their prey like a wolf does, hence the name wolf spider. These spiders are from the family Lycosidae, which makes up about eight percent of the world's spider fauna. As with all our spiders, wolf spiders are extremely beneficial. They are at the top of the food chain in the insect world and prey on pretty much any insect they are able to overpower. These pouncers leap onto their unsuspecting prey and inject them with deadly venom. A commonly encountered wolf spiders is *P. moesta*,

ID: *Adult:* brown overall; ground dweller; long, thin legs; female sometimes observed carrying blue to white egg sac. *Immature:* same as adult.

Size: *Adult:* body length 4–6 mm. *Immature:* 1–4 mm.

Habitat and Range: Throughout Ontario in a wide range of habitats.

Scouting: Search the garden and yard, around farms and any open area with debris for spiders to hide in and plenty of insects to eat.

How to Attract: Avoid using harmful insecticides.

Jumping Spiders

Family Salticidae

Boreal Jumping Spider
(*Phiddipus borealis*)

These amazing creatures are the acrobats of the garden circus. They can be seen high up in the vegetation or scampering across the ground. One identifying characteristic of a jumping spider is that, if you try to poke it, the spider will often launch itself out of sight in a flash.

Jumping spiders are in the family Salticidae, which makes up about 10 percent of the world's spider fauna. Salticidae spiders are probably the most overlooked family in Canada because of their elusive behaviour. To find these guys in the garden, head out on a warm, sunny day and scan sunny patches on tree trunks, or look for them perched in the canopy of garden plants. These spiders have two large eyes that give them excellent binocular capabilities. They can see prey or predators from far away. One neat experiment you can do demonstrates how alert jumping spiders are. Hold a pen so the tip is in front of a jumping spider and move it slowly back in forth. The spider will move its body, following the pen with its eyes.

The life cycle of jumping spiders is similar to that of other spiders. Mating occurs in spring, eggs are laid in egg sacs in late spring and the eggs hatch in summer. Jumping spiders overwinter as spiderlings, maturing and reproducing the following spring.

ID: *Adult:* stout body with short legs; female often rather drab brown; male somewhat more brightly coloured; abdomen often has colourful cryptic patterns; middle 2 eyes are large and distinguish this species from other types of spiders. *Immature:* similar to adult.

Size: *Adult:* body length 3–10 mm. *Immature:* body length 1–3 mm.

Habitat and Range: Throughout Ontario in gardens, yards and natural areas.

Scouting: Check sunny patches on tree trunks and in garden vegetation. Look on sidewalks and buildings, and in any place where they may be able to capture a meal.

How to Attract: Avoid using harmful insecticides.

Orbweavers

Araneus spp.

Shamrock Orbweaver

Folks often get excited when they encounter this large spider, especially the fully grown female, which is twice the size of the male and can be the size of a loonie. We usually encounter the orbweaver in late summer, often dangling from people's house porches. The easiest way to move an orbweaver is to chase it into a cup or jar, or if you are brave, carry it gently by hand to a nearby fence or shrub. Try to relocate it to a spot in the yard where, if it builds a new web, it will be beneficial to you. The orbweaver is harmless to humans and is often hugely beneficial to us, devouring numerous insects including plenty of pesky ones. An orbweaver commonly found in Ontario is the Shamrock Orbweaver (*Araneus trifolium*).

Mating occurs in autumn. The female produces an egg case and then dies. The egg case overwinters, often tucked away in a protective crevice. In spring after the eggs hatch, the spiderlings climb to a high spot and release silken threads. The wind catches these threads and carries the spiderlings to their new homes. This process is known as ballooning. The spiderlings build webs and begin to feed, maturing by autumn.

ID: *Adult:* plump, brown body; large, lighter brown abdomen often marked with dark brown and white, giving the appearance of a cat face (or arrow on some specimens). *Immature:* similar to adult.

Size: *Adult:* body length 6–7 mm (male) or 14–15 mm (female). *Immature:* 3–5 mm.

Habitat and Range: Throughout Ontario in gardens and farmyards; can be quite common in maturing farm crops.

Scouting: Look for huge, orb-shaped webs on fences, shrubs or porches in late summer and autumn. The spider is never far, often tucked away in a silken chamber off to the side of the web.

How to Attract: Avoid using harmful insecticides.

Northern Black Widow

Latrodectus variolus

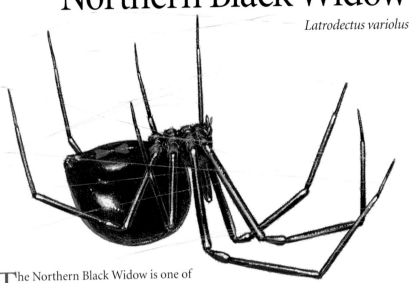

The Northern Black Widow is one of the best-known and notorious spiders, and folks are often surprised to know it exists in Ontario. This spider is a member of the Cobweb spider family (Theridiidae), which makes up eight percent of the world's spiders. It builds a rather messy looking web that basically clogs the entrance to a hole or crevice, so that any insect or small creature that enters becomes entangled.

In Ontario, black widows would be considered a beneficial species because they eat plenty of pest insects; however, they also happen to be the deadliest spiders in North America because their venom can be lethal. Fortunately, they are generally quite docile. If you work in an area where the Northern Black Widow is known to exist, wear gloves when you retrieve wood from a woodpile or move stuff around in a barn, unfinished basement or outdoor building.

Mating occurs in spring and, yes, females often devour their mates. Later that spring, an egg case containing 250 to 700 eggs is produced and placed in a sheltered location with constant humidity. Spiderlings hatch in mid- to late spring and quickly disperse. Adults overwinter and can live for up to three years. Females spend most of their lives at the nest.

ID: *Adult:* glossy, black body; long legs; red mark on underside of abdomen resembles hourglass. *Immature:* similar to adult.

Size: *Adult:* 5 mm (male) or 12 mm (female). *Immature:* 2–4 mm.

Habitat and Range: Only on the Bruce Peninsula; most often observed in sheltered locations such as animal holes, woodpiles and any other dark crevice or hole.

Scouting: Look for these spiders and their webs in abandoned badger and ground squirrel holes, woodpiles and outhouses.

Physical/Cultural Control: Gently remove webs and spiders from locations where they may contact humans or pets; otherwise, leave them alone.

Centipedes

Lithobius spp.

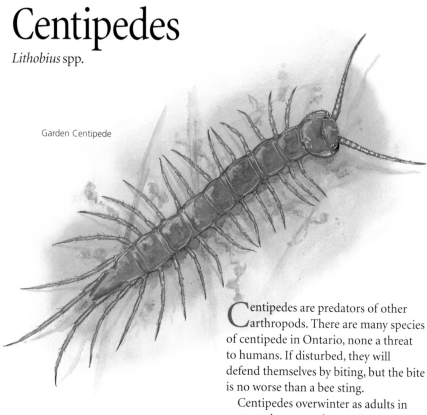

Garden Centipede

Not all centipedes live up to their name by having 100 legs. The most common centipede in Ontario has only 30 legs.

Centipedes are predators of other arthropods. There are many species of centipede in Ontario, none a threat to humans. If disturbed, they will defend themselves by biting, but the bite is no worse than a bee sting.

Centipedes overwinter as adults in protected areas, such as under rocks. They lay eggs in soil from spring onward. The immatures undergo several moults and may take as long as a year to mature. Some centipedes have been reported to live five or six years.

ID: *Adult:* many-legged, flattened, red or orange body with curved pincers and long antennae. *Immature:* resembles adult, only smaller; only 1 pair of legs per segment, which usually stick out laterally.

Size: *Adult:* 20–40 mm. *Immature:* 5–20 mm.

Habitat and Range: Widespread throughout Ontario; prefers moist, dark areas, including basements, moist soil, leaf litter and lawns.

Scouting: Centipedes are active at night and feed on insects that are smaller and slower than they are. You can often find them under stones and wood and in corners of damp basements.

Cultural/Physical Control: Remove the source of damp conditions by ensuring good air circulation and drainage and repairing leaks. Remove piles of debris or trash that serve as hiding places for centipedes. Repair cracks or holes in the foundation, window frames, weather stripping and screens to prevent entry from outside.

Biological Control: Centipedes are fast-moving, top predators of the insect world and have very few natural enemies, except mammals such as mice and shrews. Centipedes, in turn, prey on spiders and carpet beetles indoors and earthworms and insects outdoors. If you find them indoors, it means you have insects for them to feed on. Use the presence of centipedes as a wake up call to "bug-proof" your house.

Millipedes

Allajulus spp.

Although the name millipede means "a thousand legs," these arthropods, in fact, have only 30 to 100 pairs. Because they have two pairs of legs on each segment, they appear to have many more, hence the "thousand leg" moniker.

Millipedes have biting/chewing mouthparts that they use to feed on decaying vegetation. There are many species of millipede in Ontario. These arthropods serve a very useful role in breaking down material and opening up soils.

Millipedes overwinter as adults, late-instar immatures or eggs. Adults mate in autumn and lay eggs in soil or under debris. In spring, the eggs hatch and go through 7 to 10 moults before becoming adults. The life cycle may take up to two years, with adults living for four to five years.

ID: *Adult:* dark, elongate and cylindrical with legs on each of many segments. *Immature:* initially looks like white worm but grows progressively longer and darker to resemble adult.

Size: *Adult:* 25–40 mm. *Immature:* 5–30 mm.

Habitat and Range: In moist soils throughout the province.

Scouting: Millipedes are active at night, feeding on any kind of plant material that is soft, such as decaying vegetation, tender roots and mature fruit. They are often seen in mature strawberries that touch the ground. Like the armadillo, millipedes curl up to protect their soft underbelly when disturbed.

Cultural/Physical Control: Raise fruit off the ground, and remove debris and rotting vegetation.

Biological Control: These arthropods rarely pose a threat to healthy plants. Few animals prey on millipedes because some millipedes can excrete a noxious gas in self-defence.

Pseudoscorpion

Chelifer cancroides

Pseudoscorpions are essentially scorpions with a rounded abdomen and without the tail.

They are predators of small arthropods, feeding on springtails, mites and most small insects. There are several species of pseudoscorpion in Ontario, but the most common species to be found in or around the home is *C. cancroides*.

The adult female pseudoscorpion builds a nest out of leaf litter and silk in which to lay eggs. She remains in the nest and nurtures the immatures until they are in the third instar, whereupon mother and young leave the nest. It takes approximately a year to go from egg to adult, and adults may live up to five years.

Lacking the stinging tail of a true scorpion, pseudoscorpions grab prey with their claws and inject poison through an appendage on the claw. These predators are far too small to pose any risk to humans.

ID: *Adult:* light brown to whitish, round body; 2 long, clawed appendages at front. *Immature:* similar to adult.

Size: *Adult:* 3–5 mm. *Immature:* 1–3 mm.

Habitat and Range: Widespread throughout Ontario; favours protected sites such as animal nests or the shelter of rocks.

Scouting: Often overlooked because of their small size, pseudoscorpions hunt for prey in leaf litter and under bark. When observed indoors, they are usually found in the bathroom, where it is humid and warm, and they likely came in on your clothing.

How to Attract: Given that these are beneficial predators, there is no need to control them other than to gently pick up any that you find indoors and release them outdoors.

Springtails

Families Sminthuridae, Entomobryidae, Isotomidae and Onychiuridae

Springtails, or collembolans, have biting/chewing mouthparts that they use to feed on fungi and decaying plant material. Springtails have a worldwide distribution, including Antarctica. The most commonly encountered springtails are in four families: Sminthuridae, Entomobryidae, Isotomidae and Onychiuridae. The defining character of springtails is an appendage arising from the underside at the rear called a furcula. It is used to launch the springtails into the air as a means of escape from predators.

Springtails lay up to 400 eggs singly or in groups, depending on the species, in the soil or in leaf litter. Eggs hatch in a few days, and the immatures moult anywhere from three to eight times before becoming adults. Unlike other insects, the adults continue to moult, as many as an additional 40 times. Springtails live from one to five years.

ID: *Adult: Onychiuridae:* elongate and whitish with no furcula. *Entomobryidae* and *Isotomidae:* elongate, ranging from blue or purple to grey; well developed furcula. *Sminthuridae:* globular shape. *Immature:* identical to adult, but smaller.

Size: *Adult:* 1–6 mm. *Immature:* 1–4 mm.

Habitat and Range: Province-wide; most are leaf-litter or soil dwellers, though they can also be found on water, at margins of rivers and ponds and on trees; so common that densities of up to 60,000/m² have been found; may be the most numerous animal on the planet.

Scouting: In spring, as the snow is melting, you can see large masses of springtails on snow banks; it may be easier for these small creatures to travel over snow than through the rough terrain underneath. Any time you disturb soil, you should be able to see springtails. Their presence is considered a positive indicator of soil health.

Cultural/Physical Control: To prevent springtails from occasional feeding on seedlings and root hairs of young plants, let the soil dry between watering.

Biological Control: Pseudoscorpions prey on springtails, and reducing the amount of organic matter in your soil will keep springtail numbers lower. However, there is usually no need to control them. They are beneficial and also feed on disease fungi.

Harvestmen

Leiobunum spp., *Phalangium opilio*

Harvestmen have a curious habit called autotomy, where, in self-defence, they will shed one or two legs to distract a predator. The legs twitch for some time after being shed.

Phalangium opilio

Harvestmen or Daddy Longlegs have piercing mouthparts much like a spider's to prey on small insects and mites. There are several species in the genus *Leiobunum*, but the most commonly encountered species in Ontario is *P. opilio*. Harvestmen are not spiders, merely close relatives. They do not produce silk or poison.

Harvestmen overwinter in the egg stage, hatching out in spring. The immatures develop over summer, with adults noticeable in July. There is only one generation per year.

Also Known As: Daddy Longlegs

ID: *Adult:* spider-like but with seemingly only 1 body segment instead of 2, and only 2 eyes; exceptionally long, thin legs. *Immature:* identical to the adult, but smaller.

Size: *Adult:* 4–6 mm. *Immature:* 1–4 mm.

Habitat and Range: Widespread throughout Ontario; prefers grassy margins.

Scouting: Look for Harvestmen in the fringe of grass next to your home or crawling up the wall. Adult Harvestmen are most noticeable in August and September.

How to Attract: These beneficial creatures are effective predators, eating small insects and mites and scavenge dead insects and plant debris. The fringe of grass around fences and walls is both their preferred habitat and your first line of defence against insects entering your home. Keep your evil weed-whacker, the archenemy of the Harvestman, away from this fringe of grass.

Sowbugs

Porcellio spp.

Sowbugs are one of the few members of the class Crustacea (which includes lobster, shrimp and crab) to invade land. In general, insects are considered to be the lords of the land, while crustaceans rule the oceans.

Sowbugs (also known as wood lice) are detritivores, feeding on decaying plant material. Occasionally they feed on seedlings and fruit in contact with soil. The sowbugs *P. laevis* and *P. scaber* are common in urban centres and can be found in moist soils and under decaying vegetation, wood and bark. Both species of sowbug are introduced from Europe.

Female sowbugs retain eggs and young immatures in a marsupium on their underside for a couple of months. It may take up to a year for sowbugs to go from egg to adult. Adults may live up to three years.

Sowbug

ID: *Adult:* armadillo-like, flattened armour plates; bluish grey overall; 7 pairs of legs; 2 long and 2 short antennae in front, and short, paired appendages protruding out back. *Immature:* resembles adult, only smaller.

Size: *Adult:* 5–12 mm. *Immature:* 3–10 mm.

Habitat and Range: Throughout Ontario, mostly in urban areas but slowly expanding to rural areas around major urban centres and natural areas; prefers moist soil and woody debris in urban gardens.

Scouting: Sowbugs are active mostly at night and on damp, cloudy days; look for them escaping the sun under rocks and debris. Occasionally they will venture into your home.

Cultural/Physical Control: Plant seeds deeply and do not water until the first true leaves emerge. Water early in the day, and lift foliage and fruit off the ground. Remove debris that sowbugs use for shelter.

Biological Control: Being a recent introduction, they are not on the menu of many known predators.

Gray Garden Slug

Agriolimax reticulatus

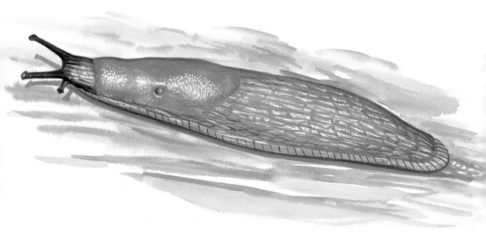

The Gray Garden Slug feeds on a wide variety of garden plants, rasping away the soft tissues of leaves and fruit. This slug was introduced from Europe and has found its way across Ontario.

Slugs lay eggs in the soil or under debris all season long. Primarily eggs, but also immatures and adults, are capable of surviving winter.

Given that slugs move slowly, they do not have a lot of opportunity to get out and meet a mate. Therefore, slugs are hermaphroditic—they have both sets of reproductive organs. However, they still have to exchange sperm with another slug. So, every slug they meet is a potential mate—no need to wander around endlessly looking for Mr. or Mrs. Right.

ID: *Adult:* grey, elongate, slimy, fleshy body; 1 long pair of antennae on upper part of head and 1 short pair of antennae on underside of head. *Immature:* identical to adult, only smaller.

Size: *Adult:* 1–3 cm. *Immature:* 5–20 mm.

Habitat and Range: Restricted to moist areas, especially pampered gardens throughout Ontario.

Scouting: Slugs are most active between 3 and 6 AM, climbing onto low vegetation. Look for the characteristic shredding of tissue by immatures and ragged holes made by adults, and for dried slime trails on soil and plants.

Cultural/Physical Control: If you put 10 cm x 10 cm pieces of plywood onto the soil, slugs will gather under the wood for protection. Each morning, collect and dispose of the slugs. You can also trap slugs in shallow pans of stale beer sunk into the soil. Check and refresh traps daily. Jagged barriers of sand, sharp rock, crushed egg shells or diatomaceous earth, or screens or bands of copper placed around plants or as a border to the garden will discourage slugs. Keep your yard clean and remove debris slugs can hide under.

Biological Control: Ground beetles and marsh flies prey on or parasitize slugs.

Earthworms

Aporrectodea tuberculata, Eisenia fetida, Lumbricus terrestris

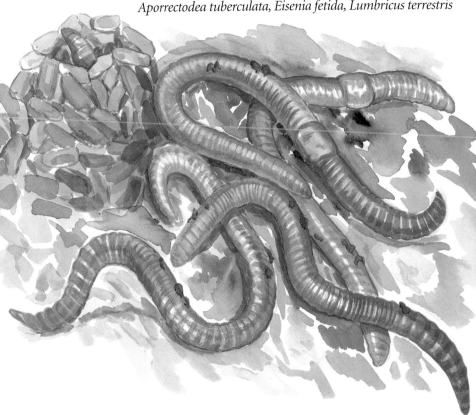

All worms consume decaying organic matter. The Dewworm (*L. terrestris*), originally from Europe, digs long, vertical tunnels as deep as three metres. It forages for food horizontally in and around the root zone, with occasional exit mounds formed at the soil surface to void waste material. The Canadian Worm (*A. tuberculata*) is very common, feeding well underground.

ID: *Adult:* elongate pink to reddish body; segmented, with collar near front end; no legs or identifiable head. *Immature:* identical to adult, but with no clitellum and smaller in size.

Size: *Adult:* 5–25 cm. *Immature:* 1–5 cm.

Habitat and Range: Urban areas and near popular fishing spots province-wide.

Scouting: Most worms are at peak activity in wet springs and again in autumn. Dewworms leave large mounds with castings (its waste) on the surface, but other worms do not make such conspicuous mounds. Burrows near the surface cause the ground to be lumpy and uneven, so lawn mowers with the blade set too low will scalp the sod. There is much debate on the merits/demerits of earthworms. Although they rapidly turn over organic matter and mix and aerate the soil, they also substantially change the local plant community by removing layers of litter that limit what can grow in an area.

Earthworms (continued)

Red Wriggler compost worms

Composters use the Red Wriggler (*E. fetida*) to rapidly break down organic matter for use in the garden.

In general, earthworms, being hermaphrodites, exchange sperm to fertilize their eggs. Eggs and sperm are cast off in a cocoon, hatching in three weeks. There are anywhere from 2 to 20 worms in each cocoon, and 20 to 40 cocoons are produced yearly. It takes approximately a year for immature worms to mature. Adult worms can live as long as nine years.

Contrary to popular belief, earthworms do not get flushed out of the soil during a rainstorm to drown on the surface. Instead, the lubricating properties of rain make surface travel possible. It is simply unfortunate if earthworms wander into a puddle (more likely, the puddle forms around them, earthworms not being known for a speedy gait) or is stranded on the sidewalk when the rain stops and the water evaporates.

Cultural/Physical Control: Top-dressing with sand and infrequent deep watering to drive roots down discourages earthworms from feeding too near the surface. Remove thatch in the lawn to disrupt their burrows.

Biological Control: Many birds and insects feed on earthworms.

References

Acorn, J. 2003. *Bugs of Ontario.* Lone Pine Publishing, Edmonton.

Barnes, R.D. 1991. *Invertebrate Zoology* (5th ed.). Harcourt Brace Jovanovich Inc., Toronto.

Borror, D.J., C.A. Triplehorn and N.F. Johnson. 1989. *An Introduction to the Study of Insects* (6th ed.). Saunders College Publishing, Philadelphia.

Buddle, C.M. and D.P. Shorthouse. 2000. "Jumping spiders of Canada." Newsletter of the Biological Survey of Canada (Terrestrial Arthropods) 19(1): 16–18.

Corbet, P. 1999. *Dragonflies: Behavior and Ecology of Odonata.* Cornell University Press, New York.

Cranshaw, W. 2004. *Garden Insects of North America.* Princeton University Press, Princeton.

Dunkle, S. 2000. *Dragonflies Through Binoculars: A Field Guide to Dragonflies of North America.* Oxford University Press, New York.

Edwards, C.A. (ed). 2004. *Earthworm Ecology* (2nd ed.). CRC Press LLC, New York.

Eisner, T., M. Eisner and M. Siegler. 2005. *Secret Weapons: Defenses of Insects, Spiders, Scorpions and other Many-legged Creatures.* Harvard University Press, Cambridge.

Eisner T. 1994. "Integumental Slime and Wax Secretion: Defensive Adaptations of Sawfly Larvae." *J Chem Ecol* 20: 2743–49.

Evans, H.E. 1984. *Insect Biology.* Addison-Wesley Publishing, Reading.

Flint, M.L. and S.H. Dreistadt. 1998. *Natural Enemies Handbook: The Illustrated Guide to Biological Pest Control.* University of California Statewide Integrated Pest Management Project Publication 3386.

Fullard J.H., M.B. Fenton and J.A. Simmons. 1979. "Jamming Bat Echolocation: The Clicks of Arctiid Moths." *Can J Zool* 57: 647–49.

Gieles, C. 1996. *Microlepidoptera of Europe.* Vol 1. Pterophoridae. Apollo Books, Stentrup.

Hopkin, S.P. 1997. *Biology of the Springtails.* Oxford University Press, New York.

Ip, D.W. 1992. *Dutch Elm Disease.* Natural Resources Canada, Canadian Forestry Service. Northern Forestry Centre, Edmonton. Forestry Leaflet 19.

Layberry, R.A., P.W. Hall and J.D. Lafontaine. 1998. *The Butterflies of Canada.* University of Toronto Press, Toronto.

Marshall, S.A. 2006. *Insects: Their Natural History and Diversity.* Firefly Books Ltd., Richmond Hill.

Metcalf, C.L., W.P. Flint and R. L. Metcalf. 1962. *Destructive and Useful Insects* (4th ed.). McGraw-Hill Book Company, New York.

Opler, P., V. Malikul. 2004. *A Field Guide to Eastern Butterflies.* Houghton Mifflin, Boston.

Pedigo, L. 1989. *Entomology and Pest Management.* Macmillian Publishing Company, New York.

Sargent T.D. 1976. *Legion of Night: The Underwing Moths.* University of Massachusetts Press, Massachusetts.

Solomon, J.D. 1995. "Guide to Insect Borers of North American Broadleaf Trees and Shrubs." *Agricultural Handbook 706.* U.S. Department of Agriculture, Forest Service, Washington, DC.

Triplehorn, C.A. and N.F. Johnson. *Borror and DeLong's Introduction to the Study of Insects* (7th ed.). Thomson Brooks/Cole, Toronto.

Glossary

abdomen: posterior-most major body region of insects containing the digestive system and gonads

anterior: the head end of the organism

borer: an insect that chews into woody tissue of plants

B.t. (Bacillus thuringiensis): a bacterium that produces a protein toxic to insects. Different strains of the bacterium affect different kinds of insects, e.g., B.t.k. for caterpillars and B.t.i. for fly maggots. B.t. is considered a very effective and environmentally friendly pesticide.

cat-facing: a type of damage caused by insects feeding on developing seeds, which results in a lack of growth hormone in the plant and a lack of growth at the point of feeding, leaving a seam or scar while the surrounding tissue continues to grow

chrysalis: a term specifically referring to the pupal stage of a butterfly. A caterpillar changes into the butterfly within the chrysalis.

complete metamorphosis: the insect life cycle that progresses from an egg through at least three larval instars and a non-feeding pupal stage, ending in the adult stage. The immature or larval stage rarely resembles the adult form. The wings only develop during the major transformation undergone in the pupal stage.

cornicle: one of a pair of small upright posterior-pointing tubes on the underside of the last segment of the abdomen of aphids

cuticle: the hardened outer shell of an insect

distal: farthest from the body

dorsal: top or uppermost surface of the body

deutonymphs: the third developmental stage of mites and ticks

ecdysis: shedding of the cuticle during the moult to the next instar

elytra: the first pair of wings on beetles that are modified into hardened wing covers

erinea: mite-induced plant hair growths

forb: a non-woody flowering plant; includes most vegetables, herbs and garden flowers

flocculence: waxy secretions from woolly adelgids feeding on conifers

frass: dry to semi-dry excrement of insects, in contrast to liquid "honeydew" secreted by aphids

furcula: an appendage at the rear of springtails, used to propel the springtails into the air to escape predators

gall: woody growth of plant tissue, usually induced by insect activity or secretions to surround and protect the insect inside

gradual metamorphosis: the insect life cycle that progresses from an egg through at least one nymphal stage and ends in the adult stage. The immature or nymphal stage resembles the adult stage, except that the wings are not completely formed but are visible as developing buds.

haplodiploidy: a form of reproduction where unfertilized females give birth to male offspring and fertilized females give birth to female offspring

heartwood: the tissue of a tree at the centre of the main stem. Little or no fluid transport occurs here, in contrast to the sapwood where there is free-flowing water transport. The heartwood and sapwood combined make up the xylem of a tree.

hermaphrodite: the adult contains both male and female gonads and sex organs. It usually must exchange sperm with another of the same species to fertilize the eggs.

holarctic: a term describing the distribution of an organism, in this case, across all landmasses north of the equator.

instar: the immature growth stage of an insect. There may be several instars between the egg and adult stages.

larva: the immature stage of an insect that undergoes complete metamorphosis

latrodectism: the clinical symptoms resulting from a neurotoxic venom from one of many spider species in the genus *Latrodectus*, which are commonly referred to as black widow spiders.

moulting: formation of new cuticle followed by ecdysis; the growth process of an insect

nymph: immature stage of an insect that undergoes gradual metamorphosis

ovipositor: abdominal appendage on females used to deposit eggs

palp: an elongated appendage found near the mouth of invertebrates. It is used for feeding, locomotion and sensory reception.

parthenogenesis: reproduction without mating; occurs in many aphids and some thrips

phytoplasma: wall-less bacteria that live in the phloem of plants and in insects. The damage they cause ranges from mild yellowing to death. Examples include aster yellows and western-X disease of *Prunus*.

proboscis: modified mouthparts of butterflies and moths, adapted for siphoning nectar from flowers

pronotum: the shoulder area immediately behind the head, often present as a hardened plate

prothorax: the first body segment behind the head, followed by the meso- and metathoracic segments

proximal: closest to the body

raptorial: a leg with an enlarged femur to facilitate grasping of prey, commonly seen in preying mantids and damsel bugs

scutellum: a triangular plate behind the pronotum; is commonly enlarged in stink bugs and plant bugs

skeletonizer: an insect that scrapes off the epidermal or surface tissues of a leaf

stylet: mouthpart adapted for piercing and sucking

tachinid: a member of the Diptera family Tachinidae. These flies parasitize other insects and are considered to be beneficial.

thorax: the second major body region of an insect, located between the head and the abdomen. It is composed of three segments with a pair of legs arising from each segment. The first thoracic segment is often strengthened dorsally and referred to as the pronotum. If the insect is winged, the first pair of wings arises from the second segment and the second pair of wings arises from the third thoracic segment.

ventral: lower or bottommost surface of the body

Where to Scout

Species	Trees	Shrubs	Herbaceous Plants	Grasses/Lawns	Leaf Litter/Soil	Ponds/Wetlands	Open/Sunny Areas	Woodlands	Roots/Crown	Flowers	Foliage/Fruit	Stems/Branches	Trunk/Bark
Dragonflies & Damselflies • Odonata													
Meadowhawks & Whiteface Dragonflies		•	•	•		•	•					•	
Mosaic Darners	•	•	•	•		•	•					•	•
Spreadwings			•	•		•	•				•	•	
Bluets			•	•		•	•			•	•		
Grasshoppers & Crickets • Orthoptera													
Grasshoppers			•				•			•			
Field Crickets			•	•			•			•	•		
Broad-winged Katydid	•	•					•	•		•			
True Bugs • Hemiptera													
Ambush Bug			•	•			•	•		•	•		
Damsel Bugs	•	•	•	•			•	•		•	•	•	•
Plant Bugs	•	•	•	•			•	•		•	•		
Stink Bugs	•	•	•	•			•	•		•	•		
Spined Soldier Bug			•	•			•			•	•	•	
Lace Bugs	•	•	•				•	•			•		
Boxelder Bug	•							•			•		
Minute Pirate Bug	•	•	•	•			•	•		•	•	•	•
Spined Assassin Bug			•	•			•			•	•		
Hairy Chinch Bug				•			•		•		•	•	
Sucking Insects • Hemiptera (Homopterans)													
Aphids	•	•	•				•	•			•	•	
Woolly Aphids	•							•	•		•		
Cooley Spruce Gall Adelgid	•							•			•	•	
Eastern Spruce Gall Adelgid	•							•			•	•	
Mealybugs			•								•	•	
Scale Insects	•	•						•			•	•	
Boxwood Psyllid		•					•	•			•	•	
Cottony Psyllid	•						•	•			•	•	
Leafhoppers	•	•	•	•			•	•			•		
Cicadas	•			•			•	•				•	
Spittlebugs	•	•	•				•	•			•	•	
Thrips, Earwigs & Lacewings • Thysanoptera, Dermaptera & Neuroptera													
Thrips	•	•	•				•	•		•	•		
European Earwig			•	•	•			•		•	•		
Lacewings	•	•	•	•			•	•		•	•	•	

When to Scout					Look For						Page Number	Species
Early Spring	Late Spring	Early Summer	Late Summer	Fall	Larva/Nymph	Eggs/Pupa	Adult	Damage	Beneficial	Pest		
Odonata • Dragonflies & Damselflies												
	•	•	•				•		•		42	Meadowhawks & Whiteface Dragonflies
	•	•					•		•		45	Mosaic Darners
	•	•					•		•		46	Spreadwings
	•	•					•		•		48	Bluets
Orthoptera • Grasshoppers & Crickets												
	•	•	•		•		•			•	49	Grasshoppers
	•	•	•	•	•		•			•	50	Field Crickets
	•	•	•		•		•			•	51	Broad-winged Katydid
Hemiptera • True Bugs												
		•	•				•		•		52	Ambush Bug
	•	•	•		•		•		•		53	Damsel Bugs
•	•	•	•		•		•	•		•	54	Plant Bugs
	•	•	•		•		•	•		•	55	Stink Bugs
	•	•	•		•		•		•		56	Spined Soldier Bug
•	•	•	•		•	•	•	•		•	57	Lace Bugs
	•	•	•	•			•			•	58	Boxelder Bug
•	•	•	•				•		•		59	Minute Pirate Bug
•	•	•	•	•	•	•	•		•	•	60	Spined Assassin Bug
	•	•	•		•		•			•	61	Hairy Chinch Bug
Hemiptera (Homopterans) • Sucking Insects												
	•	•	•	•	•		•			•	62	Aphids
•	•	•	•				•	•		•	64	Woolly Aphids
		•	•					•		•	66	Cooley Spruce Gall Adelgid
•	•						•			•	67	Eastern Spruce Gall Adelgid
	•	•			•		•			•	68	Mealybugs
	•	•					•			•	69	Scale Insects
	•	•			•		•	•		•	70	Boxwood Psyllid
	•	•	•		•		•	•		•	71	Cottony Psyllid
	•	•	•		•		•	•		•	72	Leafhoppers
		•	•	•			•	•		•	73	Cicadas
	•	•			•		•			•	75	Spittlebugs
Thysanoptera, Dermaptera & Neuroptera • Thrips, Earwigs & Lacewings												
	•	•	•				•			•	76	Thrips
		•	•	•			•	•	•	•	78	European Earwig
	•	•	•		•	•	•		•		79	Lacewings

Where to Scout

Species	Trees	Shrubs	Herbaceous Plants	Grasses/Lawns	Leaf Litter/Soil	Ponds/Wetlands	Open/Sunny Areas	Woodlands	Roots/Crown	Flowers	Foliage/Fruit	Stems/Branches	Trunk/Bark
Beetles, Weevils & Borers • Coleoptera													
Ground Beetles	•	•	•		•	•	•	•			•	•	•
Blister Beetles		•	•				•			•	•		
Flea Beetles			•				•				•		
Lily Leaf Beetle			•				•			•	•		
Leaf Beetles	•		•				•	•		•	•	•	•
Colorado Potato Beetle			•				•				•		
Sap Beetles	•	•	•	•			•			•	•		
Carrion Beetles			•				•	•			•		
Click Beetles	•	•	•	•	•		•		•				
June Beetles	•	•		•			•		•		•		
European Chafer	•	•		•			•		•		•		
Aphodius Beetles				•			•		•				
Japanese Beetle	•	•	•	•	•		•	•			•		
Lady Beetles	•	•	•	•	•	•	•	•		•	•	•	•
Multicoloured Asian Lady Bird Beetle	•	•	•	•	•	•	•	•		•	•	•	•
Bark Beetles	•								•				•
Elm Bark Beetles	•								•				
Eastern Ash Bark Beetle	•								•			•	•
Strawberry Root Weevil		•	•	•	•		•		•		•		
White Pine Weevil	•						•	•				•	
Poplar and Willow Borer	•							•				•	•
Rose Curculio		•					•			•			
Asian Long-horned Beetle	•						•	•				•	•
Poplar Borer	•							•			•	•	•
White-spotted Sawyer	•							•					•
Bronze Birch Borer	•							•					•
Emerald Ash Borer	•							•			•		•
Butterflies, Moths & Allies • Lepidoptera													
Tiger Swallowtails	•	•	•			•	•	•		•	•	•	
Cabbage Butterfly			•				•				•		
Clouded Sulphur			•				•			•	•		
Spring Azure & Eastern Tailed Blue		•	•				•	•		•			
Mourning Cloak Butterfly	•	•						•			•	•	
Painted Lady			•				•			•	•		
White Admiral	•	•						•		•	•	•	

When to Scout					Look For						Page Number	Species
Early Spring	Late Spring	Early Summer	Late Summer	Fall	Larva/Nymph	Eggs/Pupa	Adult	Damage	Beneficial	Pest		
												Coleoptera • Beetles, Weevils & Borers
	•	•	•	•			•		•		80	Ground Beetles
	•	•					•		•	•	81	Blister Beetles
•	•	•	•				•	•		•	82	Flea Beetles
•	•	•	•		•	•	•	•		•	83	Lily Leaf Beetle
•	•	•			•	•	•	•		•	84	Leaf Beetles
	•	•					•	•		•	86	Colorado Potato Beetle
	•	•					•	•		•	87	Sap Beetles
•	•	•			•		•	•	•	•	88	Carrion Beetles
•	•	•			•		•	•		•	89	Click Beetles
	•	•	•		•		•	•		•	90	June Beetles
	•	•			•		•	•		•	92	European Chafer
•	•	•	•		•		•		•	•	93	*Aphodius* Beetles
•	•	•			•		•	•		•	94	Japanese Beetle
•	•	•	•		•	•	•		•		96	Lady Beetles
•	•	•	•	•	•	•	•		•		98	Multicoloured Asian Lady Bird Beetle
•	•	•	•					•		•	99	Bark Beetles
•	•	•						•		•	100	Elm Bark Beetles
•	•	•			•		•	•		•	101	Eastern Ash Bark Beetle
•	•	•	•				•	•		•	102	Strawberry Root Weevil
•	•	•			•		•	•		•	103	White Pine Weevil
	•	•					•	•		•	104	Poplar and Willow Borer
•	•	•					•	•		•	105	Rose Curculio
•	•	•			•	•	•	•		•	106	Asian Long-horned Beetle
	•	•					•	•		•	107	Poplar Borer
•	•	•					•	•	•	•	108	White-spotted Sawyer
•	•	•					•	•		•	110	Bronze Birch Borer
•	•	•					•	•		•	111	Emerald Ash Borer
												Lepidoptera • Butterflies, Moths & Allies
	•	•	•		•		•		•		112	Tiger Swallowtails
	•	•	•	•	•		•	•		•	114	Cabbage Butterfly
•	•	•	•	•			•		•		115	Clouded Sulphur
•	•				•		•		•		116	Spring Azure & Eastern Tailed Blue
•	•	•	•	•	•		•	•		•	118	Mourning Cloak Butterfly
	•	•	•	•	•		•		•		119	Painted Lady
	•	•	•	•	•		•		•		121	White Admiral

Where to Scout

Species	Trees	Shrubs	Herbaceous Plants	Grasses/Lawns	Leaf Litter/Soil	Ponds/Wetlands	Open/Sunny Areas	Woodlands	Roots/Crown	Flowers	Foliage/Fruit	Stems/Branches	Trunk/Bark
Butterflies, Moths & Allies • Lepidoptera													
Monarch		•					•			•	•		
European Skipper			•	•			•			•	•		
Lilac Leaf Miner		•					•	•			•		
Peach Twig Borer	•						•	•			•	•	
Peach Tree Borer	•	•						•					•
Raspberry Crown Borer		•					•		•		•		
Ash Borer	•							•				•	•
Boxelder Twig Borer	•							•				•	
Aspen Twoleaf Tier & Aspen Leafroller	•							•			•		
Northern Pitch Twig Moth	•							•				•	
Codling Moth	•							•			•		
Uglynest Caterpillar		•					•	•			•		
Eastern Tent Caterpillar	•	•					•	•			•	•	•
Common Plume Moth & Many Plumed Moths		•	•				•			•	•		
Luna Moth	•							•			•	•	
Polyphemus Moth	•	•						•			•	•	
Twin-spotted Sphinx	•	•	•				•	•		•	•		
Snowberry Clearwing		•	•				•	•		•			
Garden Tiger Moth	•	•					•	•			•		
Gypsy Moth	•	•					•	•			•	•	•
Underwing Moths	•							•			•	•	
Linden Looper	•							•			•		
Speckled Green Fruitworm	•	•						•		•	•	•	
Armyworm Moth & Army Cutworm			•	•			•				•	•	
Carpenterworms & Carpentermoths	•							•					•
Sod Webworms	•			•			•		•		•		
Maggots, Flies, Midges & Mosquitoes • Diptera													
Root Maggots			•		•		•		•	•			
Crane Flies			•	•			•		•				
Fruit Flies	•	•						•		•	•		
Carrot Rust Fly			•		•				•				
Tachinid Flies	•	•	•				•	•		•	•		
Hover Flies	•	•	•			•	•	•		•	•		
Robber Flies	•	•	•				•	•			•	•	
Chokecherry Gall Midge	•	•						•		•	•		

Early Spring	Late Spring	Early Summer	Late Summer	Fall	Larva/Nymph	Eggs/Pupa	Adult	Damage	Beneficial	Pest	Page Number	Species
												Lepidoptera • Butterflies, Moths & Allies
		•	•		•		•		•		122	Monarch
		•	•				•			•	124	European Skipper
	•	•	•		•			•		•	125	Lilac Leaf Miner
•	•	•	•	•	•		•	•		◦	126	Peach Twig Borer
	•	•	•				•	•		•	127	Peach Tree Borer
	•	•	•		•			•		•	128	Raspberry Crown Borer
	•	•	•				•	•		•	129	Ash Borer
	•	•	•	•	•		•	•		•	130	Boxelder Twig Borer
	•	•	•		•		•	•		•	131	Aspen Twoleaf Tier & Aspen Leafroller
		•	•					•		•	132	Northern Pitch Twig Moth
	•	•						•		•	133	Codling Moth
	•	•	•	•	•		•	•		•	134	Uglynest Caterpillar
•	•	•			•		•	•		•	135	Eastern Tent Caterpillar
•	•	•	•	•			•		•		137	Common Plume Moth & Many Plumed Moths
•	•	•			•		•		•		138	Luna Moth
•	•	•			•		•		•		139	Polyphemus Moth
•	•	•			•		•		•		140	Twin-spotted Sphinx
•							•		•		141	Snowberry Clearwing
•	•	•			•		•		•		142	Garden Tiger Moth
•	•	•	•		•	•	•	•		•	143	Gypsy Moth
•	•	•			•		•		•		145	Underwing Moths
•	•	•		•	•		•	•		•	146	Linden Looper
•	•	•			•		•	•		•	147	Speckled Green Fruitworm
•					•			•		•	148	Armyworm Moth & Army Cutworm
	•	•	•				•	•		•	150	Carpenterworms & Carpentermoths
	•	•	•		•		•	•		•	151	Sod Webworms
												Diptera • Maggots, Flies, Midges & Mosquitoes
•		•	•				•	•		•	153	Root Maggots
	•	•	•				•	•		•	155	Crane Flies
		•	•				•	•		•	156	Fruit Flies
	•	•					•	•		•	157	Carrot Rust Fly
	•	•	•			•	•		•		158	Tachinid Flies
•	•	•	•	•	•		•		•		159	Hover Flies
	•	•	•				•		•		160	Robber Flies
•	•	•					•	•		•	161	Chokecherry Gall Midge

Where to Scout

Species	Trees	Shrubs	Herbaceous Plants	Grasses/Lawns	Leaf Litter/Soil	Ponds/Wetlands	Open/Sunny Areas	Woodlands	Roots/Crown	Flowers	Foliage/Fruit	Stems/Branches	Trunk/Bark
Maggots, Flies, Midges & Gnats • Diptera													
Swede Midge			•				•			•	•		
Fungus Gnats & Shore Flies					•	•	•		•				
Mosquitoes			•	•		•	•				•		
Sawflies, Ants, Bees & Wasps • Hymenoptera													
Webspinning Sawflies	•							•			•	•	
Dogwood Sawflies		•						•			•		
Willow Redgall Sawfly	•	•						•			•		
Raspberry Sawfly		•					•				•		
Imported Currantworm		•					•	•			•		
Birch Leaf Miners	•										•		
Pear Slug	•	•						•			•		
Ants	•	•	•	•	•		•	•	•	•	•	•	•
Carpenter Ants	•	•			•			•				•	•
Honey Bee	•	•	•				•	•		•			
Solitary Bees	•	•					•	•		•	•		
Bumble Bees	•	•	•				•	•		•			
Parasitoid Wasps			•					•		•	•		
Yellow Jackets	•	•	•		•		•	•		•	•	•	
Other Bugs of Garden Interest													
Spruce Spider Mite	•	•					•	•			•		
Eriophyid Gall Mites	•	•					•	•		•	•	•	
Spider Mites	•	•	•				•	•			•		
Blacklegged Tick	•	•	•	•		•	•	•			•	•	
Crab Spiders		•	•		•		•	•		•		•	•
Wolf Spiders			•	•	•		•						
Jumping Spiders	•	•	•		•		•	•		•	•	•	•
Orbweavers	•	•	•	•			•	•			•	•	•
Northern Black Widow					•			•					
Centipedes			•	•	•		•	•					
Millipedes			•		•			•			•		
Pseudoscorpion					•			•					•
Springtails					•	•		•	•				
Harvestman			•	•	•		•						
Sowbugs	•	•	•	•	•			•	•				
Gray Garden Slug			•		•						•		
Earthworms				•	•			•	•				

	When to Scout					Look For							Species
Early Spring	Late Spring	Early Summer	Late Summer	Fall	Larva/Nymph	Eggs/Pupa	Adult	Damage	Beneficial	Pest	Page Number		
												Diptera • Maggots, Flies, Midges & Gnats	
•	•	•	•				•	•		•	162		Swede Midge
•	•	•	•				•		•	•	163		Fungus Gnats & Shore Flies
•	•	•	•				•			•	164		Mosquitoes
												Hymenoptera • Sawflies, Ants, Bees & Wasps	
•	•	•			•			•		•	166		Webspinning Sawflies
	•	•	•		•			•		•	167		Dogwood Sawflies
	•	•	•					•		•	168		Willow Redgall Sawfly
	•	•	•		•			•		•	169		Raspberry Sawfly
•	•	•			•			•		•	170		Imported Currantworm
	•	•	•					•		•	171		Birch Leaf Miners
	•	•	•		•			•		•	173		Pear Slug
	•	•	•	•			•	•	•	•	174		Ants
	•	•	•				•	•	•	•	176		Carpenter Ants
	•	•	•				•		•		177		Honey Bee
	•	•	•				•	•	•	•	179		Solitary Bees
•	•	•	•	•			•		•		181		Bumble Bees
	•	•	•				•		•		182		Parasitoid Wasps
•	•	•	•				•		•	•	184		Yellow Jackets
												Other Bugs of Garden Interest	
	•	•	•	•	•		•	•		•	188		Spruce Spider Mite
	•	•	•				•			•	189		Eriophyid Gall Mites
•	•	•	•	•	•		•	•		•	190		Spider Mites
	•	•	•		•		•	•		•	192		Blacklegged Tick
	•	•					•		•		193		Crab Spiders
•	•	•	•	•	•		•		•		194		Wolf Spiders
•	•	•			•		•		•		195		Jumping Spiders
		•	•				•		•		196		Orbweavers
•	•	•	•		•		•		•	•	197		Northern Black Widow
	•	•	•	•			•		•		198		Centipedes
	•	•	•		•		•		•	•	199		Millipedes
	•	•	•		•		•		•		200		Pseudoscorpion
•	•	•	•				•		•		201		Springtails
	•	•	•		•		•		•		202		Harvestman
	•	•	•		•		•		•	•	203		Sowbugs
	•	•	•		•		•		•	•	204		Gray Garden Slug
	•	•	•	•	•		•	•	•	•	205		Earthworms

Index

Names in **boldface** type refer to the primary species accounts.

About the Authors

Leslie Proctor Foster

Growing up in the country, Leslie Proctor Foster showed an early interest and passion for nature that led to an Honours degree in Ecology and a Master's degree in Entomology. Her thesis work focused on field crickets, specifically their calling and mating behaviour. She has also earned a Bachelor of Education degree and taught Math and Science in elementary and secondary schools for several years. Today, Leslie is the Curator of the world-renowned Niagara Parks Commission Butterfly Conservatory and teaches at the Niagara Parks Commission School of Horticulture in Niagara Falls, Ontario. Leslie spends most of her spare time with her husband Rob and their two beautiful boys, Tie (5) and Trent (2), both of whom already show a love for nature.

Ken Fry

Ken Fry, entomology instructor at the School of Horticulture at Olds College, has been involved in insect pest management research, teaching and extension for over 12 years, including nine years as a research scientist at the Alberta Research Council. His research is focused on biological control of insect pests and integrated pest management. Ken has never met a bug he didn't like, or at least have a grudging respect for.

Doug Macaulay

Doug Macaulay's childhood fascination with insects led to a career as an agroforester and entomologist with Alberta Agriculture and Food, where he helps people farm with trees, reforest watersheds, manage woodlots and deal with insects and diseases. In his spare time, he works as an insect taxonomist, curating his collection of Alberta insects. He is also working on an identification key of the plume moths of Alberta and Western Canada, and surveying Lepidoptera and Odonata in Alberta parks in cooperation with the Alberta Lepidopterists' Guild and Alberta Parks and Protected Areas.